City Requiem, Calcutta

2003

Globalization and Community

Dennis R. Judd, Series Editor

All photographs in the book, except those in the postscript, were taken by the author in 1997. The postscript photographs were taken in winter 2000–2001.

Excerpt from "The Balcony," by Octavio Paz, translated by Eliot Weinburger, from *Collected Poems, 1957–1987,* copyright 1986 by Octavio Paz and Eliot Weinburger; reprinted by permission of New Directions Publishing Corporation and Paladin.

Lines from Part II ("Here is a map of our country") from "An Atlas of the Difficult World," by Adrienne Rich, from *An Atlas of the Difficult World: Poems, 1988–1991,* copyright 1991 by Adrienne Rich; used by permission of the author and W. W. Norton Company, Inc.

Published by the University of Minnesota Press
111 Third Avenue South, Suite 290
Minneapolis, MN 55401-2520
http://www.upress.umn.edu

Library of Congress Cataloging-in-Publication Data

Roy, Ananya.
    City requiem, Calcutta : gender and the politics of poverty / Ananya Roy.
        p.   cm. — . (Globalization and community ; v. 10)
    Includes bibliographical references and index.
    ISBN 0-8166-3932-9 (hardcover : alk. paper) — ISBN 0-8166-3933-7 (pbk. : alk. paper)
        1. Calcutta (India)—Social conditions.   2. Poverty—India—Calcutta.   3. Poor women—India—Calcutta.   4. Women in development—India—Calcutta.   I. Title. II. Series.
    HN690.C2R68 2002
    306'.0954'147—dc21

                                                                    2002009069

Printed in the United States of America on acid-free paper

The University of Minnesota is an equal-opportunity educator and employer.

12 11 10 09 08 07 06 05 04 03   10 9 8 7 6 5 4 3 2 1

City Requiem, Calcu

Gender and the Politics of Po

Anan

Globalization and Community / Volume

University of Minnesota P

Minneapolis • Lon

To my parents,
who gave me the words to always speak my mind,

and

to Nezar,
who was rendered speechless by the city but had much to say later

Contents

Preface

This is a book about poverty. But it was never meant to be about the old-fashioned subject of poverty. This is a book about Calcutta, the "black hole" of Third World urbanization. But it was never meant to be about urbanization under conditions of abject poverty.

This book started out as a research project about the reforms of the world's longest-serving democratically elected communist government: the Left Front of West Bengal. Notable for its agrarian and institutional reforms, the Left has a reputation for bringing a measure of prosperity and order to the state. Choosing to study West Bengal, therefore, did not necessarily imply studying poverty. I had grown up in Calcutta, and the city had inevitably hovered in the shadows of my interest in cities. It was thus not surprising that I would return full circle to the region, compelled to transform what was once "home" into the "field" of research. I was also eager to disrupt the vocabulary of crisis through which Calcutta is always represented. The emphasis on Left Front reformism seemed to do just that.

But my ethnographic presence in the region returned me to the question that I had most attempted to avoid: poverty. At the fringes of the city, where its concrete density faded into verdant fields of paddy, I found the rural landless seeking to stake a claim to urban livelihood and shelter. On the teeming trains that ran restlessly between southern villages and middle-class urban neighborhoods, I found desperate women carving out a grueling commute against hunger and deprivation. If the city was urbanizing at a frantic pace, engulfing large swathes of agricultural land, then the villages of the southern delta were becoming ruralized, surviving as impoverished labor hinterlands of the metropolis.

This rural-urban interface belonged to more than simply distress migrants, squatters, and commuters. It was here, in the historicized niches of the city, that the Left Front was seeking to implement liberalization, what I came to call a communism for the new millennium. What is striking about the New Communism is its territorialized flexibility, a volatile remaking of the city in and through which the hegemony of poverty is quietly reproduced.

My requiem is written as a parody of the concept of crisis-bound Third World primate cities requiring diagnosis and resuscitation. But it is also written with the sad awareness that tropes of death and dying have become standard idioms of critique, even of living, in Calcutta. My ethnographic interpretation of this death-in-life is inevitably incomplete, inevitably contradicted, evoking another sense in which I mean the idea of a requiem. As Nezar AlSayyad, my colleague and partner, has so often reminded me, a requiem is as much about the act of composition as it is about the performance of death. This study of poverty is thus marked by my intellectualist pleasures and feminist desires.

I have accrued numerous, and welcome, debts during the course of this project and production. Manuel Castells continues to provide inspiration. I remember vividly my first encounter with *The Urban Question* and *The City and the Grassroots*—as a freshman, in the gracious Mills library designed by Julia Morgan. I read, transfixed, rooted to that spot on the floor between the stacks, until the library closed, and thereafter. In many ways, this book is a return to such passions. Anno Saxenian has consistently and enthusiastically green-lighted my academic explorations, including the wayward ones. Her work on regions has informed my interests in space and place. From early on, Gill Hart has enriched this project in significant ways. My intellectual acknowledgments to her are evident in various parts of this book. Michael Watts, as always, has gone to the heart of the matter and helped me imagine New Communism in ways not fully reflected here. At Mills College, Ted Thomas taught a series of remarkable sociology courses that cemented my commitment to research and teaching in the field of urban studies.

Different phases of this research project were supported by the junior fellowship of the American Institute of Indian Studies (AIIS), as well as various grants from sources at the University of California, Berkeley, including a Simpson Fellowship from the Institute of International Studies and the Vice-Chancellor for Research Fund. The International Association for the Study of Traditional Environments (IASTE) provided an institutional home, and the Center for Environmental Design Research (CEDR) assisted with resources.

In Calcutta, the Centre for Social Science Studies was a generous host.

I am particularly grateful to my sponsor, Nirmala Banerjee, whose scholarship and activism I have long admired. My research assistant, Rita Bose, was a gem, providing camaraderie in the field. Special thanks also go to Koely Roy, formerly of Unnayan, and S. K. Bhattacharya of the Calcutta Metropolitan Development Association. It is impossible to acknowledge all of the warmth and help that I received from the residents of various settlements and villages. I hope this book presents some sense of their indefatigable spirit.

In the transition from research project to manuscript, Derek Gregory and series editor Dennis Judd provided encouragement. I remain humbled by Janet Abu-Lughod's endorsement of this project, for her transnational work on cities remains the standard to which I will always aspire. At the University of Minnesota Press, Carrie Mullen has been the shining light of this endeavor, with steadfast advice and help from start to finish. Lynn Walterick meticulously edited the manuscript and Laura Westlund graciously supervised the production process.

At the University of California at Berkeley, the faculty, staff, and students of the Department of City and Regional Planning made teaching a pleasure. I am especially grateful to Chair Fred Collignon for his support. Dean Harrison Fraker has been an exceptional advocate of my work in urban studies.

Radha and baby Ishan were there at the start of this project and have been since, continuing to provide love and support. Thursday evenings with Romi helped with the last push. Over the years, my parents have made possible my academic forays in many incredible ways, too numerous to list. My mother, as a committed educator, has imaginatively reminded me of the novelistic, artistic, and cinematic spaces of the city. My father has shared with me his brilliant satirical commentary on Calcutta and India. This book is ultimately about their city.

In everyday and extraordinary ways, Nezar AlSayyad has provided intellectual partnership. I interpret his recent statement, "You have been at it for a while now, but the city has not yet been put to sleep," as evidence of his patience and of how much we both love the cities that constitute our lives.

Berkeley, September 2001

Opening Moves

If this beginning is a beginning
It does not begin with me
I begin with it
                    I perpetuate myself in it
Elbows leaning on the balcony
                              I see
This distance that is so near
I do not know how to name it

Octavio Paz, "The Balcony"

A Beginning

The annual book fair is a well-established tradition in Calcutta, an urban ritual played out under a late-winter sun with dense lines of bamboo and cloth stalls, barely holding up to the swirls of dust stirred up by the shuffling crowds. In many ways, the fairs are meant to signal Bengal's participation in a world arena of literary production with stalls representing particular nations and their cultural traditions. Thus, at the 1997 book fair, an ill-proportioned copy of Louis Kahn's National Assembly building served to represent Bangladesh[1] and a stocky arch led to "Montmarte" where indigent local artists displayed their paintings for ridiculously low prices. Was this a world exhibition of sorts? A postcolonial articulation of the legacy of colonial museums and fairs, displaying "otherness" with commercialized certitude?

But there is more, something that marks off Calcutta as different. If the fin-de-siècle world expositions had reconstructed the preserved exoticism of the colonies, and if this symbolized the colonial power to represent

1

Figure 1.1. The Bangladesh stall at the 1997 Calcutta book fair, with a replica of Kahn's National Assembly building.

(Mitchell 1988), then, at the turn of this century, how is the clumsiness of Calcutta's stalls to be interpreted? As a snide rejection of the exhibition motif, Dostoevsky wishing to stick out his tongue, on the sly, at the edifices of the West, a desire that Berman (1982) fixes as the "warped modernism of underdevelopment"?[2] Isn't this the city where communist leaders, albeit Oxford-educated, had sought to do away with English and to recover an authentic mother tongue? Or does the book fair and its symbols tell a more prosaic story about the everyday routines of a localized regime and its visions of urbanism? Or perhaps the first interpretation—of modernism and its discontents—can be told only in light of the second—of places and their contentments.

The 1997 book fair had a French theme, with a truncated cutout of the Eiffel Tower that served as the venue's gate and complete with the French philosopher Jacques Derrida, who served as guest of honor. Derrida was as symbolic as the cardboard Eiffel Tower, his presence upstaged by a liberalizing Left Front,[3] simply eager to attract French investment to the city. Quite appropriately, then, a gigantic Coca-Cola bottle overshadowed the entrance to the French stalls.

But there was an unfortunate twist to this Bengali perestroika. A gas cylinder, which was being used to cook food, overturned and set off a fire. The sole fire truck on duty had no access to water; in fact, the fireman was

Figure 1.2. "Montmartre" at the book fair.

Figure 1.3. The Eiffel Tower as the gate at the book fair.

Figure 1.4. A giant Coca-Cola bottle blocks the entrance to the "Arc de Triomphe" French stall at the book fair.

on his tea break, and others did not arrive until the combustible mixture of bamboo, cloth, and books had created a mushroom cloud of fire and smoke. The book fair burnt to the ground. The French publishers who had arrived in the city ever so tentatively retreated ever so rapidly.

This is one image of liberalization—that of an entrepreneurial urban regime seeking to create what Harvey (1994, 376) calls the "architecture of festival and spectacle." Yet the denouement in Calcutta is a pile of charred books. Herein lies another interpretation of Calcutta's clumsy book fair stalls—that this marks Calcutta's tenuous presence on the margins of a global cartography. The fire can be seen as just another instance of Calcutta's crumbling infrastructure, the mundane inability of the city to put out a fire. Surely a requiem is in order.

Narrating the City

The idea of a decrepit Calcutta is of course nothing new. If Paris has been narrated through the figure of the flaneur, and Los Angeles through postmodern fragmentation, then Calcutta has most often been narrated as the "City of Dreadful Night," Kipling's (1920) unshakable epithet for the city. As the "black hole," Calcutta has been seen to be in constant crisis, timeless in its poverty. Not surprisingly, in seeking to imagine this unimaginable poverty, the imagery of death and dying has dominated. For example,

Figure 1.5. The book fair on fire. The photograph was taken in haste after my having just escaped the fire.

Figure 1.6. Mushroom clouds of smoke as the book fair burns to the ground.

one recent book on "Calcutta's poor" presents itself as "elegies" on the city (Thomas 1997).

It is thus that I settled on my title: a requiem. I mean the idea of requiem in more than simply a funeral for Calcutta. I also mean it as a satire on the very trope of the dying city, and as a critique of the icon of the chaotic Third World metropolis, always[6] in trouble, always needing remedy. One other note: a requiem is as much about the act of composition as it is about death.[4] In other words, it signals the crucial need to uncover the complicities that constitute the production of a city.

Such forms of reflexivity have usually taken the shape of Calcutta scholars prefacing their research by acknowledging the stereotypes of the city (Chatterjee 1990b, 27; Ray 1999, 49). But perhaps the most caustic critique, one where the stereotype itself becomes the object of investigation, comes in Hutnyk's (1996) *The Rumour of Calcutta*.[5] The rumor is poverty, the only way in which, Hutnyk argues, Calcutta is whispered about in Orientalist gossip.

Reading *The Rumour* after having returned from the field was paralyzing. I saw my research on poverty as continuous with the production of other shocking images of Calcutta, the ones Hutnyk's hippie-style tourists were seeking out. It was a panorama of misery whose darkness was only deepened by the occasional glimmers of hope: Mother Teresa in her white robes blessing the poor with her gnarled hands; Patrick Swayze as the savior in the ineluctably Hollywood film *City of Joy*. I could not shake the sense of being just another sympathetic Western visitor to the city.

But it seemed equally paralyzing not to be able to talk about poverty. Could I simply dismiss my research findings as the perversions of ontological complicity? Surely Calcutta was a great deal more than an aggregation of poverty. But could Calcutta be recuperated without taking note of this deprivation and exclusion? Would it not be equally complicit to perpetuate the Left Front myth of a *Sonar Bangla*—a Bengal of fields of gold? This is a trope with stubborn genealogy, what Greenough (1982, 12) calls a "cultural construct of prosperity," conferring moral legitimacy on social truths. Or was this an interrogation too close to home?

Hutnyk advances what has become the standard critique of representations of Calcutta: one that situates the city in a dualistic mapping of the world-system, where the periphery is produced in and through the discourse of the core. Here, the city's colonial history is seen as continuous with the contemporary moment of late capitalism and poverty tourism. Thus, as Minister of Information and Cultural Affairs, prominent CPM leader Buddhadeb Bhattacharjee[6] (1991, iii–iv) wrote the following in his foreword to a volume celebrating Calcutta's tercentenary:

> To probe the historical roots of the city's maladies, one needs to
> hark back to the days of colonial rule . . . The historic city, divided
> between the comparatively "urban" European zone and the ne-
> glected and rudimentary "native" one, was a world cleft in two . . .
> Quite apart from this, Calcutta has always had the onerous task of
> having to absorb the continuing stream of migration from the vast
> hinterland that it was made to serve . . . We certainly do have our
> quota of critics in the realm of urban development . . . There are
> those who seem to be living far away, in foreign countries, attitudi-
> nally if not physically, divorced from the realities of the situation
> prevailing here.

There are many ways in which I can unpackage this packaging of the city: that such arguments about historical continuity are blatantly func-tionalist; that discourse is presented as "cause" manifested in the "effect" of poverty; that much effort is directed toward reversing the stereotypes, leav-ing us with a city vocabulary that is formed only in opposition to the domi-nant tropes of black hole, White Town, and dreadful night.

What I am, however, concerned with is how such formulations of outside/foreign forces elide key aspects of the city's "present history."[7] Who is the normalized "Calcuttan," the subject-citizen to whom the city unques-tioningly belongs? I would argue that the Calcutta that is thus rescued from alien forces is a *bhadralok* city: genteel, gentle:

> I am moved by fancies that are curled
> Around these images, and cling:
> The notion of some infinitely gentle
> Infinitely suffering thing.[8]

The *bhadralok,* as a Bengali urban intelligentsia that emerged in the crucible of colonialism, quite obviously looms large in the historical narra-tions. But even accounts of contemporary Calcutta maintain the city as the domain of the *bhadralok.* Thus, Thomas's discussion of poverty is an elegy "on a city above pretense." Calcutta is presented as a city above pretense because, according to Thomas (1997, 164), the city cannot escape a con-frontation with poverty. Here, poverty becomes that which the anthro-pomorphized city confronts, that which exists outside of the normalized subject-citizen. The key markers of this normalization, from the glimpses of decaying *babu*[9] splendor evident in crumbling mansions, to the heartening celebration of intellectuals and *adda,*[10] work to produce a city whose legiti-mate boundaries coincide with those of the *bhadralok.* In this account of Calcutta, all other social groups can be designated as subaltern, not because they are silenced but rather because they cannot be represented within this system of narration.[11] Or, put another way, the *bhadralok* can emerge as a figure only in relation to the subaltern, speaking for those who cannot be represented. This is the *"babu-coolie"* relationship that the critical histories of subaltern studies have sought to uncover (Chakrabarty 1984, 146–48), the "double articulation of dominance" (Guha 1992) that greatly complicates questions of power in Calcutta.

So, if my opening move was to present Calcutta as the periphery of the world-system, then I now seek to re-present Calcutta at the margins, and indeed the margins of Calcutta, as much more than simply a site of powerlessness. I am interested in the specific exercise of territorialized power within Calcutta, and in how the city is itself constituted through these sociopolitical practices, through these everyday normalizations of the extraordinary.

Sidenotes to the Fair

Let me briefly indicate the nature of this territorialized power by highlighting a few sidenotes to the 1997 book fair. I have written earlier about how the fire can be seen as a symbol of the city's crumbling infrastructure, a stunning example of how and why a former prime minister of India had long ago dismissed the city as "dying."[12]

But for the ruling Left Front this label has become a badge of honor, a driving metaphor in its incredibly successful agrarian populism. I will later detail this particular rural-urban connection. For the moment, I am broadly invoking Williams's (1973) brilliant work on the discursive duality of city and countryside, which shows how in late-nineteenth-century England neo-urban imagery rested on, and manufactured, a pastoral nostalgia, precisely at the moment of great agrarian change. Put bluntly, the Left's ability to mythicize and mobilize a peasant Bengal is predicated on the narrative of a horrible urban capitalism, much of which is conveniently attributed to a colonial history and a neoimperialist present. Images of a Bengali city being exploited by a nonindigenous bourgeoisie pervade popular interpretations of urban woes, a common theme being that of the city as a "courtesan," "hired for a few hours for ten rupees, dancing in the crowd of hungry men."[13]

In other words, one of the chief ways in which power is normalized in Calcutta is through a celebration of the city's marginalization. Such discursive framings constitute what Ong (1999, 81) designates as "self-orientalization" and what Dirlik (1997, 322) interprets as the hegemonic construction of an "alternative within capitalism." The narration of the city is thus simultaneously a narration of the nation,[14] setting boundaries and securing consent for its exclusions.

However, there are two significant disruptions of this discursive structure. The first is a large body of evidence that points to deepening rural dispossession, the sense that not all is well in the Left's utopian villages. My ethnographic research is partly in this genre, and throughout this book I will detail the kinds of distress migration that have begun to emerge in the region. The second disruption is that the narrative of a monstrous urban capitalism sits uneasily with the Left's newfound interest in urban developmentalism.

Both these disruptions are acutely apparent at the rural-urban fringes of Calcutta. Indeed, the processes of peasant migration and urban liberalization literally intersect at the edges of the city. It is here that impoverished migrants have been able to stake informal claims to shelter. And it is here that there is a flurry of middle-class housing developments, on agricultural land, many sponsored by the Left Front itself. This rural-urban interface is the territoriality of liberalization, the space within which the regime is remaking itself, and the region whose boundaries are being redrawn through these rural-urban conflicts. Much of this book will be located at these margins of the city.

In order to introduce the question of liberalization, let me return to the 1997 book fair. At the fair, Derrida talked about "the state of the lie and the lie of the state" (*Telegraph*, 5 February 1997). His words, however, were not the focus of the fair, for he was upstaged by the launching of Chief Minister Basu's memoir, *With the People*.[15] It was reported that, at the so-called dialogue session, Derrida was left onstage with "a disinterested economist reading a paper," "a surly bureaucrat," and "a scampering mouse." The "global" came to Calcutta in 1997 not in the form of French deconstructionism with the potential to unravel the Left's sutured and secured meanings but rather as capitalist consumerism: the selling of books and the imaging of cities. This after all was meant to be the face of a communism for the new millennium, a communism as comfortable with global capital as with the sons of the soil. That this scripted narrative would center around Basu rather than Derrida was quite predictable. This after all was also the record-breaking twentieth anniversary of Left Front rule in West Bengal, a record of electoral stability unknown to any Indian region.

A second book was launched at the 1997 book fair, an official biography simply titled *Jyoti Basu*. Basu's biographer, Surabhi Banerjee, was a professor of English at a local university. A few months later it was revealed that he had "given" her a plot of valuable land in the highly contested rural-urban fringes. The transaction was just one of innumerable acts of territorialized patronage, albeit blatantly illegal. But this time it came on the heels of brutal Left Front evictions of informal vendors, known as "hawkers," from the sidewalks of Calcutta. These vendors had occupied the city's sidewalks for as long as the Left Front had been in power, but in December 1996, in a euphemistically titled "Operation Sunshine," they were evicted. The move was hailed internationally: *Newsweek* magazine (March 1997) headlined that the "world's worst city" was cleaning up its act. Locally, official and popular discourses cast the event as a return to a *bhadralok* Calcutta (Mitra 1997). The word *bhadralok* is appropriately polyvalent, meaning not only the distinctive elite with colonial roots that I described earlier but also "gentlemanly." Operation Sunshine sought to recover a gentleman's Calcutta. This is a city produced through nostalgia, a nostalgia that normalizes certain ways of dwelling in the city (Chakrabarty 1999). What is important is both the object of nostalgia as well as the specific moment at which nostalgia becomes a dominant technique for framing urban discourses and practices. Whose Calcutta is thus recovered?

Hawker encroachments or squatting can be broadly interpreted as a set of public claims. Kaviraj (1997, 103), for example, argues that postcolonial Calcutta has been marked by a process of democratization that established claims to the *"pablik"*—an interlingual term that captures how the original English word is pronounced in colloquial Bengali. The "quasi-claims" embodied in various informal practices can be seen as instances of the *pablik* (Kaviraj 1997, 108). In this spirit, the Left's newfound agenda of urban developmentalism can be read as an attempt to recover the "public" from the *pablik,* reinscribing space as middle class and subject to civic control.

But the "public" is an inherently contested domain. Operation Sunshine sparked a set of unceasing struggles, such that the hawker question became a lightning rod for opposition parties such as the Congress, and most notably for one of the region's most powerful opposition leaders, Mamata Banerjee. On the day that the newspapers carried headlines about Basu's gift of land, at a squatter settlement on the city's fringes, an old and wizened Congress-affiliated squatter leader insisted to me:

> They blame us, the poor. They tell us we are criminals, we are thieves. Just because we have settled this land. But what about the CPM. It's the party's cadres that illegally sell agricultural land to developers. And why should we blame cadres when Jyoti Basu has been giving away land in Salt Lake as if it is his own family property? Did you see the headlines today? He gave a plot of land to his biographer, Surabhi Banerjee. Because she wrote a nice book about him. And they want to punish us! We are just filling our stomachs.

This squatter was one of the thousands of landless peasants who had migrated to the city during the last two decades, informally settling in the rural-urban fringes and engaging in brutal battles to maintain such claims. That this squatter, along with hundreds of other families, was evicted five months following this conversation, and that these evictions had less to do with the machinations of the Left Front than with the internal rivalries of a chaotic Congress party, is a process that I will detail later.

I tell this story of the 1997 book fair, moving from the somewhat tongue-in-cheek cardboard Eiffel Tower example to the backstage struggle over land, because this ensemble of events indicates a particular historical moment. The book fair epitomizes the city as spectacle. Such spatial practices are overdetermined by their class content and by a "distinctive cultural logic" that institutionalizes postmodernism (Harvey 1994, 363–65). I will argue that the "festivals and spectacle" theme inaugurates a specific hegemony of the state, one that works through, rather than against, the rhetoric of free markets and entrepreneurship. Despite its "hollowed-out"[16] appearance, this state has a definite material basis and a marked sociocultural idiom, one that I designate as a communism for a new millennium.

If the book fair belongs to the New Communism, then my sidenotes mark the brutality of this moment, the violences that persist beneath the veneer of gentlemanly Calcutta. The sidenotes are also glimpses into a larger space constituted through rural-urban flows, a set of heterogeneous labor migration and circulation practices that span city and countryside. Here, the dynamics of agrarian dispossession are of crucial importance, in ways that belie both the pastoral myths of the *bhadralok* and the revolutionary victories claimed by the Marxist *bhadralok*. While I do not discuss West Bengal's agrarian capitalism in any detail in this book, my analytical emphasis on distress migration points to the sheer fact of rural landlessness and its gendered vulnerabilities. From domestic service to informal vending, life in *bhadralok* Calcutta is engendered on an everyday basis through feminized livelihoods.

And yet my sidenotes also indicate the paradoxical specificity of New Communism. On the one hand, the Left Front has sought to engage in a new set of developmental strategies. On the other hand, it has attempted to maintain old populisms, for example its mobilizational alliances with the rural-urban poor. This tightrope balancing, inevitably manifested spatially, has created a quite amazing impasse, most notably the unrelenting cycles of evictions and resettlement to which the poor are subject. But there is also a broader sense in which developmental projects, including those sponsored by the state, remain stalled in Calcutta. As I will explain later, the very regulatory ambiguities that have allowed the regime its territorialized flexibility have also created the basis for great political challenges—from opposition parties as well as from commercialized factions within the Left Front itself. Put bluntly, the Left is unable to capitalize on the very tracts of urbanizable land that it so savagely has carved out for itself.

Amidst the cycles of land invasions and evictions; the endless transactions on the edges of the city; the countless reformisms of this party and that; the hurrying to work of the daily poor; the street-blocking rallies; the fist-shaking wrath of squatter leaders; and the sickly sweet celebrations of last-bastion communism, there is a chilling stillness at the heart of Calcutta. It would be misguided to read this stability, as have some observers, as an indication of good governance, as a precondition of successful liberalization. Instead, what is at work is a regime seeking to reinvent its forms of hegemony, at the margins of global change, through the mythicization of a New Communism and a genteel history. If this is a book about a dying city in the dying years of the old millennium, then it is about volatility as stasis. I will visit this theme many times over in this book but I broach it here, right at the start, through the trope of a lone and paralyzed fire truck amidst the flurry of a globalized book fair in the watery sunlight of a winter afternoon.

Intentions

None of this, however, is what I had intended to investigate. At the start of my research project, even as I wandered through the stalls of the 1997 book fair, I would have never imagined that, a few years later, my reconstruction of West Bengal's "present history" would start with this event. Indeed, this book is structured around three themes, none of which I had anticipated: poverty, the urban, and gender. In order to introduce the book and its arguments, I am compelled to explain how and why I came to adopt these analytical anchors, and how they differ from my original intentions.

Poverty

The Left Front of West Bengal is the world's longest-serving democratically elected communist government. Following on the heels of a chaotic period—five different governments and two terms of emergency rule in a span of eight years (1969–77)—its twenty-plus years of unbroken rule have been rather remarkable. Indeed, the Left's performance is quite exceptional in a country that entered the new millennium, not under the grand mantle of a stable Congress dynasty, but instead marked by shifting and fragile coalitions. Amidst the fractious, and often violent, communalism that continues to ravage much of India, contemporary West Bengal also stands apart from its peers, having come a long way from its own gory Partition history. These characteristics have led scholars like Kohli (1997) to laud the state for moving from "breakdown to order."

The Left's reforms have garnered a great deal of academic and policy interest. The agrarian reforms have encompassed land ceilings and redistribution, as well as tenancy reforms, mainly in the form of sharecropping rights. Equally notable is the consolidation of the *panchayats*—village-level elected councils that, in this case, have unprecedented control over developmental resources. Such invigorated *panchayats* are widely seen as unique to West Bengal. Kohli (1987, 139) concludes, "For the first time in modern India, political institutions capable of facilitating rural development with redistribution are being developed at the behest of CPM leadership."

More recently, the state has drawn attention for a dramatic spurt in agricultural production, surpassing national growth rates after decades of stagnation.[17] There is hope that the West Bengal countryside can once again be *Sonar Bangla*—prosperous and profitable (Rogaly et al. 1995).

If the agrarian debates pose the possibility of growth with redistribution, then they also train the spotlight on a striking anomaly: the persistent poverty of the rural landless as revealed by a growing body of village-level studies. However, despite detailed research on agrarian elites (Echeverri-Gent 1992; Bhattacharya 1993), little is known about the practices of the landless (for exceptions, see Beck 1994; Rogaly 1994). What is intriguing is that the rural landless figure prominently in various urban surveys that reveal heavy flows of destitute households from rural West Bengal into Calcutta (Dasgupta 1992; Jagannathan and Halder 1988–89). Such studies indicate that distress migration is a relatively recent phenomenon, taking hold of the region during the last fifteen to twenty years, coincident with the period of Left Front rule, and that it is deeply gendered, involving new forms of feminized work.[18] My intervention in the West Bengal controversy is through attention to such patterns of migration and urban settlement.

Locating poverty thus, at the rural-urban interface, through processes that bypass the conventional categories of city and countryside, also brings to light the mutual constitution of region and regime. In many ways, the West Bengal debates have reduced the agrarian question to what Byres (1992, 7) calls Engels's "peasant question"—a concern with which portions of a differentiated peasantry can be politically mobilized. In this sense, the agrarian debates have replicated the concerns of the Left Front, remaining content with evaluating the regime on its own terms. In contrast, the idea of the rural-urban interface revives a broader understanding of the agrarian question—as an intricate set of articulations between city and countryside.

Here, the debates that explore the transition from feudalism to capitalism are useful, particularly in Merrington's (1976, 195) insistence that urbanization and ruralization be considered as two sides of the same process.[19] In other words, the agrarian question is also an "urban question."[20]

The Urban Question

One way of specifying the rural-urban interface is by taking a closer look at sectoral linkages, as in Mellor's (1976) model of dynamic rural industrialization.[21] When I first started work on West Bengal, the issue of such growth linkages was uppermost in my research agenda. Two trends convinced me of the importance of this analytical focus: the rise of market towns in certain fast-growing districts of West Bengal such as Burdwan (Harriss-White 1993), and the urbanization of Calcutta's fringes (Chakraborty 1991) that resemble what McGee (1991) identifies as the quintessentially "Asian" rural-urban, high-growth *desakota* region.

But the more closely I looked at the West Bengal context, the less evidence I saw of dynamic rural-urban linkages. Researchers like Chandrasekhar (1993) argued that nonagricultural diversification was distress-induced, signaling a failure of the Green Revolution rather than its successes. Burdwan's market towns turned out to be dominated by urban oligopolies exploiting a mass of petty traders (Harriss-White 1993). And the growth of Calcutta's *desakota* region seemed problematic: an "uncontrolled undersprawl of an unprecedented magnitude" (Ghosh 1991, 69), dotted with miserable squatter settlements (Unnayan 1996). The region was indeed a far cry from the "Asian" ideal-type of sectoral linkages and urbanization.

But such findings are in keeping with a body of research that draws attention to the political economy of growth linkages, showing how varying agrarian structures can create drastically different trajectories of nonagricultural diversification (Johnston and Kilby 1982; Mukhopadhyay and Lim 1985; Harriss 1992a; Saith 1992; Ranis and Stewart 1993). In other words, they point to the need for a direct confrontation with the issue of spatialized poverty, with how peasants get to be in the city and how they survive in differentiated ways.

How then can the matter of peasants in the city be conceptualized? The theoretical tradition that I draw upon is the idea of urban informality. I pose the issue of informality not as a challenge that unravels the modernist, formal logic of planned cities but instead as a system of spatialized practices that is fundamentally articulated with legality and formality (Collier 1976; Eckstein 1977; Castells 1983; de Soto 1989).[22] Here, I quite explicitly draw upon what are essentially Latin American concepts but present them in the specificity of Calcutta's "present history." Indeed, I am particularly concerned with what Roberts (1995) calls "sources of diversity"—how and why seemingly similar processes, such as urban informality, take on divergent forms within different contexts. Identifying the sources of diversity means taking account of the heterogeneity of rural-urban linkages, and thinking through the historicized geopolitics of cities and regions. In the context of West Bengal, this involves two related issues: the specificity of the urban, and the historical moment of liberalization.

The West Bengal debates have paid scant attention to the urban. Calcutta, while the center of a great deal of anguish, has almost always been seen as synonymous with the region's troubled industrial sector (Kohli 1987; Mallick 1993). With the possible exception of Dasgupta's (1992) study of petty trading, the "urban question" (Castells 1977)—the concrete constitution of the city through struggles over social reproduction—has not been posed. Accordingly, on the rare occasions when rural-urban linkages have been investigated (Shaw 1988) they have been conceptualized as functionally derivative rather than dynamically constitutive, a symptom of rural subsidies to urban capitalism. These neo-Marxist formulations ironically bear striking resemblance to the Left's neopopulist diagnosis of what ails West Bengal, a sense of a dreadful urban capitalism. By presupposing both the mechanisms and outcomes of exploitation, such conceptualizations of the urban subvert the question of poverty.

Part of the problem rests in the quite clumsy ways in which these understandings of the urban pose the connection between "big" development models and spatiality, what Gore (1984) calls the "incomplete relational concept of space." How are "social" categories such as peasants to be matched up with "spatial" categories such as the rural or the urban? What is the sociality of spatialized categories such as migration? Much of the work on Calcutta posits a reified urban ecology—often the "dying city" myth—from which to read off social processes. The complex and power-laden ways by which space and society come to be linked in the specific arena of the urban is thus completely bypassed.

The informality debates in contrast present a dramatically different understanding of the urban, specifically as a set of territorialized social practices. What is equally important is that these struggles over social reproduction are recognized to inevitably encompass the actions of the state, what Castells (1983) calls collective consumption. What does it mean to thus "urbanize" the state? What does it mean to study the Left Front regime, usually conceptualized as a rural presence, in Calcutta? If the politicized *panchayats* are the hallmark of rural West Bengal, what marks the institutional landscape of the city? If the "Bengali modern"[23] has been recovered—and regulated—through the Left Front trope of the peasant, then what modernities can be imagined in the metropolis?

When posed at the rural-urban interface, such questions return us once again to the transition debates. In paying attention to the interconnections between agrarian and urban change, these arguments were not claiming that city and countryside are similar. Rather, they sought to specify the nature of the urban, the city as *civitas/civis*—a body of citizens. I do not mean this urban citizenship in Pirenne's (1925) sense of urban islands of freedom or Anderson's (1979) idea of a civic democracy inherited from Western antiquity. Instead, the concept of *civitas* poses the question of the kinds of citizenship that are made possible in the city.

In the case of contemporary Calcutta, urban citizenship has to be understood at the historical moment of liberalization. In the chapters that follow I detail this new face of the regime, but let me preview two key issues. First, as I have already mentioned, while the Left Front has been long known for its agrarian reformism, more recently it has engaged in a strategy of urban developmentalism. The Left has always deftly reconciled its radical ideologies with the constraints of parliamentary democracy (Herring 1989). But in the 1990s, in keeping with India's liberalization drive, it launched a New Economic Policy (Shaw 1997), partly in order to adapt to the electoral challenges of the new millennium (Sengupta 1989, 1997).

Second, the New Communism has played out with great intensity on the ruralized fringes of Calcutta. The moment of liberalization has not only manifested itself at the level of the urban—in the city as spectacle—but has also taken hold in particular, historicized interstices within the urban. Indeed, in Calcutta, the space of liberalization is not so much the annual book fair with a French theme as it is the volatile land transactions occurring at its less visible margins. Here, as rural and urban regulatory contexts bump and collide, a new regime of spatial regulation and social discipline takes hold.[24] In this, Calcutta's messy urban fringes do not constitute a deviation from McGee's (1995, 205) "organic Asian ideal-type." Instead, their historicized specificity is indication of how urban politics is constitutive of inevitably divergent trajectories of urbanization, such that it is impossible to deduce social outcomes from seeming regularities in spatial forms.

This is not just a question of spatialized diversity but instead a consideration of the inherent "contingency" of the urban question (Cooper 1983). If liberalization is a new regime of discipline and control, then I have argued that it is not the gentlemanly "order" propagated by the Left and lauded by observers (Kohli 1992). And if contemporary Calcutta seems to be quiescent, then as Mallick (1993, 218) rightfully warns, this must not be read as stability. My research is concerned with the mechanisms through which order is guaranteed and acquiescence is secured. Here, the presence of peasants in the city does not inherently guarantee the functionalist reproduction of labor power; nor does the *desakota* automatically create new economies of growth. Rather, each is a messy and ongoing process that requires what Chatterjee (1997, 144) terms the "daily renewal of legitimacy."

In the various chapters that follow, I will detail how, at the moment of New Communism, such hegemonic consolidations are taking place in the distinctive idiom of *bhadralok* dominance. This is the "political culture" (AlSayyad 1993) that gives specific form and shape to Calcutta's urban informality. This is the social reproduction that works in and through the reproduction of social identities (Moore 1994, 90). I mean the idea of "culture" not as a frozen history but rather in the post-Marxist sense of "lived practices of domination and subordination" (Williams 1977; Willis 1977; Hall 1988), the "contingent logic of the social" (Laclau and Mouffe 1987). And yet this contingency is not necessarily subversion. As squatting cannot be interpreted as the rebellion of the urban poor—indeed the Latin American research shows how it is often a mechanism of dominance—so the unpredictability of social reproduction cannot be read as the undermining of power. Indeed, much of this book is concerned with how, in Calcutta, hegemony is fixed and policed not by transcending negotiability but instead through it, through unceasing negotiability. In the following section, I outline how and why I have drawn upon contemporary debates in feminism to delineate this insidious realm of the "social as a site of dispersed regulation" (Smith 1994, 83).

Gender as an Analytic Category

Many of the West Bengal debates have used class as the key analytic category, thereby replicating the discourses of the Left Front. Gendered research has yielded a quite different perspective on the region. Particularly evident has been the gendered differentiation of labor markets, and how this is turn is linked to inequalities within households (Banerjee 1985; Standing 1991; Rogaly 1997). In fact, paying attention to such gendered structures has been a crucial step toward rendering poverty visible (Beck 1994).

My research on the feminization of livelihood lays claim to this legacy of studying gendered poverty. I am concerned with women as primary earners as well as the devaluation of such work by the state and within households. Here, social reproduction—as the reproduction of labor power and social relations (Castells 1977, 460)—is located not in a single institution but rather in how the boundaries between state, household, economy, and community are contested (Stack 1974; Warde 1988; Laslett and Brenner 1989).[25]

Further, while much of this book is concerned quite directly with poor women, I explicitly reject "poor women" as a fetishized category, whether this is cast in the image of Third World victimhood[26] or in the new-found rationale of efficient policy targets.[27] Instead, I am interested in figuring out the ways in which the very category of "poor women" comes to be constructed. Such a framework, I hope, not only allows an exploration of gendered inequalities but also provides the possibility of using gender to theorize the concept of inequality. Another way of putting this would be to say that gender is not my object of analysis; rather, it is my analytical toolkit (Scott 1988).

How does the subject of feminism alter the subject of poverty? Feminism is clearly not a stable repository of categories that provides a consensus on the question of gender. Instead, it is marked by ongoing debates, an ensemble of "feminist contentions" rather than enduring certainties (Butler and Scott 1992; Benhabib 1995; Narayan and Shanley 1997). I am particularly interested in how poststructuralism is interpreted within feminism, drawing attention to both difference and domination (Fraser and Nicholson 1990). In Haraway's (1990, 203) elegant words, "Some differences are playful; some are poles of world historical systems of domination. Epistemology is about knowing the difference."

Poststructuralist feminism, of course, does not provide a single, fixed way of articulating the subject of poverty. Rather, it unsettles ontological and epistemological certainties, stable subjects and their authorial claims. As Butler (1992, 9) emphasizes, this critique is "not a negation or repudiation of the subject, but rather a way of interrogating its construction as a pregiven or foundationalist premise." Essentialist ideas of gender as stable roles and ideologies accordingly give way to "the multiple and contradictory positionings and subjectivities" that constitute gendered hierarchies (Moore 1994, 55).

I find such theorizations to be invaluable in thinking through the politics of poverty. This is a far cry from the functionalism of capitalism and patriarchy endlessly aiding and abetting each other (Ehrenreich 1984). Rather, the challenge of poststructuralist feminism is to show how the persistence of poverty is engendered in and through the formation of normalized subjects. The shift from "poor women" to gendered subjects is crucial at many levels. On the one hand, it allows the specter of poverty to be dislodged from the body of the woman, and indeed from the body of the poor. Instead, in highlighting the relational aspects of poverty, it makes possible a discussion that moves beyond what Jackson (1999, 90) critiques as "the analytically crude cardboard cutouts of pampered sons and patriarchs." On the other hand, the change in question from "what is the subject?" to "how is the subject regulated and produced?" (Butler 1992, 13) elasticizes the notion of politics.

For example, a gendered critique shows how the agrarian and urban questions are also the woman question, involving not so much the universal subject of Marxism as the processes through which this subject is rendered universal, and thereby hegemonic.[28] My research, for example, reveals how the Left's interventions in informal housing and work are in the idiom of a bourgeois masculinity, meant to bolster a *bhadralok* Calcutta. Politics, in this case, has been as much about the allocation of resources as it has been about the "constitution and transformation of subject-positions" (Mouffe 1992, 379).

If poststructuralist feminism alters the subject of poverty, then it also thereby reworks the community of poverty, showing how it is a process rather than a guarantee.[29] As Scott (1988, 4) points out, "The emphasis on 'how' suggests a study of processes, not of origins, of multiple rather than single causes, of rhetoric or discourse rather than ideology or consciousness. It does not abandon attention to structures and institutions, but it does insist that we need to understand what these organizations mean in order to understand how they work."

The current West Bengal debates are depoliticized not because they focus almost exclusively on the hegemony of the rural elite but because they fail to show *how* this hegemony is consolidated and challenged. When there are glimpses, as in Ruud's (1994, 1995) explication of clientelism, in Rogaly's (1994, 1998) analysis of labor management, and Bhattacharya's (1993) argument about the cultural forms of patronage, the making and unmaking of class and gender relations are revealed.

Also thereby revealed is a notion of community quite different from the romanticism that lurks in the shadows of the West Bengal debates. The village-level studies, for the most part, anticipate an ideal-type even as they discuss institutional corruptions (for example, Lieten 1996b). In the expectation of "good" institutions, they echo the Left's myth of peasant communities, of the village as an embodiment of grassroots justice. Such ideas are also congruent with current celebrations of civil society that see the practices of the poor as resistance to the oppressions of state and economy (Escobar 1992; Douglass and Friedmann 1998). In contrast, I present civil society as thoroughly implicated in state power, a "private apparatus of hegemony" that buttresses the ethical content of the state (Gramsci 1971,

264). If the community of poverty is constituted through social networks, through "family strategies" (Roberts 1994) and "ideologies of reciprocity" (Mingione 1994), then gendered analysis mandates a specification of these ideologies and strategies.

In seeking to meet this challenge, I have drawn upon post-Marxist regional histories that seek to provide a genealogy of hegemonic ideas and practices (see for example Chatterjee 1993; Chakrabarty 1994). Chatterjee (1990a), for example, has brilliantly shown how, in Bengal, at a moment of elitist struggle against colonialism, the "woman question" was resolved within the "national question," a hegemonic resolution that crystallizes in the contemporary Left Front (Basu 1992; Ray 1999). I see such analyses as creating a "present history" (Chatterjee 1997), whereby the historicized production of subjects and communities is always evident. Not surprisingly, I use the term "present history" in a second, but fundamentally related sense: as Bertaux-Wiame's (1981) emphasis that the narration of life histories is always an interpretation of the past in light of the present.

I have moved, then, from the urban question to the woman question, and to how the woman question is resolved at multiple moments within the national question. Here, as Radcliffe (1993) notes, the material geographies of poverty become inseparable from the metaphorical territory of the nation. But in many ways this is a return, full circle, to the urban question, to how hegemony is localized. In this book, I focus on two sites at which the regime takes shape and form, two embodied commodities each with a unique spatiality: labor and housing. The city that is thus recovered does not simply "contain" gender and poverty.[30] As attention shifts to the production and regulation of the subject of poverty, so is the assumption of places as "singular, bounded, static" undermined (Massey 1995, 284). The city is itself produced through the politics of poverty.

In Good Faith?

If poverty, the urban question, and a gendered toolkit are three unanticipated themes, there is yet a fourth that has sneaked in: the issue of voice. As already evident, this book has a great deal of my presence, much more than I had ever expected. I had always thought that I would be responsibly self-reflexive but within the neat boundaries of a short preface. Instead, in keeping with my focus on lived hegemony, reflexivity has turned out to be terribly messy. If this is a requiem meant to satirize the myth of the dying metropolis, then it is also a composition that recognizes the desires and pleasures inherent in narration.

Such compositions are, of course, inevitably spatialized. In many ways, my research is in keeping with what Nagar (1997, 206) designates as a "feminist ethnogeography," where ethnography involves negotiating a space of power. But the "real multiplicities of space-time" (Massey 1995, 284) that mark this project extend well beyond Calcutta. I therefore locate my ethnographic and textual negotiations in the transnational space articulated by postcolonial feminism, one that indicates "how what goes on over here" is always shaped "in terms of what goes on over there" (Grewal 1996; Spivak 1990b).

Feminist research has been inherently reflexive, provoking intimate interrogations of research commitments (Stacey 1988). But I would argue that geopolitical difference greatly complicates the question of reflexivity by introducing an "uncontainability of context" (Jones III et al. 1997, xxvii). While postmodernism confronts the geography of alterity (Barnes and Curry 1992), postcolonial feminists shift the focus to the global cartographies within which gendered subalternity is imagined and produced (Spivak 1987).

In the context of this research project, attention to such geopolitical specificities has revealed the liminal space within which I define my "insider/outsider" positionality (Zavella 1992; McDowell 1992). If I have felt the power of "Western eyes" (Mohanty 1988) during fieldwork, it was I who was often the source of the gaze. And if I had ventured into the field in the spirit of returning home to Calcutta, I was soon disenchanted of such notions.[31] Amidst the rumor that is Calcutta, "home" and "field" were often blurred, each unsettling the certainties of the other (Viswesaran 1992). Indeed, I have had to interpret my presence in the field as the seemingly paradoxical combination of embodiment and "deterritorialization" (Kaplan 1987).[32] Here, Calcutta becomes a territory from which I am displaced but which I also negotiate, dismantle, and imagine as a site of return. This is a "politics of location" (Rich 1986) that is marked by inherent ambiguity and contradiction.[33] I thus speak as a "fake" native, disclaiming authenticity but claiming the privileges through which transnational research is produced and disseminated.

In the chapters that follow, I battle my demons of "home" and "field" by making explicit the politics of knowledge that accompanies the politics of poverty. I do so in two ways: by explaining the process of research such that my concepts emerge in dialectical relation with the "field," and by inserting postscripts and prescripts that challenge the certain narratives of "fieldwork." I do not intend these disjunctures to resolve the thorny questions of authorship and representation. Instead, it is my hope that the collisions between the composition and compositional strategies, between evidentiary material and anomalous stories, will expose the construction and normalization of key categories and concepts.[34] I would also hope that these minirequiems present the sociospatiality of research without taming and reforming geopolitical difference in a singular coherence.

Confronting ethnographic disjunctures has not been easy. Such issues have at times wrought a numbing paralysis, ironically replicating the impasse that I argue exists amidst Calcutta's volatility. One of the allegories that I use to make sense of this paralysis comes from the film *Lisbon Story* (1994), directed by Wim Wenders. In this film, Wenders, who is often characterized as a postmodern interpreter of urban environments (see, for example, Harvey 1989), presents the "real" Lisbon as a "represented" city, a montage of sounds and images being put together for a cinematic audience. Toward the end, the filmmaker pronounces that he has abandoned the project of filmmaking because he is disillusioned about the corruption of images. For him, the only "innocent" image of the city is one that can be recovered without his mediation. He thus decides to strap a camera to his back, letting it shoot a set of random images as he walks through the city. His friend, the sound engineer, points out how ridiculous a project this is, and that the real challenge is to face up directly to the potential, and responsibilities, of the "magic celluloid."

In many ways, feminist reflexivity contains a similar imperative. It is the recognition that there are no "innocent" images that drives the need to hoist the camera on one's shoulder and look the city in the eye. *Lisbon Story* ends on a note of modernist innocence, mainly because, while Wenders questions the privilege to see, he does not extend this interrogation to the privilege to hear. It is the freedom of the sound engineer to roam the city that makes possible this final recovery of innocence. The privilege to hear, to even eavesdrop, is also often unquestioned in ethnographies. Rather, it is the freedom to translate into words, to represent in writing, what Rich (1984, 326) calls "verbal privilege," that is in question. But when the rights and rites of sound are scrutinized as much as is the weight of the written word or the arranged visual image, then it becomes hard to defend the impeccable credentials of ethnographer-writer as sound engineer.

And a closer look at *Lisbon Story* reveals that the modernist innocence of the ending is anticipated throughout the film. While the visual narrative abandons the possibility of "representing" the city, it maintains intact the representation of the figure of the woman—in this case, the elusive but haunting presence of Portuguese singer Teresa Salgueiro. She, in her virginal beauty, becomes the imagined, at once material and iconic, the city as woman. Through this representation is consolidated a specific hegemony:

that of a universal, knowing subject, one that despite the innovative tactics of postmodernism is secure in its masculinist and bourgeois privileges.[35]

In the chapters that follow, I resist the urge to replicate this innocence, to present my research as the random images of a camera strapped to my back or to naturalize iconic representations that maintain a *bhadralok* city. This is my way of dispelling the "rumor" of Calcutta as well as the fiction of a *Sonar Bangla,* a Bengal of fields of gold.

2

The Politics of Poverty

West Bengal, a very poor and very rural state, has vastly improved
its relative position on a broad range of economic, social, and rural
indicators. Land reforms, the development of panchayats and implementation of poverty alleviation programs through them, and
political mobilization of the rural poor, are the distinguishing features of development since 1977 which account for this progress.

**Biplab Dasgupta, "Institutional Reforms and
Poverty Alleviation in West Bengal"**

The Left Front experiment in West Bengal is now widely regard-
ed by knowledgeable observers as a failure . . . That the Left
Front was a dismal failure should no longer be a matter of debate. What is more significant is the nature of its failure.

Ross Mallick, *Development Policy of a Communist Government*

In Search of the Poor

In the winter of 1996 the central government of India announced an expansion of the Public Distribution Scheme (PDS), a rationing system that provides foodgrains at subsidized rates to urban and rural consumers. Launched
as a major poverty alleviation measure, the new intervention was specifically to target households below the poverty line, providing them with restricted quantities of rice and wheat at half the former PDS prices. As in the
case of the original PDS, the expansion was to be implemented by state
governments that were to create lists of beneficiaries for ration shops. Those
eligible for the program were to have "BPL" or "Below Poverty Line" stamped
on their ration cards and those who did not have ration cards were to be
given cards (*Anandabazar Patrika,* 29 January 1997).

It was a typical Calcutta winter. The days were short and mild, the Christmas lights on the scrawny trees lining once-posh boulevards flickered hesitantly, and a dust-laden smog settled heavily into every crevice of the city's crumbling buildings. I had just arrived in West Bengal, determined to study poverty but still grappling with how and where to start. Yoked as it was to a statewide effort to locate and identify poverty, the new PDS scheme was of special significance for me.

"Below Poverty Line"—a clear stamp identifying the poor! I had visions of a neatly classified and tagged population. Perhaps one only had to stand at the door of ration shops and sift through the stream of consumers—"BPLs, step aside please. I have some questions to ask you." But this was not to be, and a quiet controversy brewed over the identification of the poor. The Left Front government, which until now had asserted a dramatic decline in poverty rates, suddenly had a stake in claiming high rates. When the central government assessed that West Bengal had 39 percent of its population living below the poverty line, Kalimuddin Shams, the Food Minister, protested that the figure was closer to 70 percent. Shams later retreated from this statement and came to accept the 39 percent figure (*Anandabazar Patrika*, 19 January 1997).

Who constitutes this 39 percent? Reports from the districts showed that state officials did not know how to implement the scheme because they did not have any lists or records of the poor (*Bartaman*, 9 January 1997). I was struck by the irony of a communist government that claims to have made a significant dent in poverty but does not maintain any useful measures of the poor, despite the massive quantities of data that it churns out every year. The Food Minister finally announced that food offices in rural areas would use *panchayat* records that list the rural landless. He said that the state government had already been providing this group with cheap foodgrains three months a year and their eligibility could be easily verified by *panchayats* (*Anandabazar Patrika*, 19 January 1997). The problems with such an approach are of course numerous, ranging from contending definitions of landlessness to the sole reliance on *panchayats* for the choice of beneficiaries (*Bartaman*, 9 January 1997).

In the case of urban areas, particularly Calcutta, the Food Minister was less clear about how to find the poor. He argued that ration holders were already divided into A, B, and C categories based on income and that this could help determine eligibility. But sensing that these categories were problematic and that many of the poor did not even own ration cards, he went on to describe how food offices would use lists of the poor prepared by the Calcutta Metropolitan Development Authority (CMDA).[1] In areas where such lists did not exist, municipal representatives and food officers would prepare their own lists (*Anandabazar Patrika*, 29 January 1997).

Heartened by the prospect of CMDA lists, I went in search of them through the labyrinthine corridors of Calcutta's bureaucracies. In the basement of the CMDA offices, I finally discovered that the agency was conducting a socioeconomic survey of 20,000 households in order to create a database for the PDS scheme. The study was part of a genre of CMDA surveys supervised by the Planning Head, Animesh Halder. The results of the survey were not going to be available for at least a year but long interviews with Halder provided some interesting insights. Most striking of all was his admission that the study deliberately excluded all squatter settlements, studying only pavement-dwellers and slum-dwellers: "We are concerned that studying squatters will give them a false sense of legitimacy. We cannot acknowledge their presence."

The PDS lists were a tremendous disappointment as a research resource, almost useless for any serious effort to locate the poor. In the villages that I would eventually visit, the *panchayat* lists became a matter of scornful mirth for the landless. Those who needed the subsidies the most knew that they were never going to get them. "They are just pouring more oil on heads that are already soaked with oil," landless men and women commented sardonically again and again. And in Calcutta, existing surveys, ongoing research by NGOs, and sheer common sense pointed to the fact that large groups of the poor were clustered in squatter settlements, precisely the areas that the CMDA deliberately ignored.

The PDS scheme thus raised broader questions about how poverty is studied and measured. The state government's definitions of poverty were indications of how the setting of methodological limits can set the poverty agenda. I already had a sense of this from the dissonances of the West Bengal debates—that it was crucial to pay attention to the analytical frameworks within which poverty was being conceptualized. This was the politics of knowledge that inevitably informs the politics of poverty.

The Consensus on West Bengal

In 1997, the year of the ill-fated book fair, the Left Front regime celebrated its twentieth anniversary in various ways, not least through a series of publications that repeatedly proclaimed the achievements of a reasonable communism.[2] The Left's self-congratulatory discourse has long been echoed in the academic arena. Perhaps the most insistent voice has been that of Lieten (1996a, 111), who argues that West Bengal is witnessing a "virtuous cycle of higher production" with "a decrease in poverty and polarization," and that this in turn can be directly traced to the Left's reformism. But there have also been dissenters. Not only is the source of agricultural growth a matter of contention,[3] but also there are concerns about how the Midas touch of growth and reforms might have left structures of poverty and marginalization untouched (Rogaly et al. 1995). Indeed, the Left Front's critics have been scathing in their evaluation of the regime, emphasizing that the key reason for this "hunger in a fertile land" is "an agrarian structure that is both inequitable and inefficient" (Boyce 1987). Perhaps the most serious indictment has been Mallick's (1993) detailed evaluation of the Left Front's development policy, showing the persistent exclusion of the rural poor from the largesse of the state.

What is happening in West Bengal? This is the question being posed by many, including Harriss (1993). What accounts for such widely divergent evaluations of Left Front reforms? In some ways, the raucous West Bengal controversy is reminiscent of the ongoing debates that mark the agrarian question in development discourses. If there is one point of consensus in the West Bengal debates, it is that the primary beneficiaries of the Left Front's agrarian reforms have been middle peasants who own small plots of agricultural land, usually under five acres, and who actively participate in *panchayat* politics. But this is where the consensus ends. While Kohli (1987), Nossiter (1988), and Lieten (1996a) see this as a shift to a more equitable agrarian structure, others argue that middle peasants constitute a new agrarian elite enjoying economic and political hegemony (Webster 1992; Echeverri-Gent 1992; Mallick 1993; Bhattacharya 1993; Ruud 1994; Beck 1994; Rogaly 1994).

The disjuncture is predicated on radically different conceptualizations of agrarian structure. Kohli, Nossiter, and Lieten are primarily concerned with the disappearance of large landowners, assuming a unity of interests among all other peasants. Lieten (1996b, 185–86) even goes so far as to assert that the middle peasants, who form the bulk of *panchayat* membership, act on behalf of the landless. This position seems to represent what Lehmann (1986) calls "Chayanovian Marxism"—a homogenizing view of the peasantry that fails to recognize the full implications of capitalist differentiation. Such views also resonate in the Left's neopopulist construction of the agrarian question where an essentialized and homogenized peasantry is situated within a broader context of urban exploitation.

But for others, the consolidation of middle peasants is a sign, not of Chayanovian stability but instead of the emergence of a new agrarian elite. As Lenin (1899, 75) had declared that the Russian peasantry was undergoing rapid differentiation, a process that rendered "totally fictitious all average figures," so the Left's critics have argued that West Bengal's middle peasants cannot be lumped together with the large mass of agricultural wage-laborers (Bhattacharya 1993). These researchers have emphasized that the region's middle peasants are, in effect, a dominant class: West Bengal's "kulaks." And as in the case of the Soviet industrialization debate (Erlich 1967), there is vehement disagreement over whether these kulaks are the motor of capital accumulation (Harriss 1993) or whether they impede surplus extraction and growth (Mallick 1993).

What is perhaps most interesting about West Bengal's agrarian structure is that, unlike the role of kulaks in Marxist narratives, this new elite is not simply an evanescent presence in the modernist progression from agriculture to industry. West Bengal's middle peasantry has not withered away. In fact, its entrenchment raises Kautsky's (1899) question of the conditions under which the deepening of market relations coexists with the consolidation of the peasantry (Friedmann 1978). As Watts (1996) notes, such patterns inevitably point to the need to pay attention to state interventions.[4] In the case of West Bengal, this draws notice to how the Left Front has played a crucial role in reproducing the middle peasantry, especially by channeling development resources through the *panchayats* (Westergaard 1986; Herring 1989; Webster 1990; Mallick 1993).

But if the village-level studies have documented the consolidation of an agrarian elite as well as the marginalization of the rural landless, then they have also been surprisingly silent on the nature and dynamics of this exclusion. How do the landless survive? Through seasonal migration, as shown by Rogaly (1994) in his study of agricultural labor? Through tenuous access to common property resources, as revealed by Beck (1994)? By simply dropping out of the village economy through permanent migration, as suggested by Bhattacharya and Chattopadhyay's (1989) longitudinal survey of villages?

As outlined in the opening chapter, I have been interested in how and why a whole series of surveys conducted in Calcutta, for different purposes, provides glimpses of the rural landless. Specifically, the urban surveys indicate heavy and consistent flows of destitute households from rural West Bengal into Calcutta during the last fifteen to twenty years, that is, coincident with the period of Left Front rule (Jagannathan and Halder 1988–89; Chakrabarti and Halder 1990; Roy et al. 1992).

Migration is not new to the Calcutta metropolitan region. Breman (1990) has shown how the colonial state established distinct patterns of circular migration from labor recruitment areas in Bihar, Orissa, and Uttar Pradesh.[5] In addition to such patterns of mobilized migration, colonial interventions in the rural economy itself triggered migration, which the colonial state often dealt with through forcible return (van Schendel and Faraizi 1984). With increasing rural impoverishment, landlessness, and the violent destruction of crafts production, such forms of distress migration intensified (Dasgupta 1984, 1987). By the time of the 1943 famine, large numbers of starving migrants came pouring into the city from the hinterland. The Bengal Destitute Persons Ordinance allowed the colonial police to round up thousands of migrants and evict them from Calcutta. However, many remained and started a new life in water pipes and beside the railway lines (Goswami 1990, 92).

Herein lie the historical traces of two distinct streams of migration. The first, with roots in colonial labor-recruitment policy, involves patterns of circular interstate migration linked to key segments of the urban labor market through an "ethnic division of labor" (Weiner 1978). Such forms of migration are characterized by intricate systems of kin and village networks that regulate entry into urban labor markets (de Haan 1994). Indeed, it is estimated that such preferential practices were "locked in" by the early twentieth century, with Bengali migrants finding only temporary or less privileged jobs in the Calcutta jute mills (van Schendel and Faraizi 1984, 53). Recent research on intrastate migration has shown the continued difficulties of Bengali migrants in accessing Calcutta's urban labor markets (Dasgupta 1992), although they seem to have an easier time finding shelter in the city's slums (Shaw 1988).

The second stream of migration is one linked to rural dispossession. However, these flows are not as vividly depicted in the migration studies of the region. It is clear that by the waning years of colonialism, distress migration was a key feature of the regional economy. But it then drops out of sight, either because such patterns recede or because the focus of research changes. Instead, academic and public concern has been directed at the "refugee" problem—the estimated four million people who moved from Bangladesh to West Bengal between 1946 and 1971 (Chatterjee 1990, 71). The incorporation of Bangladeshi refugees into the city's labor and housing markets has a distinctive trajectory, one that involves regularized settlements and sturdy patronage, quite at odds with the vulnerabilities that seem to characterize distress migration. Indeed, the urban surveys of the 1980s indicate that, in the context of agrarian reformism, new forms of distress migration have emerged in the region.

Methodological Implications

I intervene in the West Bengal controversy by focusing directly on patterns of distress migration and urban settlement. I see my contribution to the agrarian debates as drawing attention to rural landlessness. But my work speaks more directly to the dynamics of urban poverty: how and why land-less households manage to forge differential access to work and shelter but remain poor despite such access. If the village-level studies are thin on the struggles of the rural landless, then the urban surveys are silent on the dynamics of urban poverty.

What is at stake, then, in both the agrarian debates and urban surveys is not only whether poverty is addressed but also *how* exclusion is conceptualized, measured, and represented. This chapter, then, is as concerned with the contested nature of key poverty measures as it is with sociospatial differentiation. Indeed, these contestations are neither new nor unique to West Bengal.

In 1985 the Social Science Research Council, in collaboration with the Indian Statistical Institute, held a workshop in Bangalore involving the upper echelon of social scientists working on issues pertaining to India. What was interesting about the event was that it involved both economists and anthropologists and was explicitly oriented toward discussing how and why these two groups had very different understandings of structure and change. In the workshop proceedings, Bardhan (1989b) points out that, in the India debates, macro-micro divergences are common. In other words, studies using large-scale, macro-quantitative data and those using small-scale, micro, often qualitative, data yield radically different narratives of change. For example, in the national poverty debates of the 1970s, while macro-indicators showed increasing poverty, local-level studies pointed to substantial improvements. The situation was reversed during the debate over the success of the Integrated Rural Development Program (IRDP) when macroevaluations claimed stunning benefits and village-level studies demonstrated ineffectiveness (Dreze 1990).

The West Bengal debates have turned out to be a microcosm of these larger dilemmas. During the twenty years of the Left Front regime, there has often been a disjuncture between macro-optimism and micro-pessimism. Evaluations using large-scale quantitative data such as the census and National Sample Survey (NSS) point to a fall in poverty, an improvement in the human development index, successful land and tenancy reforms, and even re-peasantization. For example, Dasgupta (1995) uses NSS data to show that, with regard to the poverty headcount, West Bengal has improved its position relative to other Indian states. Lieten (1996b, 38) reaches the same conclusion: "According to the Economic Survey 1992–93 based on NSS data, the percentage of the total population below the poverty line has shrunk fast in West Bengal (from 52.5 % in 1978 to 27.6 % in 1988)." Many of the village-level studies indicate just the reverse: a rise in assetlessness and dispossession and the failure of reforms to offset this marginalization. For example, Beck's (1994) ethnographic study of three villages shows the persistence, and even intensification, of poverty.

But such divergent evaluations cannot simply be interpreted as a contrast between macro/quantitative/economistic and micro/qualitative/ anthropological studies. In the same SSRC workshop proceedings, Harriss (1989a, 137–38) emphasizes that it is important not to conflate levels of analysis with methodologies. He points out that village-level studies can be highly economistic, using only quantitative data, or that macro studies can be qualitative, paying careful attention to political economy.

I would take Harriss's argument a step further and emphasize that there are fundamental differences within qualitative studies. What matters is the kind of primary question that is posed and the analytical framework within which this question is investigated. Take for example the striking differences between the findings of Lieten's (1996b) and Harriss's (1993) village-level studies and those of Bhattacharya (1993), Ruud (1994), Rogaly (1994), and Beck (1994). The former are primarily concerned with the virtuous cycle of agricultural production and growth and are content to take the word of "agricultural laborers and middle peasants" that they are better off (Harriss 1993). The latter are concerned with precisely the differentiation within this peasant category, and, more important, the everyday practices through which power is maintained and negotiated.

Thus, in this chapter, I am concerned not so much with presenting a grounded and qualitative conception of poverty that contrasts with limited quantitative measures as with posing a different set of primary questions about poverty. Indeed, I often present some of my findings in a quantitative format to indicate how these different questions can yield a different set of poverty indicators. In the discussions that follow, it will become apparent that these different questions are about the politics of poverty. I present poverty as negotiated access, an ensemble of struggles over resources and meanings: the ways in which landless migrants and commuters negotiate tenuous access to urban shelter through political patronage; that this is simultaneously a negotiation within households and kinship networks; that the livelihoods and incomes of these families are intrinsically shaped by gendered battles over rights and responsibilities. It is in this sense that I put forth a relational rather than distributional understanding of poverty.

Relationality involves not only contested social relations but also intricate connections and flows between spaces and places, which I seek to map through the methodological strategy of fieldwork nodes. It is my hope that such explications of the rural-urban interface break with what Burawoy (1991, 6) critiques as the "conventional correspondence between technique and level of analysis," such that the constitution of "macro" structures through the "micro-organization" of life and work is revealed. If the ethnography and life histories uncover sociospatial relations hitherto obscured in the West Bengal debates, then it is not simply because this presents a qualitative understanding of poverty but rather because of the ways in which the field of research is conceptualized and traversed.

The Logic of the Field

What does it mean to locate poverty at the rural-urban interface? In the face of labor circulation, permanent migration, and other sociospatial linkages, how are the categories of city and countryside to be conceptualized? What are the boundaries of the "field" within which distress migration can be usefully analyzed? Such were the questions I wrestled with at the start of this research project.

I realized, for example, that it is clearly possible to use a village as the springboard for studying migration but, in West Bengal, this is quite tricky. Unlike circular migration where households retain rural bases, in the case of permanent migration households literally drop out from village profiles. The urban surveys indicate that this is precisely what is happening with rural landless households (Roy et al. 1992). In the villages the only way to tell that these households are missing is through panel studies (as in Bhattacharya et al. 1989) or by relying solely on the memory and knowledge of village residents. Such trends mean contending with the methodological challenge of how to study poor households that are simply disappearing from the "public interactional arenas" where fieldwork is conducted (Appadurai 1989). In effect, it entails a rethinking of the "field" and its boundaries.

When I embarked on research, I accordingly decided to fix Calcutta as a starting point, using existing urban surveys to locate poor migrants and then trace their roots to the countryside. Such linkages, recovered through life histories and "present" histories, or ethnographies, were meant to concretize the rural-urban interface. I was also interested in what Calcutta would afford as a research starting point. How would the urban question allow a fresh understanding of the Left Front regime?

The city, however, can be an equally tricky starting point. Before I could begin to track rural-urban linkages, I had to cross my first daunting hurdle: to locate poor migrants in an urban agglomeration of eleven million. One possibility was to concentrate on a labor market segment.[6] However, given the thinness of information on such migrants, it was impossible to make a priori assumptions about their occupational profile. In fact, the urban surveys seemed to show that informal sectors such as petty trading involved not only vulnerable and poor migrants but also more well-established merchants (Dasgupta 1992). In other words, such labor markets did not provide any unique purchase on the question of poverty.

Instead, settlement patterns yielded the most promising options. The urban surveys, as well as NGO research, indicated the dominance of poor migrants in Calcutta's squatter settlements. While formalized slums seemed to house well-established migrants, often the so-called Bangladeshi refugees (Shaw 1988; Chakrabarti and Haldar 1990; Ghosh 1992), squatting involved more recent migrants from the West Bengal countryside with a tenuous hold on shelter (Sen 1992; Unnayan 1996). Such squatter settlements thus became my first means of demarcating the field, of starting somewhere.

Given the PDS case, it was obvious that squatter settlements were not on any official maps. I turned instead to a series of unofficial maps, most of them produced by Unnayan, an NGO with a long history of confrontations with the state government regarding squatter rights. A 1983 Unnayan report, updated in 1992, mapped the city, showing the occupation of "marginal land"—land bordering public infrastructure—by squatter settlements. But squatting, by definition, is a volatile process involving cycles of eviction and resettlement. In the winter of 1996, as I visited each site marked on the 1992 Unnayan map, I realized that most of the settlements had disappeared, and that it was going to be impossible to use the map as a tool for locating squatter settlements. In fact, a 1996 Unnayan report came to exactly the same conclusion, highlighting the volatile cycles of evictions and resettlements that characterize squatting.

But if the Unnayan studies were not road maps, they were at least signposts. They showed that the search for poor and recent migrants in Calcutta requires a spatial conceptualization that discards the conventional urban markings of wards and neighborhoods. An alternative conceptualization has to pay close attention to railway tracks, drainage canals, bridges, urban streams, and vacant agricultural land, searching for patches of territory that squatters can claim as their own. I thus started my search for squatters with topographical maps that listed key elements of the city's public infrastructure, systematically visiting every possible site of squatting. Given the scale of this endeavor, I soon restricted myself to the southern reaches of the city, eventually choosing three key squatter settlements as study areas (Figure A.1 in the book's appendix):

1. Jadavpur: a settlement of seventy households lining the railway tracks at a South Calcutta station. An informal market of fifty stalls also borders the settlement. The settlement has been in existence for over thirty years but has witnessed cycles of evictions. Most of the current households migrated to Calcutta during the last twenty-five years.

2. Chetla: a settlement of about eight hundred households along the putrid canals of the Port Trust in residential South Calcutta. Much of the settlement dates to the early 1980s, although there are sections that are older. Most of the families that live here migrated to Calcutta about ten to fifteen years ago and relocated from other squatter sites to the settlement during the last five to ten years.

3. Patuli: a CMDA sites and services project that had been built on the southern fringes of the city in the late 1970s and was taken over by about two thousand squatter households. The settlement of squatters started soon after the project was completed and continued all through the 1980s.

Each of these three settlements is almost exclusively composed of landless families that have migrated from rural West Bengal during the last fifteen to twenty years. Given my choice of South Calcutta locations, the bulk of migrants—about 98 percent—was from South 24-Parganas, the rural district that stretches to the south of the city. This finding is consistent with other urban surveys that also register a high rate of migrants from South 24-Parganas in the southern wards and fringes of the city (Jagannathan and Halder 1988–89; Chakrabarti and Halder 1990). The remaining 2 percent of migrant households are primarily from Bangladesh, with a few households from other West Bengal districts such as Mednipur and Purulia. In order to maintain the emphasis on South 24-Parganas, I eventually dropped these households from the study. The rural-urban interface thus finally concretized as a set of sociospatial linkages between South 24-Parganas villages and squatter settlements in South Calcutta.

But in order to map this rural-urban interface, I had to transgress the very boundaries that I had drawn. No sooner did I start fieldwork in the three squatter settlements than I realized that they were a part of complex regional processes that could not be captured in a single locality. Instead, each of my fieldwork sites was a node, an intersection of practices and exchanges that stretched across multiple institutional and physical spaces. As Breman (1989, 130) emphasizes, such an approach is very different from starting with a given spatial framework such as a locality or region. He advocates focusing on an analytical theme and following it through spatially, thereby developing an understanding of where, how, and why institutions "condense." I began to think about research as inserting myself into a given node and tracing through the flows that ultimately coalesce to give shape and spirit to the region. Let me explain this methodological strategy by using the Jadavpur settlement as an example.

Fieldwork Nodes

On my first visit to Jadavpur station, a large hub on the local railway lines in a densely developed part of South Calcutta, I was searching for migrants who might have squatted along the railway lines. As I headed southward toward the station, leaving behind the jostling throngs of roadside markets and picking my way through the piles of rotting garbage that lined the tracks, I came across a cluster of makeshift huts. On closer examination, it turned out to be an informal market that operates mainly in the evenings. In the morning, the *bazar* was deserted, an eerie landscape of gunny sack bundles of stored merchandise. Through the maze, an old woman, her teeth rotted and stained, her body bent and misshapen, beckoned to me. I followed her to the shade of a cluster of stalls where some merchants were having their morning *panta bhat,* stale rice soaked in the starchy cooking water. She whispered, "I live here, but my son and daughter-in-law live in Jamunanagar. My son is ill and he does not work. My daughter-in-law comes here every evening to help me cook and sell snacks."

I had never heard of Jamunanagar and so I sat down on a bale of rice to hear more about the place from Kartik Naskar, a rice trader. Naskar was a slender and aging man. While we talked, he picked through a filthy pile of husk and dust, gleaning for paddy, his ribs straining against his sun-wrinkled skin. Over cups of sickly sweet tea that drew the interest of scores of fat black flies, he told me about his village in Canning, South 24-Parganas, life as a landless laborer, and migration to Calcutta eighteen years ago. He lived in a shanty along the railway tracks near the station until he was evicted seven years ago. Pointing to the new bridge that was suspended over the tracks, Kartik said:

> They were building Sukanta Bridge, and we had to move. We
> had supported the CPM for years and so Kanti*babu*[7] took us to
> Jamunanagar. We were each given a tiny plot of land. There are
> no jobs there and so we still come to this market every day to earn
> a living . . . You should go to Jamunanagar and see for yourself. It
> is over there, to the south.

Over the next few months I was to spend a great deal of time in Jamunanagar, which turned out to be a CPM-sponsored resettlement colony of almost a thousand households tucked away in a lush tract of land in the eastern fringes of Calcutta.

Also on the southern horizon, just across from market, was a squatter settlement lining both sides of the meandering railway tracks. The western strip of the settlement consisted of precarious shacks barely five feet from the roaring trains. It had no electricity, running water, or toilets, and residents were worried about the constant threat of evictions. The eastern strip was more formalized. Residents paid a small monthly fee for electricity that was provided to them by the local CPM bosses. They scoffed at the idea of evictions and most of them had extended family, a second home if you will, in Jamunanagar or a similar resettlement colony. During the course of fieldwork, I was to learn that these differences had to do with variations in patronage networks, with residents of the western strip failing to replicate the intergenerational political ties maintained by those of the eastern strip.

But in both settlements the grimness of male unemployment and the dependence on female earnings through domestic work was overwhelmingly apparent. Gray-haired Nokul Mondol leaned against his shack and described how, as a landless laborer in his village in Dakhin Barasat, South 24-Parganas, he found work for at best three months a year. He moved to Calcutta but here too could not find regular work and after a few years simply stopped looking. Krishna Adhikary was abandoned by her husband and moved to the city with her children. She now works as a domestic servant and lives with her mother on the western side. Her two brothers each have a small plot in Jamunanagar. She asked, "But if you think my plight is bad, what will you say when you see the hundreds of women who have to commute every day from our villages?" Nokul Mondol stumbled across the tracks to join our conversation, this time a little drunk: "Take your camera and go to the top of Sukanta Bridge. Every morning you will see thousands of women alighting at Jadavpur Station. They are like countless rivers. There are no women left at home in our villages. They are all out of place."

His words stayed with me as I retraced my steps back past the station to the market. It was late afternoon by this time and the sun cast long, deep shadows in the *bazar*. In the recesses were hordes of women, many of them sitting on the bundles of stored merchandise or resting against the bamboo poles that propped up the stalls. A train arrived at the station and suddenly, in the flash of an eye, many of these women disappeared. It began to dawn on me that these were the daily commuters whom the migrants had brought to my attention. During the coming months, I would learn that these women come from landless households in rural South 24-Parganas and commute on a daily basis to work as domestic servants or vegetable vendors in Calcutta. As I was to realize during the course of fieldwork in South Calcutta stations and in "commuter" villages in South 24-Parganas, their restless movement back and forth between country and city makes it hard to find or study them. My first afternoon at Jadavpur would turn out to be a fortuitous discovery—that the best opportunity to talk to commuter women is in the late afternoon at local stations when they are waiting to return home, usually gathered in shady waiting places close to where the "Ladies Only" compartments of southward trains stop.

Jadavpur is a fieldwork node. It yielded unanticipated linkages such as commuting and working daughters as well as unimagined geographies such as the resettlement colonies. These new and "grounded" categories also entailed a rethinking of my original categories, an analytical journey that revealed the logic of the field. Figure 2.1 is a crude representation of the idea of a fieldwork node.

This analytical diagram delineates two forms of the rural-urban interface, each implicated in the other: one is composed of distinctively gendered processes of permanent migration and daily commuting; the other involves patterns of rural-urban settlement in turn linked to questions of

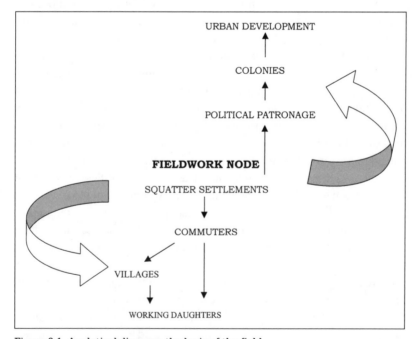

Figure 2.1. Analytical diagram: the logic of the field.

state, patronage, and the territorialized imperatives of liberalization. Unlike conventional migration studies where numerous places are linked to a central point through one type of process, fieldwork nodes such as Jadavpur point to how a few key rural-urban sites are linked to each other through a diversity of sociospatial processes. And unlike conventional studies of urban neighborhoods, Jadavpur's "field" shows that squatting, while initially condensing in discrete settlements, is only fully articulated in a restless geography of regional change. The multiplicity of these linkages raises the question of how the local is formed and transcended, stabilized and disrupted. This means thinking about localities as processes and about poverty as inherently relational. It is in this sense that fieldwork nodes are "places" in the space of poverty: "articulated moments in networks of social relations and understandings" (Massey 1993, 66).

In order to take account of such localizations of poverty, I eventually added the following research sites to my initial three squatter settlements:

1. Resettlement colonies: There are numerous colonies dotting the eastern fringes of Calcutta. The squatter settlements had linkages with three in the southeastern fringes: Jamunanagar, Sahid Colony, and Mukundapur (Figure A.1 in the appendix). All three colonies were established by the CPM during the last twenty-five years and have been used as sites for the periodic resettlement of squatters. These colonies also became a springboard for studying processes of urban development in the city's southeastern fringes.

2. Commuting: At the urging of my squatter informants, I decided to study commuting as a specific manifestation of the rural-urban interface. While there are numerous forms of commuting that tie Calcutta to the surrounding countryside, I conducted research within a narrow band: landless or near-landless peasants engaged in daily commuting. In keeping with my focus on South Calcutta, I chose five railway stations at which to establish contacts with commuters: Jadavpur, Dhakuria, Baghajatin, Garia, and Kalighat. Given the South Calcutta locations, 100 percent of the commuter men and women I studied came from villages in South 24-Parganas. As in the case of squatting, it soon became apparent that I was studying a set of linkages that had intensified during the last twenty years. The overwhelming majority of commuters whom I researched had started work in Calcutta during the last twelve to fifteen years. But the breathless

pace of commuting also meant that it was impossible to conduct any life histories or lengthy interviews with commuters at these stations. Furthermore, unlike squatter settlements or resettlement colonies where I could interview every member of a household or kinship network, in the case of commuters I had access to only individuals. Thus, in order to study commuter households and to situate them within a broader social context, I decided to conduct fieldwork in a commuter village, Bayarsin, of Taldi Gram Panchayat in the Canning block of South 24-Parganas (Figure A.2 in the appendix).

3. Working daughters: My search for commuter villages had first taken me to a village called Tetultola in the Mathurapur I block of South 24-Parganas (Figure A.2 in the appendix). On arriving in Tetultola, I realized that it was too far from any railway stations to allow daily commuting. But I soon discovered that a large number of Tetultola's 135 households, most of them landless and destitute, had forged other urban linkages: working daughters. These are young girls, ranging from ages seven to twenty-one, who are sent off to work as full-time maids in Calcutta, rarely returning to the village during their years of wage-earning work. Working daughters thus became an important part of my attempt to specify the rural-urban interface and its gendered dimensions.

It is important to note that I did not study each of these new categories with the same detail as I did the three fieldwork nodes of squatter settlements. I had continuous presence in the three squatter settlements and one colony, Jamunanagar, for a year. During the last four months of this time period I also began to investigate the transformation of the city's southeastern fringes. By contrast, my contact with commuters was more intermittent, usually in the late afternoons at South Calcutta railway stations as they waited for the trains. I spent a month intensively studying some of Bayarsin's commuter households. My stay at Tetultola was only a few days, and while I maintained contact with some of the working daughters in Calcutta, I do not include them in my presentation of findings, except when clearly specified. The details and limitations of these various strategies are discussed more fully in the methodological appendix.

Fieldwork Techniques

The thinness of secondary sources had meant that I could broach the issue of poverty only in terms of a very broad research question: how do the rural landless survive at the rural-urban interface? But, as I have already noted, this fuzziness turned out to be extremely valuable, allowing me to work with a flexible spatial concept and to eventually take note of all kinds of socio-spatial flows that defied conventional analytical boundaries. In particular, I have been keen to avoid what Sayer (1991, 301) identifies as a key fallacy of locality research, the sense that unique sites are seen as independent of one another, an assumption that informs much of the West Bengal debates. In defining discrete urban neigborhoods and neatly bounded villages, the urban surveys and agrarian studies have conceptualized a hierarchy of neat aggregation: households combining into villages, villages combining into districts, neighborhoods combining into cities. I have sought to present spatial interdependencies such that this is a sense of place constructed through "interaction rather than through closure" (Massey 1993, 146).

A crucial part of this methodological framework is also how the rela-tionality of poverty is recovered and understood. I started at the fieldwork nodes with a range of structured methods, conducting close-ended inter-views and organizing information through detailed questionnaires and tallies. I soon began to rely heavily on open-ended interviews. I thus present information on eighty-seven migrant and seventy-two commuter households. These are households that met specific methodological crite-ria: (a) that I had been able to collect detailed, and often quantitative, in-formation on such issues as income, consumption, migration, land owner-ship; and (b) in the case of migrants, that I had been able to conduct open-ended interviews with at least two adult members of the household, and often with children as well. I had to relax this second criterion in the case of commuters because it was often impossible to establish contact with all household members. I partly resolved this problem by conducting fieldwork in Bayarsin, where I had more prolonged contact with various members of each household.

While these qualitative methods gave me a general profile of the set-tlements, some of the most crucial moments in fieldwork were beyond their ken. Here, ethnographic methods including life histories became cru-cial, throwing the spotlight on the unanticipated categories and unimag-ined geographies that could be glimpsed at fieldwork nodes. I thus inter-pret the interview data in light of intensive ethnographic fieldwork with thirty-two—twenty-five migrant and seven commuter—households.

If the more structured qualitative methods outline the contours of poverty, then the ethnographic methods capture its sociospatial dynamics. In other words, ethnographies and life histories render the "everyday world as problematic," revealing the "extralocal determinations of experience that do not lie within the scope of everyday practices" (Smith 1989, 161).

As will become apparent in the following two sections, what characterizes this methodological strategy is not simply the use of ethnographic techniques but rather their deployment to interrogate the limits of quantitative indicators as well as structured qualitative methods such as surveys and open-ended interviews. It is the disjunctures between the static representations and dynamic narratives that point to the politics of poverty. In such cases, as Bourdieu (in Bourdieu and Wacquant 1992, 27–28) notes, the "truth" resides not in the "ordinary oppositions between theory and research, between quantitative and qualitative methods, between statistical recording and ethnographic observation, between the grasping of structures and the construction of individuals as social censorship," but "precisely in the relations between realms of practice thus arbitarily separated."

Poverty Indicators

What is poverty? How can it be measured? My subjects frequently talked about *abhab*—deprivation or scarcity.[8] But how is *abhab* to be understood and interpreted?

Perhaps the most common operationalization of poverty is the poverty line, which measures all households that fall below an established cutoff point. In India, national poverty lines were first set in 1958 establishing minimum per capita consumption expenditures for rural and urban areas (EPW 1993). Since that time, National Sample Surveys of consumption expenditure have provided national and state-level poverty headcount ratios. However, the poverty lines have been subject to great controversy, particularly regarding the use of price deflators and state-level variations. Thus, for the period 1977–78 to 1987–88, while Planning Commission figures show large drops in rural and urban poverty, other estimates demonstrate much smaller declines in poverty (Minhas et al. 1991; EPW 1993, 1752).

As summarized in Table 2.1, poverty estimates for West Bengal have been subject to similar controversies.[9] The differences between the three estimates of poverty are dramatic. Particularly striking are the high estimates of rural poverty yielded by Minhas et al.'s use of statewise deflators. With regard to urban poverty, the Expert Group estimates are considerably higher than the other two for 1983–84 and 1987–88, but it is the Minhas et al. estimate that shows an increase in urban poverty during this period. The 1987–88 state-level poverty figures of the Expert Group and Minhas et al. are also much higher than Planning Commission estimates.

In the West Bengal debates, poverty counts have been used primarily to

Table 2.1

Contrasting estimates of proportion of population in poverty, West Bengal

Years	Planning Commission	Expert group	Minhas et al.
		Rural	
Early 1970s	64.0 (1972–73)	61.4 (1973–74)	76.67 (1970–71)
1977–78	58.3	57.0	—
1983–84	43.8	51.0	65.87
1987–88	30.3	33.4	57.19
		Urban	
Early 1970s	35.9 (1972–73)	33.8 (1973–74)	33.07 (1970–71)
1977–78	34.5	37.9	—
1983–84	26.5	39.8	28.84
1987–88	20.7	33.6	30.63
		State	
Early 1970s	56.9 (1972–73)	54.5 (1973–74)	65.88 (1970–71)
1977–78	52.2	52.0	—
1983–84	39.2	47.9	55.92
1987–88	27.6	33.5	49.81

Sources: EPW 1993; Minhas et al. 1991.

buttress favorable evaluations of the Left Front regime. Dasgupta (1995) and Lieten (1996a) point to a decline in rural and urban poverty during the 1980s, emphasizing that the state greatly improved its performance compared to national averages. Village-level studies have sought to counter this view by presenting evidence of continuing poverty. However, the divergences in poverty estimates, summarized in Table 2.1, show that even the use of large-scale quantitative data can point to persistent, if not rising, poverty in the state. In other words, what matters is not only the scale or type of data used but also how categories are defined and operationalized. Dasgupta and Lieten rely exclusively on Planning Commission estimates as does the Statistical Bureau of the Government of West Bengal (*Statistical Report* 1994–95). Minhas et al.'s (1991, 1673) acerbic conclusion about the Planning Commission's national poverty estimates is thus equally applicable to the West

Bengal figures: "The massive reduction in the incidence of poverty in 1987–88, as reported by the Planning Commission in 1990, is once again largely a consequence of the peculiar statistical artefacts *[sic]* used by the Commission."

In fact, the Minhas et al. calculations show that not only was rural and urban poverty much higher in West Bengal than estimated by the Planning Commission but also that poverty levels in the state continue to be higher than national averages. In terms of total and rural poverty, these estimates rank the state as one of the poorest in the country.

Apart from these ongoing disagreements, there are also rather obvious problems with the poverty line. There is now a vast body of research that severely critiques the use of an absolute measure of poverty, of a cutoff line that does not capture the intensity and duration of poverty, and of a measure of consumption expenditure that ignores intrahousehold differences and nonmarket transactions (Lipton 1988; Guhan and Harriss 1992; Gaiha 1992; Chambers 1992, 1995; Bhalla and Lapeyre 1997; Kabeer 1994, 1999). Such critiques point to the need to find other measures of poverty. Here, I focus on the issue of landlessness, which is at the heart of the whole question of distress migration and commuting.

What Does It Mean to Be Landless?

As I have noted, there are ongoing disagreements regarding West Bengal's agrarian structure. One group of researchers, in keeping with the Left Front's claims, argues that the regime's reforms have ended landlordism and drastically reduced rural inequalities. A second group counters that the West Bengal countryside is marked by severe inequalities, including the rise of a new elite comprising mainly peasants with mid-sized landholdings.

The same divergence was echoed in squatter settlements and party offices in curious ways. Many high-ranking CPM party cadres, for example, refused to acknowledge that there are any landless migrants and commuters. When asked about squatter settlements, they insisted that all residents own land in their villages. In sharp contrast, migrants and commuters described themselves as landless. In life histories and interviews, an overwhelming majority emphasized that their desperate bids to forge urban strategies of survival were necessitated by the lack of land. Such disjunctures have become the very stuff of politics in settlements such as Patuli. Squatters claim rights to regularized plots on the basis of being landless. Neighborhood bosses seek to exclude those whom they insist own rural land: "We know who they are; we know their villages, and we can verify this information through our *panchayat* sources."

Neither the academic nor political disagreements are surprising because the very category of landholdings remains in dispute in West Bengal. In fact, the government of West Bengal does not produce a single reliable indicator of rural landlessness. The Agricultural Census measures distributions only in agricultural landholdings, completely bypassing the landless who have dropped out of the landholding structure. The landlessness data presented in the annually published *Economic Review* and summarized in the recent *Statistical Report* (1994–95) pertain only to rural households without homestead land and thus present extremely low counts. When ownership is restricted to cultivable or operational agricultural land, the estimates are considerably higher. For example, in the 43rd Round of the National Sample Survey, the first measure shows landlessness in 1987–88 at 9.6 percent for West Bengal and 11.1 percent for India. The second measure of cultivable land shows landlessness to be at 39.6 percent in West Bengal and 35.4 percent in India (*Sarvekshana* 1990).

Table 2.2
Contrasting estimates of rural landlessness, West Bengal

Type of household	1971–72	1981–82
Households without operational agricultural land	30.94%	22.14%
(Submarginal holdings)	(19.79%)	(38.51%)
Households without either agricultural or homestead land	9.78%	17.21%

Sources: National Sample Survey 1971–72, 1981–82; Westergaard 1986.

Table 2.2 shows how these different conceptualizations have produced divergent estimates of changing patterns of landlessness in West Bengal. Based on the ownership of homestead land, landlessness, according to the National Sample Survey of 1971–72, was only 9.78 percent. However, based on the ownership of operational agricultural land, landlessness was 30.94 percent. The 1981–82 NSS round shows an increase in the former to 17.21 percent and a drop in the latter to 22.14 percent. But much of the gains in the ownership of operational agricultural land come through a jump in submarginal holdings, from 19.79 percent to 38.51 percent. These figures indicate that the West Bengal land reforms, when effective, have mainly redistributed tiny parcels of land.

Such trends are borne out by Boyce (1987), who by using an occupational category instead of landholding measures, shows that, between 1951 and 1981, agricultural laborers as a percentage of West Bengal's rural labor force increased from 21.4 percent to 44.4 percent. He also emphasizes that during the same period, tenancy as a percentage of operated area dropped from 28.6 percent to 16.5 percent. Boyce thus characterizes this landscape as "disarticulated," consisting of small and fragmented holdings and a large proportion of "functionally landless" households.[10]

The controversy over landlessness has carried over into the evaluation of land reforms. Favorable evaluations of Left Front reforms invariably use the homestead measure of landlessness. For example, Dasgupta (1995, 2696) echoes the official government position in ranking West Bengal first in terms of the distribution of surplus land in India, stating that one million acres have been distributed to two million beneficiaries. What this grand statement obscures is that most of this land has been distributed in tiny and uncultivable parcels, often as homestead land. While Lieten (1996a) argues that the distribution of homestead land is a harbinger of change, other village-level studies using the ownership of agricultural land as a measure are less optimistic. From Bandyopadhyay's famous evaluation of land reforms (1985) to studies by Harriss (1993) and Beck (1994), landlessness figures persist at about 40 percent of village populations, with land redistribution having only a minimal impact.

My findings are in keeping with these estimates. Table 2.3 shows that

Table 2.3

Rural landholdings, migrant and commuter households

Landholding	Migrants	Commuters	Total
Operational agricultural land	2 (2.30%)	6 (8.33%)	8 (5.03%)
Redistribution	1 (1.15%)	1 (1.39%)	2 (1.26%)
Homestead only	70 (80.46%)	51 (70.83%)	121 (76.10%)
None or rural squatters	14 (16.09%)	14 (19.44%)	28 (17.61%)
Total	87	72	159

Source: fieldwork, 1997.

Note: Average operational landholding is 1.69 *bighas*. Average redistributed plot is 1.5 *bigha*. One *bigha* equals one-third of an acre.

about 5 percent of the migrants and commuters whom I interviewed own operational agricultural land. The benefits of redistribution through land reforms have been negligible, accruing to only 1.26 percent of the households. In the case of both operational and redistributed land, holdings are extremely small with an average of slightly over 1.5 *bighas*.[11] This is what Boyce (1987) refers to as "functionally landless," emphasizing the non-viability of such plots. For example, all eight commuter households who own operational land are unable to cultivate paddy. Instead, they grow vegetables to sell in city markets. What is most striking in Table 2.3 is the large number of migrant and commuter households that own only homestead land. If these households are excluded from landownership counts, landlessness for these groups is at 93.71 percent. On the other hand, if these households are included, landlessness drops to 17.61 percent.

The controversies over landownership have also become crucial in determining how political power is understood in the context of rural West Bengal. Take, for example, Kohli's 1983 survey of *panchayat* membership. He emphasizes that the majority of members had holdings between two and five acres (Kohli 1987). Mallick (1993, 140) reinterprets the same survey to show that an overwhelming majority of these small and middle peasants used hired labor and that none of them used only family labor. Acharya's (1994, 233) study of *panchayat* candidates, culled from West Bengal government reports, highlights the dominance not only of owner cultivators but also of teachers. How does this occupation fit the categories of landholdings? To this effect, the much-quoted Mukarji-Bandyopadhyay (1993, 16) report on *panchayats* broadens the idea of "middle peasants" to a "middle category of society"—constituted of small and middle peasants as well as schoolteachers.

I emphasize this issue of the *panchayats* to not only underscore how slippery the concept of landownership can be but also to point to the inherent limitations of quantitative measures. While the categories of *panchayat* membership have been endlessly debated and deconstructed, the more useful understandings of power in rural West Bengal have emerged from investigations of how *panchayats* work. It is here that one gets a sense of not only who owns how much land but also what it means to own this land. Bhattacharya (1995) and Ruud (1995), for example, have shown how the "middles" establish and maintain rural hegemony. Mukarji and Bandyopadhyay's (1993) careful documentation of the practices of *panchayats* also reveals the true implications of the dominance of the middle peasantry. They show the phenomenal growth of money controlled by these bodies, the lack of financial accountability, and the cozy alliances between bureaucracies and *panchayats*. While none of these studies speaks directly to the issue of poverty, they begin to sketch the contours of the larger rela-tionalities within which marginalization must be understood.

Profiles of Urban Poverty

If the question of land has come to be of paramount importance in the West Bengal agrarian debates, then the issue of housing has made its presence felt in much of the Calcutta surveys. In fact, housing has come to be seen as an indicator of standards of living (Bhattacharya and Chattopadhyay 1989, 54). From the findings of the National Sample Survey to census data, re-searchers have emphasized the persistently high levels of informal housing in Calcutta, an indicator, they argue, of the city's stubborn poverty. In 1966 the *Basic Development Plan*, drawn up by a distinguished panel of foreign and national consultants, stated, "Everywhere the picture so far as housing is concerned is one of deficit and deterioration. Overcrowding, congestion, insanitation, squatting—on public pavements, municipal refuse dumps, and indeed on any vacant site" (1966, 4).

Contemporary Calcutta seems to have changed little since this 1966 description of a "metropolis in crisis." Nath's (1994, 301) census-based es-timate of slum-dwellers in metropolitan cities shows that, in Calcutta, in 1991, 4.4 million people, or 39.8 percent of the city's population, lived in slums, a 15 percent increase since 1981. While all Indian metropolitan cities experienced similar increases, Calcutta had the highest number and pro-portion of slum-dwellers. Bose (1994) further points out that the 1991 cen-sus undercounted homeless and squatter populations. He estimates that the undercounting was approximately 10 percent in cities with populations of 100,000 and over and about 5 percent in other urban areas.

But like the measures of rural landownership, the urban data on housing has its own peculiar set of problems. Most important, it conflates very different kinds of housing under the broad category of *kutcha,* or informal dwellings, as in Ghosh's (1991, 144–45) summary of CMDA data, which shows how informal building far outpaces formal construction in Calcutta. But this broad rubric of informality tells us little about the spatial circuits of housing as a commodity. For example, it automatically relates socioeconomic status to housing. But, as in the case of Calcutta's pavement-dwellers, this connection can be rather weak. CMDA surveys, for example, show that the city's pavements are occupied by a wide diversity of groups, including many circular interstate migrants who wish to minimize con-sumption expenditures (Jagannathan and Halder 1988–89). In other words, they simply are not as poor as other pavement-dwellers.

Further, the idea of a generic informal housing, of a metropolis in housing crisis, fails to examine the varied conditions under which housing is acquired and negotiated. An obvious case is the difference between Calcutta's slums and squatter settlements, the former with regularized rights to land, and the latter with tenuous and revocable claims to residence. In both instances, rights and claims have to be negotiated and maintained, but the parameters within which such contestations take place are drastically different.

Table 2.4

Urban housing conditions: Migrant-squatter households

Type of household	Number of households	Percent of total
Squatters with infrastructure	33	37.93
Squatters without infrastructure	39	44.83
Resettlement colony	15	17.24
Total	87	

Source: fieldwork, 1997.
Note: Average resettlement plot is 1.4 *kathas.* One *katha* equals 720 square feet.

In Table 2.4 I summarize the housing status of the eighty-seven migrant households in my study, showing how each type of squatting represents a particular set of rights and claims. The 17 percent living in resettlement colonies have not only access to infrastructural services but also the promise, albeit fragile, of secure tenure and ownership. It is also important to note that while squatter settlements in general have dismal living conditions, almost 38 percent of study households were living in settlements with infrastructure, mainly in the form of electricity, drinking water, and toilets. Table 2.4 is provocative because it signals the struggles over housing that make possible this differentiation within the broader category of squatting.

Yet these variations are at best what Appadurai (1989, 254) terms a "distributional profile," capturing "outcomes of social processes rather than the structure of those processes themselves." In order to capture the politics of poverty, I had to move from structured qualitative methods, or profiles of poverty, to life histories, open-ended interviews, and ethnography, or the dynamics of poverty. It is to these that I now turn.

Negotiated Access to Urban Land

In this section I draw on life histories and ethnographic encounters to detail the process of migration. But before I do so, it is important to draw attention to one important aspect of the form of these life histories. I had initially expected the life histories to reveal agrarian differentiation in great specificity. But over and over again, in different settlements and different contexts, my subjects repeatedly focused on urban struggles, ignoring many of my questions about their villages and rural employment. On 20 February 1997, a couple of months into fieldwork, I wrote my frustrations in my field journal:

> I abandoned both the questionnaire and life history today. I had first found the questionnaire to be a static tool, unable to capture change or interpretations of change. It was useful only to jog the memory—often my memory—to obtain certain detailed information. But the life history method requires a certain privacy that is lacking. I can't get people to contemplate on their rural histories. I am getting a great deal of rich detail about urban life but little about agrarian conditions even from recent migrants. And my constant prodding seems to be at odds with the very idea of life histories.

I was initially concerned that the thin descriptions of rural life had to do with the urban setting of the research project. I was clearly an urbanite asking questions in the immediacy of the city. During initial fieldwork encounters, my subjects would often not tell me the exact names of their villages and would be surprised when I would insist on knowing. What did it matter? Did I even know their village? Weren't they all the same to me? And always hovering in the background, and often pushing their way to the fore, were expectations of help in navigating urban bureaucracies—procuring ration cards, birth certificates. These interactions were predicated on a detailed accounting of specific aspects of urban life. In other words, these life histories were, as Bertaux-Wiame (1981) emphasizes, inevitably "present" histories: the past interpreted in light of the present.

But after a while I began to realize that there was a particular form and structure to the life histories, to the manner in which they frame the moment of migration. This was especially evident in the case of the thirty-two migrant and commuter households that I studied in greater depth. Here, as in the other life histories, agrarian histories are discussed in broad brushstrokes, often with a sense of tremendous resignation. In contrast, the negotiation of access to urban shelter is presented in detail. In these discourses, if the institutions of the village, such as the *panchayat,* are presented as impenetrable, then the urban is constructed as a realm of political relationships and claims, of dealing with the *sarkar* or state. I thus present a few excerpts from different life histories to present the moment of migration as it is framed by squatters: as a transition from rural marginalization to urban participation, from being victims of structures to being political agents.

Nokul

I first met thirty-nine-year-old Nokul late one spring afternoon in Jadavpur. He was leaning against his shack on a set of makeshift wooden crutches. He looked as if he were about sixty years old. As the trains roared by on the tracks only a few feet away and the stench from the stagnant pond intensified with the heat, he began to talk about the settlement and the possibility of eviction. "No, start from the beginning. Tell me where you are from," I insisted.

> **NOKUL:** My village is in the Dakhin Barasat block of South 24-Parganas. I had lived all my life there. My brother and mother still live there. My father died about five years ago. As far as I can remember, we never owned any agricultural land. We had a small homestead plot. My father did not own any agricultural land and we all live crowded in the small homestead. Every time I go back it is as if I cannot breathe. It is like a heavy hand on my heart. It is crowded here in this tiny shack with all of us—I have four children, you know—but it not as crowded as in the village. I watched my father work as an agricultural laborer. But there was no work for me. There is only one crop a year in our village. It has been that way since I can remember. Three months of work per year and then hunger, terrible hunger. My father started migrating to Hooghly district for work during the lean season. We would not hear from him for months. He had no way of sending us money. Many of the men in our village would do this. But we remained hungry. He would usually come back with some money and we would buy some rice. When I turned seventeen, my father took me with him to Hooghly. We worked in villages where they were growing vegetables. But there were so many of us. We did not always find work. And then I had a family to take care of. I left as soon as I could, fourteen years ago . . .
>
> Yes, I go back once a year for about two or three days. Just to see what's left of my family. My brother works as an agricultural laborer. When there is work he gets Rs 35 a day with one meal of *panta bhat*. His wife does not work. There is no work for her . . .
>
> Vested land? Sure the *panchayat* gave people land. Five

households in my village got land—tiny plots of land—they will be perhaps able to build a second hut on it or grow some vegetables . . .

I came to Calcutta with my entire family ten years ago. We lived on the railway platform for a few days. At that time, no one chased us away from the platforms. Now if you sit there for too long, some party or union will come and ask you for *chanda* [dues]. I found work doing *jogar* [casual construction labor] after about ten days. When we were living on the platform, I noticed all of these shacks built nearby. We began to gather together material—tarpaulin, discarded plastic bags, old tires. We would often have to fight for them, sort through the piles of garbage. But we built a shack. I guess it was more of a tent than a shack. The party took care of us . . .

Which party? The CPM. They have a club nearby—over there down that street. They would come to us during elections. We always voted for them. And they promised us that they would not evict us. But then, about seven years ago, they came to us and said that we would have to move. The *sarkar* [government] was building a bridge. This one that you now see. They told us to move our shacks next to the tracks. We met with the club leaders every day. I remember this so clearly. We were scared. But they kept reassuring us. One day, a *neta* [leader] came and he told us that if we moved to this strip of land by the tracks, no one would be able to harm us. The land belongs to the railway and they had no clubs or people to evict us. And so we moved. The other side of the tracks already had older shacks. They have electricity and now the party is building toilets for them. We don't have any of this. But perhaps we will. The party is good to us, but not to all of us . . .

Why do I say this? Because half of the families who lived in the old settlement got land in a colony—land that they own. They still come to this area to work. I meet some of them. But others like me got nothing. I don't know why. Why this stepmotherly treatment?

Sahapada

I came to know Sahapada's family well over the course of the eight months during which I frequented the Chetla settlement. They lived at the end of a pencil-thin alleyway that wound itself between tight shacks and filled up with smoke, excrement, and garbage on a daily basis. By the time I met thirty-four-year-old Sahapada I had already spent quite a bit of time at his home, with his wife, Nibarani, and their two young children. Nibarani, who works as a domestic servant, had talked to me at great length about her work, the rhythms of her daily life, and her children. But each time I talked to her about her village and the settlement, she asked me to talk to her husband. "I don't know how to talk about these matters," she would gently respond. "They are men's issues."

> **SAHAPADA:** You want to know about Mathurapur? Are you sure? What is there to tell? My father owned two *bighas* of land. But we were four brothers. Each of us had a family. What is there to tell beyond that? We got one more *bigha* of land. Vested land. The *zamindar* [landlord] never allowed us to take over that land. He used to own hundreds of *bighas* of land in our village and neighboring ones. He must have bribed the *panchayat*. He even hired his own strongmen. They would threaten us. He asked us for Rs 2000 but we did not have that kind of money. There were talks of murders in the neighboring village. My father said that we should be satisfied with what we have. Is this what you want to know? The *sarkar* has no way of getting to the villages, of getting to us, and so we have come to it here . . .
>
> I came to Calcutta twelve years ago. I have two sisters and we sold our two *bighas* of land to marry them off, for the family honor. Now three of my brothers have also moved to Calcutta. There was nowhere for them to even live in the village.
>
> I first rented a room in Kalighat. But I had to pay Rs 100 a month. Where could I find this kind of money? I sell "Pepsi"[12] for a living. And so I heard about this place through the local club. I paid Rs. 2000 to the club in dues and bought this shack from someone who was moving out for another Rs 1000. That was all of the money I had brought with me from the village and from selling my wife's jewelry. Now, this place is ours. We don't have any running water. My wife complains about this every day. I go to the club every day. Party leaders come there at least once a week. They can't provide us with water. The women just don't understand. This is port trust land. The port trust authority has to provide the taps. What can the CPM do? They are trying. Last year, they got us electricity. Here, see, we were able to pull these lines and run a bulb. The club does good work. They hold a big celebration once a year, during the festivals, with the money they raise. We all come together as a community. I stopped going to the village. What is the point?

Dhiren

Dhiren's "quarter" was unlike most of the others at Patuli. Not only was it one of the larger ones with two rooms, it also had a bed, television, and radio. Twenty-four-year-old Dhiren lived in one of the rooms with his wife and two young children. His nineteen-year-old unmarried brother lived in the second room. Dhiren comes from a village in the Diamond Harbor block of South 24-Parganas district.

> **DHIREN:** Sure, in my village, the "original poor" got land. The real poor. But what can the *sarkar* do? There isn't enough land to get rid of poverty. I came to Calcutta eight years ago. I was very young. I worked hard in *jogar* and saved some money. I thought I would go back to the village and start a shop maintaining bicycles. But business was terrible and I came back three years ago. I then focused on finding a place here. Some people from my village were living in these quarters and I took over an empty one. You want to know what my village is like? Ask all of the poor women who commute every day on those god-forsaken trains. They don't have a place like this . . .
>
> I still keep my ration card in the village. My parents use it to get some cheap foodgrains and survive. It is one of the few ways in which I can take care of them.
>
> I have to be honest with you. In my village, I was hardcore CPM. As I said, they looked after the original poor. But here, I have to be Congress. They are in charge of this settlement now. They have filed a case on our behalf in the High Court. I send my brother to help the club whenever possible. This is his duty. We are fighting a war against the CPM here. The *sarkar* is not guilty but it has to be pressurized.

Kartik

I introduced Kartik earlier in this chapter. He was the forty-two-year-old gaunt rice trader who had a stall in Sandhyabazar, the informal market at Jadavpur station. He was also the first to draw my attention to the existence of "colonies" like Jamunanagar. Over time, I came to know Kartik and his family in both Jadavpur and Jamunanagar. If in Jadavpur Kartik had outlined his roots in a landless and destitute family, in Jamunanagar he historicized his settlement in Calcutta.

> **KARTIK** (in Jadavpur): *Desher maya*[13]—that's what I had. I had watched my father being poor and hungry all of his life. But I loved my village. When they said that they were going to build fisheries, I believed the *panchayat*. So what if there was no agricultural work? This was Canning. We could have fisheries. Many small farmers began selling their land to the fisheries. We had even less work now. And the fisheries were all taken over by relatives of *panchayat* members. None of us got even a job. And in the process we lost

whatever common land the village had. We could not catch any fish, could not even bathe in what once belonged to all of us.

(in Jamunanagar): I never return to the village. It is a savage place. This is now *desh*. This place. When I came to Calcutta fifteen years ago, I had a great deal of strength. For two years, I pulled rickshaws, pulled hand carts. But then I got TB and my body broke. My wife worked in *jogar*, but she made such little money. I had heard about Sandhyabazar and managed to get a stall. The CPM gave me a card. They allowed me to build a shack nearby. There was a huge fire about twelve years ago and we lost everything we had. Everything. We just sat there by the tracks and watched. But we rebuilt.

And then one day, seven years ago, Kanti*babu* came to us. Do you know him? For us, he is the party. Without him, the CPM would be nothing. He told us that the *sarkar* was building a bridge and we would have to move. But he promised us land, a new *desh*. I don't think I believed him but he came with trucks that brought us here. I remember when Kanti*babu* came to check on us. He came up to me and put his hand on my shoulder, and said, "Kartik, do you trust me now?" I remember it clearly as if it was only yesterday.

Framing the Moment of Migration

What do these excerpts from life histories of Calcutta squatters reveal? How do they speak to issues of rural marginalization and urban access?

The life histories, buttressed by my data on a total of eighty-seven migrant households, indicate a flurry of distress migration from the villages of South 24-Parganas into Calcutta during the last twenty years. Unlike the circular migration of single males, this seems to involve the permanent movement of nuclear households. While such flows are coincident with the period of Left Front rule, it is impossible to conclude that the regime "caused" such distress migration. Instead, the life histories point to the fragile survival of landless and near-landless households where a range of events, from dowry payments to property divisions, can trigger distress migration. In such cases, a homestead plot seems to be of little use, directly contradicting Lieten's (1996a, 113) claim that "obviously insufficient to make a living, homestead land is none the less of enduring importance, both in checking migration, and in providing a secure living space."

Perhaps most striking about the life histories is that they indicate not how the Left Front affected the lives of these poor households but instead how untouched their fates were by state and party. The narratives reveal the obvious limits of redistribution in a land-poor state, the sense of there not being enough vested land to go around, of redistributed plots being ridiculously small. But more important, they show the widespread dismissal of *panchayats* as inevitably and undeniably corrupt, distributing resources to a favored few, interpreted by the migrants as taking place behind the backs of the *sarkar,* or state. This is particularly evident in Kartik's story of the fisheries—of deal-makings by *panchayat* members and the loss of common lands to which the poor had enjoyed customary access. This was a narrative that I heard repeated over and over, particularly in the context of the southern reaches of South 24-Parganas, where fisheries are becoming an important means of nonagricultural diversification.

The question of the fisheries highlights the issue of employment, or rather the lack thereof, in the villages of South 24-Parganas. Most of the West Bengal village-level studies have chosen to focus either on high-growth districts such as Burdwan or on high-profile poor districts such as Mednipur and Purulia. South 24-Parganas is more of a middle-range district, with its proportions of agricultural wage-labor (49.6 percent in 1981) and tenancy (17.8 percent) closely approximating state averages (44.4 percent and 16.5 percent; Boyce 1987; *Economic Review* 1994–95).

A chief constraint in South 24-Parganas has been irrigation, and in 1981 irrigated plots were only 21.5 percent of gross cropped area as compared to 45.5 percent for the state (Boyce 1987). This is amply evident in the life histories, where migrants repeatedly noted the prevalence of single-cropping and the seasonality of agricultural work. On the matter of wages, the life histories neither support Mallick's (1993) contention of falling real wages nor support Harriss's (1993) or Lieten's (1996b) findings of Left Front support for wage action. In effect, they bear out Webster's (1990) conclusion of "static agrarian relations."

In sharp contrast to the resigned descriptions of inevitably oppressive agrarian structures, the life histories provide animated details of how access to urban shelter is negotiated. And these details provide important insights into the dynamics of squatter settlements. In the case of Jadavpur, the narratives of Nokul and Kartik reveal an uneven and volatile geography of patronage. Nokul's family, like thirty-five others, were relocated by the CPM onto land owned by the railway authority, a public agency with weak local presence and thus unlikely to press immediate evictions. But Nokul is aware that families like Kartik's did a lot better than his: they were granted plots of land in the colonies, the opportunity to create a new *desh* under the watchful protection of party stalwarts. Sahapada reveals the growing commercialization of access to the Chetla settlement and the mediation of the settlement club in such transactions as well as in the provision of infrastructure. Dhiren bravely and forthrightly frames the migration moment as a switch in loyalties from CPM to Congress, an indication of Patuli politics as well as of his personal sense of newfound political agency.

These narratives, while quite different in the details of how access to urban shelter was negotiated, are strikingly similar in three respects. First, they all point to the fundamental importance of the political sponsorship of squatting as well as the fragilities of such patronage.

Second, the life histories point to a specific sociospatial relationality that was unanticipated in the separate sets of rural and urban landownership and housing data. In particular, they indicate the connections between Tables 2.3 and 2.4, pointing to the ways in which the rural landless come to live in squatter settlements. On the one hand, the relationality points to migration as a transition to unprecedented political and economic access—this is how migrants frame the moment. Compare, for example, Table 2.4's count of redistributed land in the urban colonies, a hearty 17 percent, with the meager 1 percent of rural beneficiaries in Table 2.3. On the other hand, this access is particularly poignant because it occurs under conditions of fragile dependence. Such connections mark Calcutta's squatter settlements as fundamentally different from the city's slums, which are characterized by high proportions of small and middle peasants as well as by regularized urban access. They thus indicate the specificity of distress migration, a set of sociospatial relations that remain unnoticed in much of Calcutta's surveys, with their focus on slums.

The third commonality has to do with the form of the life histories: that they are all stories told by men. I was often unable to get women to talk about migration and settlement histories. After a particularly harrowing day in the Chetla settlement, I wrote:

> I cannot get the women to talk about politics. I know some of them well by now—Boolan, Nibarani. They act as if they don't even know the names of different parties. Or that they don't care. And then of course they lead such harried existences—I catch them between morsels of boiled rice and the tugs of hungry children. I trail behind them as they collect water, wash clothes, wash children, and above all, earn money.
>
> It is with the men that I have a lot of quiet time, that we can ponder issues of state and party. I am always sure to find them at the club playing cards or just chatting. Talking about politics seems to reinforce their sense of themselves as guardians of the community.

What is striking then about these narratives of migration is not just their content but also their form and idiom. As Bertaux-Wiame (1981, 259) notes, if the "facts of the story" reveal "social relations in action," then the forms "reveal the shape of the mind . . . for it is through ideology and culture that interpretations are given to the real conditions of existence." In the rest of this section, I will build on what is revealed by these migration/male histories: that the negotiation of access to urban land is simultaneously a negotiation within households.

Swapan and Sumitra

I came to know Sumitra and Swapan, a middle-aged couple and migrants from South 24-Parganas, in the context of the Patuli settlement. I had initially conducted separate life histories with them and they had echoed the broader pattern of Swapan, relating the details of their migration and settlement history. But one afternoon, two months after I had first met them, as I sat with them in their one-room quarter, the sun streaming in through fading posters of past Congress rallies, they indicated a different, and contested, interpretation of this history.

> **SWAPAN:** Yes, we migrated from Sarbaria near Basanti ten years ago. We own a homestead plot with a little hut. Since no one lives in it now, I go back to check on it every six months.
>
> **SUMITRA:** I am from Gorijala near Diamond Harbor. Before I migrated here I had to migrate to his village after our marriage. My father was a landless laborer. I worked all my life. Not work that I got paid for. But I tended cattle, made cowdung cakes. All alongside my mother.
>
> **SWAPAN:** She doesn't want to know about your stupid household duties as a child. I have already told her about the village. And it's all the same. Everywhere you go in our *Sonar Bangla*—no work, smaller and smaller plots of land. Rs 40 a day and *panta bhat*. That is where things stand now. But only when there is work. And when there isn't, at times rich peasants are kind. Those who own 5–6 *bighas* of land will at times give some rice so that we don't die.
>
> **SUMITRA:** I got married when I was fifteen. My fate. From one landless household to another. All my life I have been foraging, searching—for vegetables, firewood, anything of value.
>
> **SWAPAN:** As if your family had dowry money for anything else.
>
> **SUMITRA:** Well, my father gave you a bicycle and a watch, didn't he?

SWAPAN: Yes, as if that can feed our stomachs. Twelve years ago, I started working as a porter in Sealdah. I would commute on the local trains. And I saw these quarters from the train. No one seemed to occupy them. And so I got off one day at Garia station and walked here. A few weeks later I packed up my family and moved.

SUMITRA: No, you noticed the quarters because my mother was working as *jogar* in a construction site nearby. She told us about it. She even came and looked at the quarters. We owe this to her. That's how my sister moved her. See that *kuji* over there. That is hers. She lives there with her husband and her two children.

SWAPAN: We are all allowed to live here because of my connections with the club. They respect me. That's why your sister could build this *kuji*. We had a meeting three days ago with Congress leaders. They will give us ownership of these quarters. We will finally be rewarded for our loyalties.

There are many important aspects to this contested reinterpretation of migration and settlement histories. Sumitra's attempt to cast the process of migration as one of older lineage, dating to the moment of marriage, raises questions about a whole set of practices that are well beyond the scope of this study. Equally interesting is Swapan's assertion of the similarity of all villages—they are all equally oppressive—a homogenization that is in keeping with the form of these life histories.

However, the aspect that I want to draw attention to is the disagreement between Sumitra and Swapan regarding access to the Patuli settlement. Sumitra emphasizes the importance of feminized kinship networks. In fact, such networks are strikingly apparent in Patuli and seem to have made possible its expansion and entrenchment. They are even apparent in the physical structure of the settlement. The first round of migrants had occupied the one- and two-room core units, with families often spreading out over multiple units. When the core units ran out, new migrants began squatting in makeshift expansions on the front yards of their relatives. These tentlike shacks came to be known as *kujis* or "hunchbacks," and each ensemble of core unit and *kuji* came to symbolize the ties of kin.

Many of these intergenerational kinship networks are maintained and nurtured by women and are especially crucial in the face of polygamy and male abandonment. Such networks are also apparent in the connections between Jamunanagar colony and Jadavpur settlement, where families have managed to maintain access to different plots of land through stretched kinship networks. Such claims are what Indra and Buchignani (1997) call "extended entitlements," or what Agarwal (1990) calls "social security."

Figure 2.2. A Patuli *kuji.*

In contrast, Swapan asserts the importance of his participation in settlement politics as the chief reason for their ability to establish access to Patuli. His dismissal of the role of kinship networks is ironically borne out by the dynamics of many of Patuli's families, such as Sakila's clan.

Sakila's Clan

Sakila Bibi and her husband, migrants from Lakshikantapur, moved into their two-room core unit in Patuli twelve years ago. They had migrated to Calcutta thirteen years ago and had initially rented a room near the Park Circus railway tracks. They had found out about the vacant Patuli quarters while doing *jogar* in the area. About a year ago Sakila's eldest daughter, Rekha, got married and moved in with her husband. In a *kuji* precariously propped up in Sakila Bibi's front yard lives her sister, Ambiya Bibi, and her three young children. Ambiya was abandoned by her husband ten years ago and migrated to Calcutta, seeking shelter at Patuli. When I first met the family, Ambiya's eldest daughter, Amirjan Bibi, had just migrated to Calcutta with her baby daughter and husband in tow. A new tent made of bamboo splinters and discarded cloth bags was rapidly being built on the last piece of vacant land in Sakila Bibi's plot. During each of my numerous visits to Patuli, Amirjan proudly showed off the progress on her *kuji,* posing with her daughter in it when it was finally completed, just in time for the monsoons.

Figure 2.3. Amirjan and her baby posing in their completed *kuji*, Patuli settlement.

As in the case of Sumitra and Swapan, life histories with various members of Sakila's clan revealed the ways—albeit contested—through which kinship facilitated squatting. However, it was only through an ethnographic presence that I was able to observe the dynamics of such networks. If life histories revealed the relationalities of poverty—the ensemble of rights and claims—then the drama of fieldwork pointed to the processual and volatile nature of such claims.

As Amirjan's *kuji* was being constructed, so the conditions for its dismantlement were brewing. The settlement was facing the possibility of formalization, with generous promises being made by the Congress party. One afternoon, Ambiya took me aside, confiding: "They are drawing up lists of names. They came the other day and took Sakila's name, Rekha's name, and my name. But they did not take Amirjan's. They said that she hasn't been here long enough." A few days later, Sakila rendered her opinion: "They will give only one quarter to each family. But we have become such a huge family. We can't all live cramped in this one quarter. Rekha shares her earnings with me. Ambiya and Amirjan don't. So how is one to define one's family?"

Over the next two months the conflict over formalization intensified. As the party drew up lists, it sought to eliminate those who supposedly owned land in the village. The contested definition of landlessness that has haunted the West Bengal debates became a key instrument of exclusion.

SAKILA: Ambiya is poor. I know that. Her husband left her. But Amirjan is married to a boy who has land. They should move back to his village.

(Later that afternoon)
AMBIYA: We all have equal rights to this place because no one has any rights at all. We are all squatters.

(Still later that afternoon)
AMIRJAN: What land? My husband's family has a tiny homestead— one hut for eight people. I would rather live out here on the open fields. We don't talk to Sakila anymore.

The battles within Sakila's clan were repeated in numerous Patuli families. During the negotiation of formalization, only 900 quarters were available for 2,500 families. The proliferation of claims provided tremendous fuel for a growing factionalism within the Congress, leading to evictions. However, they also revealed the shakiness of kin and village networks during moments of crisis. The promise of formalization in Patuli proved to be one such crucial juncture with colliding claims to patronage and territory. Here, households and extended networks underwent drastic change, shrinking, recombining, and even dissolving. Such vulnerabilities are also evident in the case of commuter women, many of whom describe how male abandonment has ended their possibilities of ever forging access to urban shelter.

Reena

I first met Reena in Bayarsin village in Taldi *Gram Panchayat* early one spring evening. The heat of the late afternoon was already unbearable. She was lying sprawled out on the porch of a mud hut, having just finished a two-hour commute back from Calcutta. Three children clamored around her while she wearily breastfed her youngest, a two-year-old girl, and tearfully chided her five-year-old son. The young girl, left under the charge of the boy, had nearly drowned in one of the village ponds that day.

I had come to Bayarsin looking for a base village in which to study a few commuter households. Hitherto I had studied commuters in the madness of Calcutta stations and railway trains, but I wanted to be able to situate them within a rural context.

Bayarsin is part of Taldi *Gram Panchayat,* a collection of four villages, which in 1991 had a total population of 31,981. The head of the *panchayat* estimated that 60 percent of the population did not own any operational agricultural land, and that a large proportion did not even own any homestead land. This was particularly apparent in Bayarsin, where about one-third of the households squatted on the banks of a stream or *khaal*. Almost every single one of these *khaaler paar* households survived on the earnings of commuter members, mainly women. The panchayat head put it this way: "Women of all ages from eight to sixty commute. In some cases, young girls are sent off to the city to work as servants. There are hardly any women left in our villages. When we try to hold a meeting here, or to start a program for women, it is useless, because there is no one to attend."

I had initially chosen Taldi because it was the site of a major World Bank fishery project. But the scheme was stalled because the *panchayats,* with a few exceptions such as Taldi, repeatedly failed to meet the selection criteria of the Bank, submitting lists that were blatantly corrupt. And even in Taldi, *panchayat* officials expressed the realities of the World Bank project, saying that if successful, it would benefit only forty men and women, thus having little impact on employment.

It is not surprising, then, that the matter of fisheries is of little concern for Reena. Twenty-two years old, she has been commuting for two years. Her husband abandoned her and now has a second wife. Homeless for all of this time, Reena lives on the narrow open-air porch of her uncle's boarded-up hut.

> I have been working since I was fifteen. As a domestic servant in Calcutta. This same grinding commute to the city. My family did not own any land and my earnings were important. At least my employers would feed me so that I would not have to come home and eat anything.
>
> I got married when I was seventeen. I had thought that I would not have to work. But my husband refused to work. He refused to even look for work. My parents had given him a bicycle as dowry and so I thought that we could save money and buy a van to attach it to the bicycle. I would give him my earnings but he spent them. I don't know on what. There wasn't even money to buy milk for the children. I was getting tired, so tired. One day, at Dhakuria station, I collapsed. There were some other women from our village who brought me home. This incident allowed me to convince my husband that we should move closer to Calcutta. We decided to rent a room in Champahati[14] for Rs 75 a month. Other families were doing that—the women on the trains had told me about it. I was earning about Rs 300 a month. Rents were too high in Calcutta . . .
>
> Squatting? We did not dare consider it. We did not know anyone who lived in a squatter settlement. We did not know where to

start to get access to one of those places. I guess if my husband had been smarter. But none of this matters, for suddenly one day, three years ago, he was gone. Rumor has it that he is living with a woman in Dhapa.[15] After all this time, the irony is that he moved to Calcutta. And I am left here. All my honor was gone. I took my three children and moved to Narendrapur.[16] My sister and brother-in-law lived there. My sister works as a domestic servant and my brother-in-law does *jogar*, but he always manages to find steady work. I was pregnant and since my husband abandoned me in this condition, they were worried about gossip. I would have had an abortion if I had the money or the time. But the pregnancy was too far advanced. I wished that the child would die. But she didn't. Her misfortune and mine.

When I came back to Bayarsin, I had nowhere to live. A distant uncle of mine allowed me to live out here, on the porch of his boarded-up hut. Regardless of cold, heat, or rain, this is where my four children and I live, in the open. I leave at 4:30 every morning and return at 5 in the evening. They take care of each other. There is no one to take them to school. No one to feed them.

The last time I talked to Reena, it was at Baghajatin station. I was surprised to see her there because she usually commuted to Dhakuria station. She was carrying a huge bundle of twigs:

I came here to collect these. At least here there is some open land near the station. In the village, I can't find fuelwood anymore. I have to beg with other families to forage on their lands. Or we have to buy everything. Here in the city, at least, one can go through the garbage of the rich and find a few things to sell to the recycling plant. One can pick up a fallen branch and take it home to light a fire. One can't do that in the village.

She told me that she forages for fuelwood in the city at least once a week. In order to carry these bundles back on the crowded southbound trains, she has to take a northbound train to the Sealdah terminal, board an empty southbound train, and then head to her village. It is an excruciatingly long ride on the overflowing trains. Reena was extremely restless that afternoon, scanning the station while she talked to me: "Whenever I am in Calcutta, I look for him. At every station. At times I see someone who resembles him. At times, my tired eyes are mistaken. And my heart begins to pound thunderously."

Reena's story draws attention to a few key issues. It confirms the fragile vulnerabilities of the rural landless that emerged in the other life histories. Particularly striking are the limitations of agricultural wage-labor. At Calcutta's railway stations, when I would ask women commuters like Reena why they were commuting, they would always respond that this was a silly question. Another woman from Bayarsin put it thus: "If there was work in the villages, would we come this far? Across all this distance. All these stations. The only women who can afford to stay at home are those whose husbands have salaried jobs and those who have been given land by the government."

Equally evident was the steady attrition of access to common property resources. Reena's attempt to collect fuelwood in the city, a practice that surprised me, was quite widespread. In fact, Beck (1994) estimates that such sources of livelihood, involving activities such as the collecting of fuelwood, gleaning for paddy, and fishing in ponds, constitute a crucial source of income—between 19 percent and 29 percent—for poor households, and particularly for poor women. Commuting then allows access not only to urban work but also to common property resources no longer available in villages.

But perhaps the most important aspect of Reena's story is the implication of male abandonment. Like many commuters, she felt that squatting was out of her reach but that the renting of a room in towns near Calcutta was a welcome possibility. The disappearance of her husband completely undermined that option. Her short stay with her sister points to the fragility of feminized kinship networks and the quick erosion of these claims. Reena's case poignantly reveals the ways in which the negotiation of access to urban shelter is simultaneously a negotiation within households.

Negotiating Household Income

The negotiation of households as a crucial component of the politics of poverty draws attention to two issues. The first is that households as contested aggregations matter, and that while they need to be deconstructed, the conditions under which they are formed also need to be examined. Second, this means that seemingly straightforward poverty measures such as household income or consumption are in fact slippery concepts. In this section, I take on this latter issue, showing the importance of problematizing such aggregate measures.

In Table 2.5 I present two measures of the household income of the migrants and commuters in my study. Income 1 is based on the earnings of all household members while Income 2 is based on the contributions of all household members to household income. The difference between the two measures has to do with variations in individual expenditure. A large part of the income-contributions gap is constituted by male earnings that are diverted to other households as well as those that are spent on individualized consumption.

If household income estimates demonstrate the labor market vulnerability of household types, then the income-contributions gap reveals relations within the household. Table 2.5 indicates that in the case of both migrant and commuter groups, female-earner households have the lowest per capita incomes while multiple-earner households have the highest per capita incomes. The low income levels of both male- and female-earner households are related to the labor market vulnerability of these groups, and in the case of the latter, gendered occupational and wage differentials. It is only in the case of multiple-earner households that these effects are somewhat offset, but average income levels still remain below poverty lines.

The emphasis on an income-contributions gap raises the issue of intrahousehold vulnerabilities, which resonates with widespread criticism of the poverty line for its failure to take into account the intrahousehold distribution of resources (Guhan and Harriss 1992, 20). A growing body of research on work burdens and access to resources within households shows the persistence of gender inequalities (Sen 1988; Harriss-White 1990; Bardhan 1993). Feminist theorists such as Agarwal (1995) have urged the use of alternative measures of poverty. In a study on regional variations of poverty in India, she uses sex ratios, female labor force participation rates, and fertility rates in combination with poverty rates to assess the statewise vulnerability of poor women. In the case of West Bengal, she finds that despite a fair degree of progress during the 1971–1991 period, the state still demonstrates high vulnerability for poor women, echoing a larger regional pattern of gender discrimination.

I take on these issues more fully in the following chapter, where I emphasize how the feminization of livelihood is a crucial dimension of the persistence of poverty. Here, I want to focus on the income-contributions gap, which is so evident in multiple-earner and male-earner households. The life histories provide a rather vivid picture of such gendered differences.

Sundari and Gobinda

At the Jadavpur settlement I spent a lot of time in Sundari's shack, sitting atop a great high bed that filled most of the room. It was their prized possession. Stretched across the walls were rusted wires from which hung a few tattered clothes—two saris, three shirts, a few clothes for the children. I would usually find Sundari alone in the afternoon between 1 and 3 P.M., between her two shifts of domestic service, as she would cook the afternoon

Table 2.5

Monthly income of migrant and commuter household types (in rupees)

Households and income	Migrants	Commuters	Total
	ALL		
Number of households	87	72	159
Average household size	4.7	4.8	4.7
Average household income 1	797.36	710.49	757.39
Per capita income 1	*169.61*	*148.71*	*159.93*
Average household income 2	682.47	632.98	656.60
Per capita income 2	*145.17*	*132.48*	*138.64*
	Multiple earner		
Number of households	59 (67.81%)	25 (34.72%)	84 (52.83%)
Average household size	5.0	5.2	5.1
Average household income 1	949.32	1014.40	968.69
Per capita income 1	*189.22*	*193.59*	*190.56*
Average household income 2	792.87	867.80	815.18
Per capita income 2	*158.04*	*165.61*	*160.36*
	Female earner only		
Number of households	24 (27.59%)	40 (55.56%)	64 (40.25%)
Average household size	3.8	4.5	4.3
Average household income 1	427.50	506.13	476.64
Per capita income 1	*111.52*	*112.47*	*112.15*
Average household income 2	425.83	504.18	474.80
Per capita income 2	*111.09*	*112.04*	*111.72*
	Male earner only		
Number of households	4 (4.60%)	7 (9.72%)	11 (6.92%)
Average household size	5.3	4.7	4.9
Average household income 1	775.00	792.86	786.36
Per capita income 1	*147.62*	*168.18*	*160.19*
Average household income 2	593.75	594.64	594.36
Per capita income 2	*113.10*	*126.14*	*121.07*

Source: fieldwork, 1997.

Notes: "Multiple earner" category includes all wage-earning work by children. Income 1 equals all income earned by household members. Income 2 equals actual contributions to household pot.

meal in a kitchen that cantilevered over a filthy pond. I also got to know her husband, Gobinda, well and would usually find him at the local haunt of the men in the settlement: a card game in the shadows of the new bridge that spanned the railway tracks. In the case of Sundari and her family, one of my seemingly innocent research questions was a matter of great strife: what is the household income?

> **SUNDARI,** 20 February 1997, in her shack: Income? What income? My husband left Joynagar twelve years ago. I stayed behind with our three children. There was work for only a few months a year in the village. We owned a little homestead plot. Nothing else. He said that he was going to come here and build a life for us. But he soon forgot about us. Four years! Four years went by and he did not send us a rupee! We were starving to death. I finally refused to be hungry anymore and came to Calcutta with the children. I eventually found work in three houses, cleaning floors and washing clothes. Now there is income.

> **GOBINDA,** 3 March 1997, at a card game: I came by myself to Calcutta twelve years ago. Sundari does not know how hard it was for me. She lived in the peace and quiet of the village. Here, I would work from morning until night. Whatever I earned, I had to save so that we could build this shack. And then when I had enough, I brought her and the children to Calcutta. Like a queen.

> **SUNDARI,** 3 March 1997, in her shack: Look. This is all that I could buy today. This handful of spinach. That is what I have to feed five people with. How? Gobinda hasn't given me any money for the last two weeks. My employers are supposed to pay me on the first of each month. But in two houses, they always delay payment until the 10th. Some days when Gobinda finds work, he will come and put ten or fifteen rupees in my hand. How much does he make? I really don't know.

> **GOBINDA,** 14 March 1997, in the settlement: It is impossible to find regular work. In the village, we had work for three months a year. Here, we have work two or three days a week. When I find work, I earn Rs 40 a day. At times even Rs 50. But I have to eat. That costs about Rs 10. And then a few *bidis* [local cigarettes]. I have to keep money aside for the card game. If I give it all to Sundari, it will just disappear.

This ethnographic glimpse into Sundari and Gobinda's family reveals that the concept of household income is rather slippery. Not only were Gobinda's earnings quite unstable but his contributions varied according to his individualized consumption.

Equally important was that Sundari did not really know how much Gobinda earned or what the extent of the income-contributions gap was. In order to address this methodological challenge, I made sure that for the eighty-seven migrant households in my study I interviewed all adult members and as many working children as possible. This did not mean that in all cases these interviews yielded "correct" responses. Perhaps at times the men boasted of how they defied their wives. And perhaps at times they wanted to be seen as good husbands, especially in the eyes of someone whom they often assumed was a social worker. However, in as many cases as possible, I conducted a second round of interviews to see if income and contributions estimates had drastically changed. In the case of commuters, such methodological strategies became more tricky. It was often impossible to interview all members of a household. Part of this problem was resolved by using Bayarsin as a base village. In the case of both landless migrants and commuters the ethnographic study of a smaller group of households clearly helped to understand the ongoing process of household contestations over income.

Ethnography was particularly important in revealing how what was being negotiated within these households was not just income or contributions but rather the very meaning of such practices. In other words, as in the case of migration and settlement narratives, the gendered divergences, as well as the reportings of such, point to the construction and reworking of social identities.

Purnima and Sudarshan

Purnima and Sudarshan have lived in the Chetla settlement for fourteen years. Purnima runs a small recycling business out of their shack in Chetla. On my first meeting with her, she was talking me to about her business.

> Our only source of livelihood is from this recycling business. I collect scrap metal. At times I pay the neighbor's children to sort through the garbage heaps. I then sell it to an agent in Mahabirtola. Sudarshan has been mostly unemployed for the last ten years. He used to work a few days a month but now he doesn't even do that.

At this point, Sudarshan, in a red shirt and silver chain, appeared and Purnima fell silent:

> What do you want to know? About my work. I am *bekar* [unemployed]. I am proud to be *bekar*. I am a singer, an artist, and why should I perform if I am not appreciated? I have traveled all around Bengal, singing. But who will understand me in this place? But I take

care of my family. Take a look around you. The television, the stain-
less steel dishes, the radio, the bed. How many of these things have
you seen in this settlement? These are all things that I have provided
for my family.

I will return to Sudarshan in much greater detail in the following
chapter: to his assertion of "*bekar,* and proud of it" as well as his claim of
providing for his family despite his unemployment. Here, I want to signal
the ways in which the very idea of work is interpreted in a gendered idiom.
As evident in the case of Aarti's family, such interpretations mark not only
negotiations between husbands and wives but also intergenerational rights
and claims.

Aarti's Family

Aarti's family was one of the oldest in Patuli. Her husband, Amal, worked as
a laborer on the project. When it lay vacant after construction had been
completed, like other squatters he took over a unit and brought his wife and
children in from the village. This was eighteen years ago. Aarti now works
two shifts as a domestic servant in three houses earning Rs 475 in total.
Amal still does *jogar,* earning about Rs 20 a day. But the work is extremely
unstable and by the time I met him, he was spending most of his time in the
local club.

> I have been here for so many years. At first I did not care about poli-
> tics. But then the CPM started torturing us. And we had to turn to
> the Congress for protection. I work closely with the Youth Congress
> now. We have filed a High Court case and we have to work hard to
> win it. It is more useful than trying to find *jogar* work every day. And
> what's the use? Half the days I have to come home empty-handed.

Like many other squatter and commuter households, Aarti's family
struggled to survive on her meager earnings and Amal's occasional contributions. But then, four months after I first met them, an important change
occurred. Their fifteen-year-old daughter, Taru, started earning. Taru had
worked alongside her mother since she was twelve, but she now found
work as a domestic servant in two houses, earning Rs 150 per month. When
she first told me the news, Aarti was quite happy: "Now that Taru will be
working, I will have some breathing space. Finally, there will be a steady
source of income coming into the family."

That same day, I accompanied Taru as she went to buy a few vegetables from the bazar, specifically to ask her about her new jobs. "I have been
working all my life. I take care of the two younger children. I cook. Now, I

will be doing a different version of the same kind of work." She shrugged, sighing deeply. It was as if the weight of centuries was on her shoulders.

Two months later, the situation was a great deal more fractious in Aarti's family. Taru had started keeping back thirty rupees from her monthly Rs 150 as pocket money. One day she suddenly announced to her mother that she planned to keep Rs 50 back. "I need to buy some clothes," she said quietly. Aarti was in a fit of rage: "Fifty rupees. Does no one care about this household? Who does she think she is? I tell you having daughters is impossible. If she doesn't give me this money how will I ever pay for her wedding and for her dowry? If only I had only sons and no daughters."

Taru, washing a pile of clothes outside the quarter, was dreamily humming the tune from her favorite Hindi movie, *Raja Hindustani*: "In my dreams you are the only one, in my arms you are the only one." Her bright pink dress was the only spot of color in the grim landscape.

A month later Aarti informed me that Taru had just taken on a third cleaning job and was earning an additional Rs 75 a month. This time, Aarti was full of complaints about her two sons, one twelve and the other fourteen: "They never go to school. They spend all of their times wandering the settlement. I don't dare tell them anything. They can earn but they are not interested. Nowadays, one cannot discipline boys. They are not like our daughters. We are helpless."

The intergenerational conflicts within Aarti's family reveal the important role of working daughters, who, like their mothers, are often able to find work as domestic servants. But the contestations between Aarti and Taru show that the contributions of daughters are not guaranteed but are instead secured through ongoing discipline and control, techniques that do not seem to extend to sons with the same force. Herein lies Aarti's ambivalence: she would rather have sons to avoid dowry payments, but she also knows that Taru is likely to be the only steady source of livelihood in the family. For mothers like Aarti, daughters are simultaneously assets and liabilities. For daughters like Taru, there is no alternative to work.

Relations of Poverty

I have argued that the West Bengal studies—both the agrarian debates and urban surveys—have coalesced around a limited range of primary questions and a circumscribed analytical framework. Behind the rowdy strife, there seems to be surprisingly calm agreement, a legitimated consensus, on the object of research and how that object should be located and understood. In deconstructing institutions such as households, and in transgressing the analytical boundaries of conventional localities, I have sought to pose a different set of primary questions, most notably the question of persistent poverty.

The life histories of landless migrants and commuters do not settle the contentions of the West Bengal agrarian debates in any substantive way. Instead, I see their chief contribution as an analytical emphasis on rural landlessness as well as on the social formation that, following Holmes (1989), can be called a worker-peasantry. Such "mosaics of productive arrangements" (Holmes 1989, 8) are not transitional but rather indicate a specific articulation of region and regime, family and economy, city and countryside. As Koppel (1991, 48) points out, these linkages must be understood on their own terms and not simply as derivations or reflections of urban and rural realities.

My research points to the social heterogeneity of the rural-urban interface, such that different rural origins are linked to distinctive urban sites through the differentiated processes of migration and commuting. Thus, interstate migrants seem to find a place in the labor lines of West Bengal's remaining factories (de Haan 1994; Fernandes 1997) or on Calcutta's pavements (Chakrabarti and Halder 1900) and Bengali middle peasants show up in the city's regularized slums (Shaw 1988). In sharp contrast, the rural landless negotiate urban labor markets through feminized strategies of livelihood and gain access to tenuous squatter settlements through masculinized processes of political patronage. These are issues that I will take up in great detail in the following chapter.

It is important to note that I do not see the rural-urban interface as an aggregation of these categories. As I detailed earlier, I restricted my study to the linkages between one rural district, South 24-Parganas, and the southern wards and fringes of Calcutta. Even in the case of this district it is unlikely that I exhausted all of the various urban survival strategies of the rural landless. Instead, I have been more concerned with explicating the dynamics of such rural-urban linkages, arguing that they provide a fresh perspective on contemporary West Bengal. Thus, what is generalizable from such a study is not the regularities or typifications of rural-urban linkages but rather sociospatial relations: the ways in which "social plots" are also "time-space paths" that "lack simple areal delimitations" (Crang 1992, 533). This methodology is in keeping with what Sayer (1991, 297–98) designates as a generality that explains the particularities of place: "differentiation, particularity and perhaps uniqueness arise through the interdependencies between objects or places, between the whole and the local."

While the life histories indicate that distress migration and the related feminization of the urban labor market have taken place during the last twenty years, that is, during the period of Left Front rule, I do not argue that these rural-urban linkages are "caused" by the regime. In fact, I find this question of causality to be rather limited, although this is precisely the way in which the Left Front has most often been evaluated in the West Bengal debates. Unlike much of the West Bengal debates, I do not see such findings as grounds for being either scornful or mindful of the limits of reformism.[17] I am instead interested in understanding how the regime is formed at the rural-urban interface, in these gendered practices of power. Poverty, in this case, is not a local effect of the regime. It is the localization of the regime. It is my hope that such understandings provide fresh insights into not only the case of West Bengal but also how poverty is conceptualized and located in space.

Poverty *is* how it is defined. The legitimized content of poverty is determined by the instrument and categories of measurement. This is sharply evident from the competing discourses of poverty that I have presented. Indeed, the field of poverty studies is constituted of widely differing representations of poverty. A recent piece by Ranis et al. (2000) abstracts the process of poverty in an intricate flowchart of Human Development that, at the end of the line, spits out Economic Growth. Herein is a quintessential example of how poverty has come to be viewed as an integral part of the new "efficiency" paradigm of development (Jackson 1996), promising untapped reserves of social capital and sweat equity. The American urban poverty debates provide yet another conceptualization of poverty: a moral discourse of behavioral pathologies that anticipates a punitive state pushing and prodding the worthless poor into hard work (Wacquant 1997).

In my ethnographic interpretation of poverty, I have been inspired by Sen's (1981, 1992) work on capabilities and entitlements. Concerned with achieved consumption or well-being, Sen conceptualizes capability as the combination of resources and agency. Capability is in turn determined by capital assets or endowments and by entitlements, which are legal and legitimate claims that an individual or group can make on resources. As Kabeer (1994, 140) points out, the idea of entitlements is inherently relational, invoking "a complex system of claims, which are in turn embedded within the social relations and practices that govern possession, distribution, and use in that society." In this analytical framework, poverty can involve the loss of endowments as well as an erosion of entitlements. Some of this is amply evident in the case of distress migrants and commuters. For example, while kin networks constitute a crucial entitlement, they also dissolve in the face of crisis. Such findings are somewhat at odds with the great emphasis that has been placed on social networks in studies of migration and the informal sector (Smith 1990; Mingione 1994).[18] But they are in keeping with other research that shows how rural landlessness might itself weaken household structure and kin networks (Bardhan 1993) and how such attritions intensify at moments of crisis such as seasonal unemployment (Kabeer 1994) and famines (Agarwal 1990).

Not surprisingly, much of the work on entitlements has taken explicit account of gendered inequalities in capability. Sen (1990) himself has extended the concept to map the distribution of well-being within households. My research shows how poverty is constantly negotiated within households, for example, around the issue of income contributions or around the question of "work." Such findings help complicate the idea of "family strategies" that have often been invoked by studies of the informal sector (Portes et al. 1989; Roberts 1994), showing how livelihood strategies hinge on the systematic use of gendered resources. Similarly, they undermine the Chayanovian notion of peasant households surviving through self-exploitation. As critiques of Chayanovian theory have pointed out, not only do such models mask the differentiation of the peasantry (Goodman and Redclift 1981; Lehmann 1986); they also mystify gendered processes of exploitation (Deere 1990). As Bernstein (1988) suggests, in such cases it might be more useful to see the class places of capital and labor as existing within households, implemented through gendered techniques of power.

But households are inherently contested units, constituted through a "welter of age-sex conflicts" (Harrison 1977, 137; see also Rogaly 1995). In other words, entitlements are constantly subject to negotiation and challenge. The capability approach has a bit of trouble dealing with this dynamism. For example, Sen (1990) implies that the bargaining of entitlements happens on the basis of "perceived legitimacy," a sort of altruism.[19] But as Jackson and Palmer-Jones (1999, 565) note, such altruism "may not be essential or even socialized goodness" but instead an active negotiation of class and gender hierarchies. An ethnographic conception of poverty reveals the making and remaking of such claims. It shifts attention from needs to the discourse over needs (Fraser 1989); from poverty to the politics of poverty and the politics of poverty studies; from domestic work to the domestication of livelihoods; from households to the boundaries of households.

In order to capture such processual aspects of poverty, Appadurai (1984) extends Sen's ideas by introducing the concept of enfranchisement: the ability to shape entitlement mappings through participation in decision-making processes. Agarwal (1990) takes this a step further by analyzing empowerment: the ability of an individual or group to legitimately ensure that decisions relating to entitlement are taken in its favor. Thus, female earners in migrant and commuter households can be seen to be insecurely entitled to household resources, and inasmuch as they are unable to command control over levels of male contributions, they are also disenfranchised and disempowered.

But at Calcutta's rural-urban interface the issue of gendered poverty cannot be simply posed within households. Rather, as I will later argue, the hegemony of persistent poverty must be understood as the knotting of family and regime, a congealing of class and gender hierarchies. If, as Sen (1981, 435) notes, land ownership is an endowment, then land titles are entitlements, representing the rights and claims that are embodied in sociopolitical relations. It is clear that such entitlements are differentiated by gender, with the benefits of agrarian reforms, be they land titles or sharecropper deeds, having gone overwhelmingly to male heads of households (Basu 1992; Agarwal 1998). My research shows that, in urban arenas, the negotiation of both de jure and de facto land rights remains primarily a male and masculinist enterprise.

However, in thinking about poverty as relational as well as processual, the question of *how* entitlements are defined and pressed becomes paramount. Thus, the vulnerability of Calcutta's squatters has to be understood in the context of a liberalizing regime exhibiting a territorialized flexibility that renders all land rights tenuous and fragile. The rural-urban poor can be thought of as lacking endowments but possessing entitlements, but such that the mechanisms of enfranchisement leave them disempowered. Appadurai's (1984, 495) statement is equally applicable to Calcutta's squatters: "The rural poor of South Asia, over the last century, appear to have traded a situation in which they were entitled without being enfranchised for one in which they are partially enfranchised without being securely entitled."

In Conclusion, a Story

During the course of my fieldwork, one sultry evening in July 1997, I accompanied a high-ranking Congress party worker, Sachin Mukherjee, to the Patuli squatter settlement. I had already completed six months of fieldwork in the settlement and knew many of the families well. It was late in the evening when we arrived in Patuli, and I had decided to take my car accompanied by the chauffeur employed by my family, Ponchu-*da*.[20] On previous visits I had always parked the car a distance away and then walked to the settlement. This time, Mukherjee insisted that we drive into the heart of the settlement. We inched our way down narrow asphalted roads and through the milling crowds cooling off from the day's heat, parking the car in front of a ramshackle teashop. Within minutes the ubiquitous hordes of children were clambering all around the car. I walked off toward Block L with Muk-herjee, leaving Ponchu-*da* waving angrily at the children and constantly circling around the car to inspect for any signs of mischief.

When the crowds had gathered around him, Mukherjee introduced me: "She is a visitor from America, the richest country in the world, a coun-try on whose aid the entire world survives. She owns a house here in Cal-cutta and a car. We came here today in her car."

He pointed to the car in the distance, and there sure enough was Ponchu-*da,* silhouetted against the last vestiges of twilight, flailing his arms at a group of prancing kids. Mukherjee then turned to me and asked, "How much is a maid's salary in America?" I stuttered to explain that there weren't that many maids in the United States and that I definitely did not employ one. But before I finished, he continued, "Well, it must be at least $500 a month." Singling out a young woman in the crowd, he asked, "Ruma, you work as a maid, don't you? How much do you earn a month?" "Four hun-dred" came the quiet answer. "Well, if you were a maid in America, in her country, you would make fifteen thousand rupees a month—imagine that!"

By this time, I was mortified. During the course of my fieldwork in Patuli, I had explained my research project in great detail to each of my sub-jects. I had told them where my family lived, that I grew up in Calcutta, and that I now studied in the United States. But suddenly I felt as if I had be-trayed them, as if I had lied. I had not told them that I was being financed by a hefty research grant. I had taken care to dress shabbily and to hide the car. My subjects had assumed that I came from a middle-class Calcutta family, and I had left it at that. Ethnographies are always performances (Murdock 1997, 188), and I had always been conscious of my own performative strate-gies. But I now felt that I had deceived my subjects.

Here it was—the burden of my class position suffocating me with ex-istential weight. Did it matter that my parents owned an old, middle-class, and small house; that the car was a cranky Ambassador; and that Ponchu-*da* was still on the payroll simply because he is a family fixture? Did this in any way bridge the yawning gap that had opened up between me—American visitor—and them, poor Bengalis barely scraping together two meals a day? Betrayal, Viswesaran (1994, 90) writes, "rather than signaling the impossi-bility of a feminist ethnography, can more appropriately be read as allegory for its practice." But what sort of allegory was this? And what sort of feminist practice was thus revealed? I recalled how Diane Wolf (1992b) had written—with refreshing candor—about all the misrepresentations she had engaged in during the process of fieldwork. But this was of little consolation to me at that moment. I felt that I had failed my subjects in so many ways. All of those requests for ration cards and birth certificates, the pleas of help with evictions and tubewells, what about those?

With these thoughts racing through my head, I stood quietly to one side while Mukherjee continued with his political speech. Suddenly, a group of young squatter men, perhaps sensing my discomfort, struck up a conversation with me. "Are there people like us there?" asked Ranjan, a lanky twenty-year-old with twinkling eyes. He continued, "I have heard that there are lots of homeless in America. How can that be the case? Why doesn't the government simply allow them to simply take over vacant land like we have? Aren't they citizens? Don't they have rights?" In the face of all my explanations, he insisted, "If one is a citizen, one can't be homeless."

The standard comparative measure of poverty is the poverty line, evaluating living conditions against established norms of consumption. I have emphasized that what is needed is not simply a comparative or distributional concept of poverty but rather a relational and processual understanding of deprivation. It is thus that I have presented poverty as the negotiation of the rural-urban interface, condensing in key nodes such as squatter settlements. However, there is another crucial aspect of poverty's relationality that I have quietly bypassed, and it is this that Ranjan's interrogation raises.

Deprivation, in this case, was a concept forged in a geopolitical context. I was appalled by the living conditions of squatters in Patuli and other settlements, deeply saddened by their lack of access to what I took for granted as basic goods and services. When in Calcutta, I lived in a home that required two or more domestic servants such as Ruma to keep it spotlessly clean. My earnings in the United States, while negligible by American standards, were phenomenally high compared to the incomes of my subjects. But I was so overwhelmed by these contrasts that I often failed to notice the intricacies of other comparisons. Squatters in Patuli and other settlements felt that they were better off than they had been in their villages, that they were at least rid of chronic hunger. Ranjan and his friends believed that they were better off than the homeless in the United States, more secure in the one-room, half-built housing units that their families had illegally occupied twelve years ago. And then of course there was Ponchu-*da*, protecting the rusting family Ambassador from the grubby hands of what he considered the city's unkempt masses, quite resentful of what he perceived to be a free ride by the squatters on public resources.

Ranjan's question is inherently transnational, linking the Third World squatter's patched-together home with the shopping-cart-pushing, shelter-searching men and women who struggle on another continent. His claim to shelter was a claim to a universalist conception of citizenship. Accordingly it eroded the privileges of American democracy by highlighting the humiliations of homelessness. I, who had so arrogantly measured out Third World poverty, now had to peer through a different looking glass.

Yet there is more to the Ranjan story. For in framing it as evidence of squatter entitlements, I run the risk of romanticizing poverty, of failing to take account of the brutalities of enfranchisement that mark the Calcutta landscape. Exactly ten days after Ranjan so defiantly asked me those questions, he and 2,500 other squatter families were evicted in an unforgiving demolition drive. The very negotiability that had made possible his claim to shelter and citizenship had also sealed his fate. The disjuncture between Ranjan's question and the spatial evictions that soon followed brings to light the paradoxical relationalities through which the process of poverty is lived. The squatter's claim to citizenship is precisely this: a claim that is always staked but never fulfilled, outside of any framework of enforceable rights.

If this is the politics of poverty, then it cannot be separated out from the politics of knowledge. As Willis (1977) notes, the constructs that researchers use to define poverty will inevitably be middle-class, disassociated from the fragile vulnerabilities and brave insecurities that they rarely experience themselves. Perhaps it is in this sense that I have presented Ranjan as both heroic subaltern and pathetic dupe. Understanding poverty as negotiated access inevitably involves negotiating such minefields of meaning.

The Patuli encounter made me think of the mandate for reflexivity as involving much more than simply a presentation of the intimate self. Instead, I came to grapple with Bourdieu's (Bourdieu and Wacquant 1992, 36–39) insistence on the need to unmask the "intellectualist bias which entices us to construe the world as a spectacle." This injunction is perhaps more intimate than the intimate self, for it contains the epistemological and authorial claims that undergird the social ontologies of research. In the landscape of Calcutta, this meant that it was no longer enough to ponder my "insider" status and how my "field" of research was in fact a "home." I now also had to confront the ways in which I was an "outsider," for whom the "home" was ultimately a "field," a spectacle that could be rationalized and evaluated and abandoned with considerable ease. The politics of poverty had revealed its geopolitics of difference.

> I promised to show you a map you say but this is a mural
> then yes let it be   these are small distinctions
> where do we see it from is the question
>
> Adrienne Rich, "Here is a map of our country"

3

Domestications

> **Domestic** [Latin *domesticus,* pertaining to the house, from *domus,* a house, home.] 1. Belonging to the house or home, pertaining to one's place of residence and to the family. 2. Pertaining to one's own country; not foreign. 3. Made or produced in one's own nation or country; native. 4. Domesticated; tame, not wild. 5. Home-loving; fond of home and home duties.
>
> **Domesticate:** to tame, to live in a family. 1. Originally, to cause to be at home. 2. To accustom to home life; make domestic. 3. To cause (animals or plants) to be no longer wild; tame. 4. To civilize.
> **Webster's New Universal Unabridged Dictionary, 1983**

Domestic Body-Space

The House on Stilts

Mala lives in a house on stilts suspended over a murky pond. On sunny days the rippling water underneath speckles the dark interior of the shack with a kaleidoscope of colors. The youngest of her children, a three-year-old girl, would like to capture these shards of light in her tiny hands. But she contents herself with watching the dancing of the light from the safety of a high bed that occupies most of the one-room home. She is scared of this place, particularly of the large gaps between the bamboo strips that make up the floor. When the shack was first built, she refused to enter it for months, convinced that she would fall through to the water. Mala still carries her around in her lap. Mala's shack is the last in a series of about fifty shanties that line the western side of the railway tracks at Jadavpur station. There is no infrastructure in this settlement—no running water, no toilets, and no electricity. The railway tracks are ominously close, and when she is away,

79

Figure 3.1. The see-through floor of the house on stilts, Jadavpur settlement.

Mala often has to tie some of her children to the post of the bed to ensure that they do not get run over by the trains.

I introduced Mala's husband in the previous chapter—the middle-aged Nokul on crutches. Nokul used to do *jogar* but now does not work. He talks about his battered body as a sign of how impossible it is for him to work—that he has completely withdrawn from the labor market. "I used to do *jogar* when I first got to Calcutta. But the work was unstable. I tried to find work pulling handcarts, or unloading lorries. But all of the work was taken . . . I thought of petty trading. But I had no money. When I had the accident, I gave up. What more can this tired old body do?"

Mala works as a domestic servant in three houses. Here is how she describes her work:

> I work two shifts every day, from 5:30 A.M. to 1:30 P.M., and then
> again from 4 P.M. to 7 P.M. The houses are all within fifteen minutes'
> walking distance of here. In each house, I sweep and mop the
> floors, wash the dishes, wash the clothes. In two houses, they give
> me tea and at times a snack. I earn a total of Rs 500 per month.
> There are no days off. I am expected to be at work seven days a
> week. If I miss more than two days of work per month, my employ-
> ers deduct the amount from my wages. If I am sick, I try to send my
> oldest daughter to substitute. She is only nine but she helps . . .
>
> Each afternoon, I rush home to bathe and feed the children.

We usually have *panta bhat* in the afternoon. I take a bath, line up for water at the tubewell, and then I am off to work again. At night, I buy whatever vegetables we can afford, return home and cook . . . Nokul is never at home. He is always with the other men of the settlement, smoking or playing cards . . .

How did I start on domestic work? Well, after we moved here, I had to find work for us to survive. I didn't know how to do anything else. In those days, it was easier to find work. Now, I want to add one more household but I can't find work. There is so much competition from all of these women who come on the trains. They are so poor. They will take any rate . . .

We have four children. I don't know what will become of them. I often think of taking them to an orphanage or a mission, turning them over to the kindness of strangers.

On my last day of fieldwork, almost a year after I had come to know her, I went to see Mala. The dust kicked up by the trains was particularly harsh that afternoon. The local CPM cadres—boys, really—had come visiting the night before and had posed the threat of evictions. They had made it seem that the railway authorities were interested in taking over this land to make way for temporary markets for hawkers who had been evicted from the central city. Mala was worried. She only wanted to talk about her village, about its soothing breezes and fresh air. "I just want to rest my weary body against that soft and cool earth," she said. The last time I saw Mala she was sitting by an open window, shrouded in darkness, watching the refuse of the settlement float in slow motion under her hut. I wanted to bid her goodbye but a passing train drowned my voice, rattling the shack with tremendous force. Mala and her family live on the edge, suspended over an abyss of uncertainty and bottomless poverty, the house on stilts a sad but apt metaphor for the vulnerabilities of their lives.

Life on the Fringes

I also introduced Sumitra and Swapan in the previous chapter, migrants who have lived in Patuli for the last ten years. Over time, they have expanded their one-room "quarter" through informal but neat additions. Here is an indication of their livelihood strategies, recorded over the course of multiple interviews.

> **SWAPAN,** January 1997: For the last ten years, I have been working *jogar*. Every morning, I go and stand in one of many designated corners for construction *sardars*.[1] They come and hire us depending on whether or not work is available. When I first came here,

Figure 3.2. Life on the fringes: Swapan and Sumitra's Patuli unit with an extension built with material gathered from construction sites.

there wasn't much work. But during the last five years, all of these houses have started coming up. And look at all of these apartment buildings. See those five-story buildings over there—they are for government workers. I worked on them.

A couple of months later, things were less rosy:

SWAPAN, March 1997: I haven't found work for the last fifteen days. We were working on these houses about one mile north of here. But the project has been stopped. And I don't know when we will be hired again. The *sardar* said that a High Court order came blocking construction.

SUMITRA: When we first moved here, I used to also work *jogar.* But six years ago, as all of these middle-class houses started to appear, I started looking for work as a domestic servant. It does not pay much. But at least it is steady work. Look at Swapan—he doesn't find work for weeks at times. I now work two shifts in three houses and earn Rs 475 a month.

In June 1997 Swapan told me that he was again working on a regular basis.

The monsoons are coming. Another week or so and they will be here. And during the rains, all construction comes to an end. I might

be unemployed for months. But recently, there has been a frenzy
of construction in the settlement itself. A lot of allottee houses.
I know that they involve evictions of people like us. But I need the
work. Maybe I am building the means of our own destruction. But
in the meantime, we are filling our stomachs.

His words were an eerie indication of things to come. In August 1997,
along with hundreds of other families in Patuli, they were evicted from the
settlement, their unit demolished by government bulldozers.

Trapped on the Trains

I first met Kanchan on a spring afternoon at Dhakuria railway station. As
the sun gathered strength above us, we huddled in one corner of the station
and talked. She was a new commuter. I could discern that immediately from
her shy movements, lack of companions, gentle strides, and hushed tones.
Kanchan is twenty years old but the ravages of time are already being etched
on her face. She has been commuting for only a year but she says that it
feels like a lifetime.

> My husband used to work earlier in Calcutta as a daily laborer
> hauling loads at Sealdah station. We managed. But three years ago,
> he stopped working and remarried . . . His second wife lives and
> works in Calcutta and he shuttles back and forth between city and
> village, dividing his time between his two families . . .
> Money? He gives me some from time to time but he has too
> many responsibilities now. I had to start working. My father-in-law
> is getting old. He doesn't have much work. I have two young chil-
> dren. Who is going to feed them? I leave the house at 4 every morn-
> ing. It is about a one hour walk to Canning station, another two
> hours on the train, about half an hour more to the two houses where
> I work. I spend about two hours in each house, washing clothes and
> dishes. I earn Rs 125 in each. I take the 2 P.M. train home . . .
> I try to rush back. I don't waste time or money eating any-
> thing. I have to go home, do the *bazar*, and cook for my children . . .
> How did I start commuting to Calcutta? Well, other women
> in my village were doing it. They told me they could help me find
> work. I started coming with them.

Over the course of the next few months, I would meet Kanchan on a
regular basis at Dhakuria station as she would wait for the afternoon train.
She would talk mainly about how much she hated commuting—fighting off
ticket checkers, the pressing crowds, the aggression of other women commuters, the grueling walk to and from the station, often through knee-deep

mud. While recounting the details of her backbreaking days, she often turned cynical in describing her husband. Once, after having not seen him for a month, slowly massaging her chapped and bleeding feet, she said: "I guess his livelihood is that he now lives off two women. I come to the city to fill my children's stomachs. He comes in order to rest and have fun. He has become a *babu*,[2] just like those whom I work for—they are all *babus*."

Just at that moment her train rolled in and her brave words evaporated. She seemed visibly to shrink, cringing to make herself as tiny as possible before merging with the swell of commuters.

The last time I met Kanchan, seven months after I had first talked to her, she had just lost her job in one of the households. She had been ill and had missed three consecutive days of work. She was now commuting with an older woman from a neighboring village who works in four houses and has been commuting for the last twelve years. Kanchan did not want to talk about the rather severe blow to her livelihood but her friend did: "That's how insecure we are. We miss work for some reason or other. Our bodies give out. Or the trains don't work. And we are fired. It is like living with a gun to our head. There are hundreds of others to take our place."

Introducing the Question of Gender

The rural-urban interface of Calcutta is constituted on an everyday basis through migration and commuting. While such processes are characterized by great heterogeneity, I have focused on the particular vulnerabilities of the rural landless, arguing that despite urban access to shelter and work, they remain persistently poor. The life histories detailed in the preceding chapter, as well as the three brief glimpses of employment histories provided here, point to two key dimensions of this persistent poverty. First, distress migrants come to live under conditions of fragile dependence in squatter settlements. Second, migrants and commuters have low levels of household income, which are related to seasonal and long-term employment trends, as well to patterns of male abandonment and polygamy that have eroded male contributions to the household pot.

In this chapter I take on both these issues, showing how these two vulnerabilities are negotiated through gender hierarchies. By focusing on the employment histories of migrant and commuter households, interpreted in a regional context of deindustrialization, I show how women have come to be primary earners in these families. The "feminization of livelihood" involves not only the central role of women earners but also the ways in which wage-earning work in "feminized" occupations perpetuates their vulnerable status within households.

Figure 3.3. Trapped on the trains: commuter women on the southbound journey, Dhakuria station.

If the feminization of livelihood was what I had initially set out to study, I soon realized that this was only one piece of the poverty puzzle. The dynamics of squatting revealed a logic of double gendering that inextricably links the feminization of livelihood to the masculinization of politics. By this I mean not so much the exclusion of women from political realms as the masculinist idiom of political mobilization—one that valorizes male unemployment and feminizes women's wage-earning roles. Such historicized forms of masculinist patronage are reproduced on a daily basis through the negotiation of subject-positions. It is thus that home and community are constructed and the dependence of squatters on fickle-minded political parties is secured.

I use the idea of "domestication" as a polyvalent, organizing concept to detail the logic of double gendering. In defining gender as an analytic category, Scott (1988, 43–44) presents four interrelated but analytically distinct elements: culturally available symbols; normative concepts that set forth interpretations of the meanings of the symbols; social institutions and their politics; and subjective identity. The multivalency of the concept of "domestication" allows attention to all four elements, revealing a terrain of material and symbolic contestations that points to the politics of poverty. There are four dimensions of domestication in particular that I detail.

Migrant and commuter households survive primarily through the work of women as low-paid domestic servants. Domestic work, as a point of production, continues to be defined by both domestic workers and outsiders as a feminized realm, an extension of women's work in their own private families. Domesticated bodies are thus docile bodies, moving ceaselessly across space but held in place by the weight of enormous responsibilities. This is the first instance of domestication. It renders the masses of breathless women workers invisible, legitimizes their low wages, and perpetuates their absence in party and policy discourses.

The second instance of domestication is a realm of masculinized politics in which poor migrant households negotiate access to urban shelter through male participation in masculinist patronage networks. It is here that high rates of male unemployment are legitimated and even glorified. And it is here that poor men are domesticated. As I will emphasize, this is apparent in the stark disjunctures between settlement histories as proud, male histories and the poignant realities of these settlements.

I use the term "domesticate" rather than "domestic" because I wish to emphasize that the livelihood, space, and identity of poor men and women are not naturally "domestic." They are domesticated within fields of power. In the case of Calcutta, the gendered coding has roots in the cultural history of the region, specifically in the nationalist moment of the late nineteenth century, when domesticity became inseparable from the domestic (Grewal 1996), inextricably linking issues of national autonomy to the civilizing of women (Chatterjee 1990a). The discursive placement of women in a bounded home, anchoring an entire hierarchy of global differences that pivots on the private/public binary, is the third instance of domestication.

If domestication is about creating images of familiarity, the discourses of working women politicize this familiarity, thereby disrupting domestic imperatives. The negotiation of domesticity inside and outside the *domus* is the fourth instance of domestication. Commuter women like Kanchan position their husbands and sons as *babus*, likening them to their employers, oppressors in not only gendered but also class terms. In doing so, they advance a formidable critique of masculinist power, an issue I will return to later in the book.

I emphasize the idea of domestication because its various dimensions point to the politics of poverty: how poverty persists through the contingent and open-ended contestation of social identities. There are sites at which the logic of double gendering congeals, and squatter settlements are prime expressions of such "moments of articulation."[3]

The Feminization of Livelihood

There is now a massive body of research on the gendered dimensions of globalization. It is not my intention to attempt a summary of this rich and varied material. Instead, I want to acknowledge my intellectual debts through a clarification of certain analytical concepts, specifically the feminization of livelihood.

The idea of feminized work has most often been used in conjunction with theories of globalization to indicate the large numbers of women workers who are being incorporated into the global labor force. My use of the term is similar, although, in the Calcutta context, such changes have had little to do with global investment, which is neglible in the region, and much more to do with patterns of informalization in an economy struggling at the margins of global change. Thus, the rise of feminized livelihoods has gone hand in hand with distress migration and daily commuting, both processes linked to rural landlessness.

However, there is much more to the feminization of work than simply increasing numbers of women workers. The phrase has been analytically used to indicate the feminization or downgrading of work itself, hence McDowell's (1991, 408) provocative statement that "we are all becoming 'women workers' now." Standing (1999) interprets the flexibility of global labor as an expansion in disposable, low-paid, part-time jobs, a social construction of work that is deeply gendered. In the case of Calcutta, I am concerned with the feminization of the urban informal sector. On the one hand, there is a growing segmentation of specific labor markets, such as the petty trading of perishables, with women workers constituting the most vulnerable segments (Dasgupta 1992). On the other hand, there has been a feminization of entire occupations, such as domestic work, which have also become increasingly casualized (Banerjee 1985).

If, as Burawoy (1985) notes, production politics encompasses both relations *of* production and relations *in* production, then the feminization of work also signifies the deployment of a gendered logic of regulation at the point of production. Feminist research has uncovered such processes of supervision and management in the context of assembly-line work (Ong 1987; Salzinger 1987; Hossfeld 1990; Wolf 1992a) and in the self-disciplinary "family strategies" of informal work and piece-rate production (Fernandez-Kelly and Garcia 1989; Benton 1989; Wilson 1993). Here, domestic service has emerged as a particularly intimate point of production where Taylorist time-space routines merge with personalized invocations of the "family ethic" in the regulation of work (Dill 1988; Constable 1997). While recognizing the crucial importance of such processes, I did not research feminized relations in production. Studying the practices of domestic service required a host of new and sensitive research relations with employers that were beyond the scope of this project. The experience of work was instead recuperated through narratives, and while this method revealed the meanings ascribed to work and earnings, it was often limited in detailing domestic service as an occupation.

The analytical force of the idea of feminized work rests in its immediate undermining of the false binaries of work and household, production and social reproduction, public and private. There are two aspects of this process that I have taken on in my Calcutta research. The first involves studying the gendered struggles within households that contest the meaning and value of work and determine control over earnings. In this, the vulnerabilities of migrant and commuter women resemble what feminist theorists, in the context of the United States, have termed the "feminization of poverty": the rise of women-headed households trapped in feminized, low-paid jobs with disintegrating social networks and declining intrafamily transfers (Ehrenreich and Piven 1984).

The second dimension has to do with the articulation of family and regime, the ways in which the state as ideological and material entity shapes the feminization of work. Indeed, some of the most provocative research on domestic service links it to the role of the state, whether it be racialized U.S. welfare and immigration policies that channel minority women into domestic service (Nakano Glenn 1992; Romero 1992; Chang 1994) or the international context of nation-states carefully managing this exploitative labor market (Bakan and Stasiulis 1997; Pratt 1997; Yeoh and Huang 1999). In the case of Calcutta, I will argue that the patriarchy of the state, as evident in masculinist patronage, maintains the discursive marginalization of the "woman question" (Basu 1992; Ray 1999), and thereby consolidates the gendered hierarchies that produce "domestications."

The Regional Context of Male Unemployment

The life histories frame the moment of migration as a transition from the inevitable oppressions of agrarian structures to an urban arena of negotiated possibilities. One of the key issues raised repeatedly by migrants is the tremendous limitation of agricultural employment, particularly in the context of single-cropping districts like South 24-Parganas. And yet the employment histories point to the fact that steady access to urban work is equally problematic for migrant men. Such urban patterns of unemployment need to be situated within a broader regional context of deindustrialization. Since this is an issue that has been discussed in greater depth in other studies (Mitra 1963; Banerjee and Ghosh 1988; Khanna 1989; Banerjee 1996; Ray 1996), I will highlight only a few relevant points.

Once India's premier industrialized region, West Bengal's fall from glory has been seemingly irreversible. Ravaged by the tailspin of a national recession and widespread political instability, the region witnessed a massive capital flight that started in the late 1960s and continued through the 1980s. Despite the Left's attempt to keep labor on a leash through careful monitoring of unions (Kohli 1987; Mallick 1993), the loss of industries and investment could not be checked. By the late 1980s, West Bengal had slid to eleventh among twenty-five states with respect to state domestic product, and unemployment rates were some of the nation's highest. Even during the 1990s, when the Left attempted to liberalize, growth rates remained substantially lower than national averages, with the state garnering less and less of nationwide investment (*Economic Review* 1996–97).

Particularly worrying about the West Bengal economy has been its moribund manufacturing sector. Khanna (1989, 959) shows that the share of West Bengal in the country's value of industrial output shrank all through the 1980s, such that the state's industrial output level in 1987 was slightly lower than in 1965. The declines have been for registered as well as unregistered manufacturing (Mohan and Thottan 1992, 105), indicating a pattern

Table 3.1

Index of industrial production (base: 1980 = 100)

Region	1990–91	1992–93	1995–96
West Bengal	125.39	130.31	158.72
India	212.60	218.90	283.30

Source: Economic Review, Government of West Bengal, 1996–97

of deindustrialization (Banerjee and Ghosh 1988). While the Left Front claimed record increases in industrial production in the 1990s, as Table 3.1 indicates, it seems more likely that growth was modest, with West Bengal lagging far behind national averages.

The obvious manifestation of this sluggish manufacturing sector has been the grim decline in industrial employment (GOWB 1989; Ray 1996). There was little improvement in the 1990s, with the *Bartaman* (1997 series) reporting that in 1995 the number of unemployed adults in the state was the highest in the nation. Indeed, as evident from Table 3.2, the Left's New Economic Policy seems to have seen a measure of success only in tertiary sectors like trade and hotel services. In the following chapter, I will discuss the ways in which the Left Front is sponsoring housing and commercial de-

Table 3.2

State domestic product by selected industry of origin, West Bengal (in rupees crore, constant 1980–81 prices)

Industry	1980–81	1987–88	1994–95
Agriculture	2640.60	3761.67	4784.10
Manufacturing, registered	1166.79	1291.52	1608.77
Manufacturing, unregistered	849.90	1059.82	1472.64
Construction	736.51	874.43	1204.54
Fisheries	283.85	348.26	548.41
Trade, hotels	1181.53	1612.55	2319.75
Real estate	748.82	876.20	1315.07

Source: Statistical Abstract, Government of West Bengal, 1994–95

velopment on the fringes of Calcutta. But here I want to emphasize that even these seemingly dynamic sectors have turned out to be problematic in terms of their employment effects. Swapan's account demonstrates the seasonality and informality of the construction industry. Indeed, as I will detail, residential and commercial construction in Calcutta has turned out to be volatile, subject to drawn-out legal battles and halts. Such trends have boded ill for the employment possibilities of migrant households.

Table 3.3 summarizes the employment findings of the 43rd Round of the National Sample Survey (1987–88). The NSS figures show high rates of urban unemployment in West Bengal for men, and particularly for women. Though not included in this table, female unemployment rates adjust downward when subsidiary status employment is included (*Sarvekshana* 1990). As expected, the inclusion of underemployment sharply increases unemployment rates. Also noteworthy, in the case of West Bengal, is the high rate of female unemployment, particularly in urban areas. This is in keeping with Fernandes's (1997, 38–40) finding that Calcutta's industrial sector is the domain of male workers such that women are the first to face retrenchment, a practice supported by trade unions.

Table 3.3

Usual principal status unemployment and underemployment rates, 1987–88

Population	Unemployment	Unemployment + underemployment
	West Bengal	
Rural male	3.0	24.3
Rural female	10.6	12.1
Urban male	9.0	22.1
Urban female	21.4	24.0
	India	
Rural male	2.8	22.2
Rural female	3.5	12.7
Urban male	6.1	15.5
Urban female	8.5	20.3

Source: National Sample Survey, 43d Round, 1987–88, published in Sarvekshana, 1990.

Note: Underemployment is determined by the proportion of usually employed reporting availability for work, additional work, or alternative work.

The NSS estimates are strikingly different from the findings of my study. Table 3.4 presents the employment profile of migrants and commuters in the 15–65 age group. At 92.45 percent, the female work participation rate is extremely high, particularly given West Bengal's low rates of female labor force participation (Banerjee 1985; Standing 1991). My findings also show that 100 percent of women in the 15–65 age group are employed. This is in sharp contrast to the high female unemployment rates in the NSS estimates. However, as in the case of the NSS survey, over 20 percent of women in the labor force are underemployed, that is, seeking additional or alternative employment.

Table 3.4

Employment profile of migrants and commuters (age group, 15–65 years)

Gender	Unemployment	Underemployment	Labor force participation	Total
Male	18 (14.29%)	14 (11.11%)	101 (80.16%)	126
Female	0	34 (21.38%)	147 (92.45%)	159

Source: fieldwork, 1997.

Notes: The total count for male earners does not include "not present" men. Unemployment corresponds to NSS usual principal status. Underemployment includes those actively seeking additional or alternate employment.

In my findings, male unemployment rates run at over 14 percent, considerably higher than the 9 percent NSS figure. Further, this 14 percent unemployment rate has as its base a male work force that is already eroded by high levels of labor force withdrawals, as indicated by low work participation rates. Since the NSS estimates do not provide data on labor force participation, it is not possible to compare this specific finding. Another important issue to raise here is that my estimates exclude "not present" men, that is, men who have either abandoned their households or are primarily involved with a second household, as, for example, Kanchan's husband. In these cases, it was impossible to ascertain the employment status of these men and they are thus not included in the calculations. However, "not present" men constitute over 20 percent of all male adults in the 15–65 age group and their inclusion or exclusion can have a significant effect on estimates.

The divergences between the NSS statewise data and my employment findings point to the specific labor market position of migrants and commuters. Bardhan's (1989a, 1498) analysis of similar 1977–78 NSS data for West Bengal echoes these divergences between general trends and the labor market characteristics of poor, urban households. He shows that poor households had unusually high levels of labor force withdrawals for adult males. In contrast, women had high labor force participation rates and lower unemployment rates. Such patterns are also confirmed by Roy et al.'s (1992) study of distress migration, where only 31.3 percent of the families had employed males while 100 percent had employed females.

Table 3.5

Female labor force participation rates

Village	1991 census data	1997 fieldwork data (age group, 15–65 years)	1997 fieldwork data (including workers younger than 15 years old)
Tetultola	30%	40%	65%
Bayarsin	24%	85%	90%

Source: Census of India, 1991; fieldwork, 1997.

But the divergences between the NSS estimates and my findings also raise the issue of categories and counts, particularly in the case of women workers. Especially problematic is the case of female commuting, which seems to be notoriously underestimated. Table 3.5 indicates the discrepancies between my rural employment data and 1991 census data for the village of Bayarsin in Taldi *Gram Panchayat,* South 24-Parganas. While the census shows a work participation rate of 24 percent for women in the 15–65 age group, my fieldwork indicates a rate of 85 percent. These working women were, without exception, commuters who participated in labor markets in Calcutta. Given their rural residence, it is unlikely that they are being counted as a part of the urban labor force. On the other hand, they seem to be bypassed in rural counts as well, either because they are assumed to be subsidiary workers or because their commuting makes them less visible in rural settings. Another problematic issue is that of working daughters. In the village of Tetultola, Mathurapur Block, South 24-Parganas, a large number of households had at least one, if not two, daughters working in Calcutta as full-time domestic servants. As indicated by Table 3.5, such workers are bypassed by census counts.

The counting and classification of women workers continues to be the grist for a mill of fury in India (Banerjee 1989) and raises important questions about how census and NSS categories are conceptualized and operationalized. In fact, as Chandrasekhar (1993, 214) points out, in many cases there are striking divergences between census and NSS data on women's employment, particularly in the categories of subsidiary and marginal work. My findings show that such data sources are marked by systematic exclusions that misrepresent the very structure of employment in poor households and render working women invisible. Indeed, if I have talked earlier about the domestication of the rural-urban poor, then the manner in which feminized work and feminized subjects are written out of the official profile of the region is a key aspect of discursive and material power.

Informalization

Given the broader context of regional deindustrialization, it is not surprising that much of the employment increases in Calcutta have taken place in the informal sector. However, I am also concerned with the increasing feminization of the informal sector. By this I mean three trends: the feminization of key informal occupations like domestic service, a growing casualization of informal work, and gendered differentiation within the informal sector, with women workers being confined to the most vulnerable and casualized segments of the labor market.

Table 3.6 presents my employment findings for distress migrants and commuters. Such occupational profiles are markedly different from those of regularized slums and thus point to the distinctive character of squatter settlements and daily commuting. For example, the CMDA's 1988 survey of almost 8,000 households in Calcutta slums showed poverty head count ratios of only 42.39 percent (Chakrabarti and Halder 1990). In these slums a high number of male clerical and sales workers with regular wage-earning jobs made possible these higher incomes. The median per capita monthly income for these households was over 50 percent higher than for those reliant solely on casual work (Chakrabarti and Halder 1990, 79; see also Shaw 1985).

Such differences in occupational profiles have important methodological implications. Much of the micro-level research on poverty in Calcutta has been conducted in formalized slums. As I have discussed earlier, the CMDA refuses to study squatter settlements because of their illegal occupation of public land. However, as evident from the labor market data, poverty estimates based exclusively on slum populations fail to capture the

Table 3.6

Occupational profile of migrants and commuters (age group, 15–65 years)

Type of employment	Male	Female
Domestic work	0	110 (74.83%)
Jogar (casual construction)	37 (44.59%)	7 (4.76%)
Vegetable vending	18 (21.69%)	23 (15.65%)
Rickshaw puller	8 (9.64%)	0
Agricultural wage—labor only	4 (4.82%)	0
Other	16 (19.28%)	7 (4.76%)
Total employed	83	147

Source: fieldwork, 1997.

gendered vulnerability of squatter groups. Calcutta slums are not only composed of a more well-established migrant population but also include *thika* tenants or middlemen who rent out slum properties while residing in others (Ghosh 1992), accumulation patterns that distinguish slums from the class and gender dynamics of squatter settlements. The occupational profile of distress migrants and commuters indicates that they are incorporated into casualized segments of the informal sector such as *jogar*, which are subject to great seasonal variations.

Table 3.6 reveals some important gendered dimensions of poverty. For example, it shows the importance of domestic service as a source of livelihood for the rural-urban poor. This is in keeping with 1991 census data, which indicate that this is one of the few growing sources of employment in the Calcutta metropolitan region. But it is also clear from Table 3.6 that domestic service is a "feminized" occupation, overwhelmingly composed of women workers. This was not always the case in the region. Until recently, circular migrants from Bihar, Uttar Pradesh, and other parts of West Bengal worked as domestic servants, and many of them were men (Banerjee 1985). The changing gender composition of domestic service is then related to the rise of distress migration and signals what Harriss (1989b, 249), in his review of urban labor markets in India, describes as an increasing trend toward casualization and feminization.

Such forms of casualization are evident in domestic service, which has undergone a shift from live-in to daytime workers and from monthly wages to piece-rate work. The growing presence of commuter women is a key dimension of the casualization of domestic service; Banerjee (1985, 113) dates this to the mid-1970s. My research shows that, within domestic service, commuter women like Kanchan consistently earn lower wages than squatter women like Mala and Sumitra. These patterns are in keeping with Breman's (1996, 264) diagnosis of an informalized workforce that is "kept in circulation" at the "massive bottom of the economy." Also relevant here is the emergence of new modes of labor such as working daughters who, as evidenced in Table 3.7, earn considerably less than other domestic servants. I will return to this issue later in this section.

Table 3.7 indicates significant gender variations in earnings within occupations such as *jogar* and vegetable vending. The differences in "other" occupational earnings indicate men's access to higher-paid niches of the informal labor market such as rickshaw pulling and porterage. Women, for the most part, are limited to occupations such as begging, recycling, and rag-picking. Indeed, the heterogeneity of the informal sector points to the

Table 3.7

Wages of migrants and commuters by urban occupation (all earners, in rupees)

Type of employment	Daily wage	Monthly wage
Domestic work		
Part time, 15–65 years	16	416.45
Full time, younger than 15 years	8.53	221.88
Jogar (casual construction)		
Male	35	544.59
Female	20	357.14
Vegetable vending		
Male	45	645.00
Female	25	473.19
Other		
Male	—	679.17
Female	—	453.57

Source: fieldwork, 1997.

Notes: Domestic work is a monthly rate occupation; daily rates are based on days worked per month. *Jogar* and vegetable vending are daily rate occupations; monthly rates are based on days worked per month. The "Other" category includes a range of informal sector occupations.

impossibility of speaking about a singular presence of peasants in the city. For example, Dasgupta's (1992) survey of petty trading reveals a wide range of incomes and asset holdings. Can these various class groups—from well-established traders with strong political and economic connections to vulnerable itinerant traders barely eking out a daily existence—all be seen as part of the same reserve army of labor?

My research confirms Dasgupta's (1992, 17, 241) argument about gendered segmentation, which shows that poor women constitute the most vulnerable of petty traders, with little access to credit or secure locations.[4] It also confirms Breman's (1996, 5) cautionary note about how self-employment in the informal sector often disguises wage dependency and deep vulnerabilities. In keeping with Breman's (1985, 328) emphasis on the sociopolitical mechanisms through which labor market segmentations are created and maintained, I am also interested in the ways in which Calcutta's informal market is constituted through the everyday negotiation of class and gender hierarchies. Let me briefly explain by discussing one informal occupation: petty trading of perishables.

The broad category of rural-urban commuters is composed of diverse groups, of which poor women seem to constitute a rather large proportion. Given the complete lack of data on commuters it is hard to ascertain the precise composition of this amorphous category. Villages like Bayarsin indicate that, in landless households, women are the main commuters. However, at the South Calcutta railway stations it soon becomes apparent that poor men also commute, although in much smaller numbers. One of the informal labor markets that is shared by male and female commuters is the petty trading of perishables, specifically fruits and vegetables. As indicated by Table 3.7, there are striking gendered differences within this sector.

Why do male vegetable traders earn so much more on a daily basis than women traders? First, a majority of male vendors own some land, usually a couple of *bighas*. Some of the produce they sell in Calcutta is grown on this land. The female vendors all come from landless households. Second, the male vendors buy their goods from village markets, often banding together in groups to rent a van, a pattern also noticed by Dasgupta (1992). The female vendors, without exception, buy their goods from the wholesale market at Sealdah. The women said that they cannot buy from the village markets because they do not have enough capital to do so and can only afford to buy small quantities at Sealdah. This is how Maya, a commuter from Diamond Harbor who has been selling vegetables in Chetla market for the last nine years, described the process:

My husband works a few months a year as an agricultural laborer. We rely greatly on my income . . . Every day I take the 4 A.M. train in, go directly to Sealdah, buy vegetables from the wholesale market, take the train to Kalighat station, walk to Chetla market, and then sell them there. I only buy as much as I can carry. And I usually don't have much money to buy a lot of vegetables. I pay Rs 7 per day for my stall to the "union" at the market. I usually earn between Rs 20 and Rs 25 a day after paying for all my expenses.

Maya's account was repeated by many women commuters as well as by merchants at the Sealdah wholesale market. At the market, agents confirmed that women traders had little access to credit and usually bought in small quantities while male traders bought in bulk. Jyotsna, a commuter from Budge Budge who sells vegetables at the Dhakuria station, described the wholesaling structure when I accompanied her to the Sealdah market:

You see those merchants over there. The ones up there in those offices. Well, they look more like cages. But they sit there with their money boxes, leaning against white cushions, and chewing *paan*. Just watching everything. To buy from them one has to buy a huge quantity, I think fifty kilos. Then they sell goods to a group of middlemen. To buy from them one has to buy at least five kilos worth of each vegetable. We can't even afford to buy this amount. And so we go to these traders here who let us buy whatever we can afford. But all of the payment has to be in cash. Those who buy larger quantities from the merchants buy on credit. But we are poor, and even though some of us having been coming here every day for years, they still don't trust us.

The narratives of male commuters contrast rather obviously with those of women like Maya and Jyotsna and indicate the ways in which they buy vegetables on credit at village markets or in bulk at Sealdah. But the more significant aspect of male narratives is the gendered idiom in which they characterize the very experience of commuting.

If women commuters cite deprivation or *abhab* as the reason for commuting, male commuters define commuting as a matter of choice. I remember one particular young man from Lakshikantapur who sells vegetables at Baghajatin market. He has been commuting for the last five years and when asked why he started, he answered, "I was bored in the village. I am sure there was work, but I wasn't interested in looking for it. I wanted to come to the city. Here, I can have as many wives as I want to. If one has only one wife, one's life is over. I am free. I earn money and I spend it all. On whatever I want."

Figure 3.4. Male vegetable vendors at the Baithakkhana wholesale market at Sealdah.

Figure 3.5. Female vegetable vendors selling their goods on the side of the street, Chetla.

While most commuter men did not point to the existence of steady employment in their villages, they did indicate a tremendous flexibility in how they spent their incomes. In comparison to women traders, who spent an average of Rs 2 per day of their average earnings of Rs 25, the men spent an average of Rs 18 of their Rs 40 earnings. In fact, for many of the male commuters, the stations were sites of socializing with other men, for playing cards, and smoking a few *bidis*. Long after women commuters had rushed back to the villages to take care of the "second shift,"[5] they would linger on the platforms.

Particularly striking were the divergent ways in which commuter men and women framed the question of migration. While commuter women lamented not being able to live closer to work, often blaming the laziness of their husbands, or, like Kanchan, detailing stories of male abandonment, the men situated the ideal of family firmly within the moral community of rural Bengal. If the women described the grueling rhythms of their household responsibilities, the men constructed narratives of harmonious domesticity. In most cases, their wives did not work, and they were particularly proud of this fact, defining their rural residence as synonymous with maintaining patriarchal power. Gopal, a commuter from Canning who was a permanent fixture at Kalighat station every afternoon, is a case in point:

> I have been commuting to Calcutta for fourteen years to sell vegetables at Chetla market. But my wife and children stay in the village. That is the proper place for them . . .
>
> Did I ever think of moving here? Would I bring my family to this den of evil? Absolutely not. Look at all of these women coming from the villages. I know the villages are in an awful state. Only people and no work. For work, we have to come to Calcutta. Calcutta throws food away and in the villages we are on our hands and knees, searching for food . . .
>
> But it's not right that all of these women come to the city every day. They are ruining our society. They have left their homes and are now roaming the city. It is a moral catastrophe.

Gopal's narrative becomes particularly interesting when ethnographically interpreted within the changing context of his life. During the five months that I met with him on a regular basis at Kalighat station, he took on a second wife in Calcutta and started spending every other night in the city. By the time my fieldwork drew to a close, he was returning to the village only three times a week. When asked if his first wife would have to start commuting, he was indignant: "That would be an insult to me."

I highlight these aspects of commuting to reveal the gender differentiation of petty trading and to emphasize the ways in which these labor market processes are linked with the negotiation of gendered identities. Here, the feminization of work is not simply a reflection of regional structures but is instead deeply implicated in the making and remaking of gendered subject-positions, in the contingent articulation of home and work, city and countryside. What is distinctive about male commuters is the ways in which they can deftly balance the sexual freedoms of the city with the domestic order of their villages, how they mediate these contradictions by constructing themselves as male heads of household. Nowhere perhaps is this more apparent than in the "domestication" of working daughters: the ways in which obedience is secured simultaneously in the household and in the workplace.

The Domestication of Daughters

Noyon comes from a poor, landless family in Tetultola in the Mathurapur block of South 24-Parganas. Her father used to be a sharecropper but, in 1981, lost his claims when the land he used to cultivate was confiscated from the landowner by the state. Many of Tetultola's households suffered a similar fate. The matter has been awaiting a court decision ever since. Over the years, agricultural work also became increasingly scarce. In 1987 Noyon's parents decided to send two of their daughters to Calcutta to work as full-time domestic servants. Noyon was seven, her sister was nine.

Noyon works for a middle-class urban household of six. She is the sole servant and is responsible for all chores. When I asked her about her wages, she was rather bewildered: "I do not really know what they are. One of my parents comes to Calcutta once every three months and collects the money directly from my employers. I do not care how much it is. I just want to live with them and take care of them."

For Noyon, her employers are family. For the last ten years she has known no other. She can barely find her way around her village when she visits once a year and she has lost touch with most of the families there. In fact, when visiting her parents she is eager to return to the city, worried about how her other family is faring.

Noyon is now seventeen. Her parents have already made the arrangements for her sister's wedding to a local boy. It is now her turn. Although dowry has been long banned, it remains a commonplace practice. In these poor rural households, the asking rate is usually Rs 20,000 and a bicycle. These demands are suspended only if the bride is beautiful. The boy chosen for Noyon has taken a keen liking to her photograph. "Perhaps we will be lucky and they will take her for free," her mother said to me as we drank from freshly plucked tender coconuts.

In search of women commuters, I had come to Tetultola with Noyon, introduced to her through other domestic servants. But the village turned out to be too far away from railway stations to allow daily commuting. Instead, in this village of predominantly landless households, a different form of gendered urban linkages had taken shape. For the last twelve years, a growing number of Tetultola's 135 households have been sending one, if not two, young daughters to work in Calcutta on a full-time basis as domestic servants. While the wages of these girls are shockingly low, they are a crucial part of the livelihood of these households and are usually transferred directly from employers to parents.

During my short stay in Tetultola I established contact with four other working daughters who happened to be visiting their families. While I came to know these and other working daughters in much greater detail back in Calcutta, that first meeting remains of particular significance. As I sat on the porch of a mud hut talking to working daughters by the flickering light of a small kerosene lamp, I realized that none of these young girls knew each other. They were all from the same tiny village, many of them were related to one another, had played with each other as children, and were now in the same city, often in the same neighborhood, but passed each other by on the streets as strangers. Pratima, a fourteen-year-old, said to Noyon:

Figure 3.6. Working daughters on a visit home, Tetultola village.

"Didi, I have been watching you for a few years now. I see you at times from the balcony while you are walking to the *bazar*. But I wasn't sure who you were. And I hardly go anywhere so I never had a chance to talk to you."

Noyon was clearly moved by the fact that Pratima, a distant cousin and fellow villager, had lived only six houses away from her for the last four years. How could she not have known?

The working daughters of Tetultola are sent off to Calcutta at a young age, usually six or seven. They spend their adolescent years working long hours and enjoying few freedoms in the city. It is thus that the social repro-duction of urban, middle-class households is made possible through the production of a deeply gendered form of ruralized labor. Employers define the jobs as *raat diner* (of day and night) indicating that they are getting a full-time domestic worker who will be on call at all times. The young girls and their desperate landless agricultural families define the jobs as *khao porar* (that which provides food and shelter). It is in the disjuncture be-tween these two namings that the nature of this work becomes clear.

For the working daughters, the site of employment often contains within it the promise of the family, to the extent that many of them don't collect wages on any regular basis. In response to what they often saw as my most needling question, "How much do you earn?," they would often respond with the argument that they had generous employers who were saving up money to give to them at the moment of marriage, as dowry. In this fantasy of domesticity—and I stress fantasy rather than ideology—the employer has become the paternalistic father, fulfilling gender and genera-tional responsibilities. Noyon, for example, repeatedly expressed surprise and even annoyance at my questions: "But I don't know why you keep asking about my wages. Yes, it is *kaaj* [work] but don't we have to work to take care of our own households? We have duties and chores. This is no different."

This is a statement not so much about domestic work but rather about the ways in which work, and working subjects, are domesticated—rendered of the *domus*, contained, tamed. I emphasize the fantasy of do-mesticity because I do not want to imply that working daughters are inher-ently obedient, overdetermined by their structural location in hierarchies of class and gender. Instead, a growing body of feminist research calls for a conceptualization of working daughters as social agents rather than as passive victims of global capitalism (Wolf, 1992a). This means thinking through the conditions under which coercion is implemented and consent is secured (Ong 1991). In the case of domestic service, the "illusion" of do-mesticity is an important regulatory device (Dill 1988), creating conditions similar to what Hsiung (1996, 127) notes in her study of Taiwanese satellite

factories: "the transformation of conflict between the classes into a disagreement within the family."

Although they are not a part of the central focus of this study on migration and commuting, I thus raise the issue of working daughters because
they indicate the processes of social reproduction. In particular, Noyon's
words point to the ways in which the negotiation of gendered identities—in
this case, of being a good daughter—are implicated in material struggles
over livelihood and survival:

> What makes households distinctive is not that they produce people
> and therefore reproduce society, but that they—along with many
> other institutions—produce specific sorts of persons with specific
> social identities, and particular rights and needs . . . The produc-
> tion and reproduction of social identities is the key to understand-
> ing social reproduction (Moore 1994, 93).

Yet the domestication of working daughters also has its disruptions.
As in the case of male commuters, the urban experience bears the promise
and threat of sexual and social freedoms. In Noyon's household, there was
an eerie silence about her sister, Sita, once a working daughter, who had returned to the village a year ago. The conditions of her return were a mystery.
Noyon's mother briefly explained to me that while working in Calcutta, Sita
had suddenly disappeared. Her employers did not inform the family for
over two months and then kept insisting that she had run away, possibly
eloped. Sita finally showed up in a Park Circus slum, eight months later.
Noyon seemed reluctant to discuss the incident, saying that she hoped
whoever had abducted her sister will eventually do right by her. Their father's words were decisive:

> We have to send our daughters to the city to feed our stomachs.
> They are liabilities but they are also assets. Look at what Sita did to
> us. I can't tell you what happened because I don't know myself. But
> it cannot be right. And it is not as straightforward as she makes it
> out to be. It's the city life that did this to her.

Such discursive framings are not unique to the Calcutta context.
Feminist researchers have shown how sexuality is often deployed as a key
trope in public discourses about the feminization of work. Thus, Ong's
(1987) study of factory daughters in Malaysia's electronics sector reveals the
manner in which young girls were portrayed as immoral "micro-devils."
Wright's (1999) analysis of the maquila murders shows how working girls
were seen not only as variable capital, expendable and disposable, but also

as sexually promiscuous and thus deserving of violent assaults. The casting of consumerist desires and urban freedoms as sexual corruption is a distinctive gendered critique of capitalist transitions. But it is also an idiom of critique that can reinforce hegemonic paradigms, a point I will return to later. Thus, in most of these cases, the feminization of work has gone hand in hand with intense regulation of the time-body rhythms of working daughters at the point of production as well as the point of social reproduction. Ong (1990) demonstrates how, in the context of a state-sponsored Islamic revival, factory daughters were subject to close supervision by multinational companies that allied with parents. Constable's (1997) research on Filipina domestic servants in Hong Kong indicates that as public discourses expressed concern about the sexuality of these workers, the Filipina community responded through strict codes of self-discipline that replicated the regulatory practices of employer households.[6] In the case of Calcutta, at the behest of parents, working daughters have been severely restricted in their movements. The inherent isolations of domestic service have been thus greatly intensified.

In the myth of the *Ramayana,* another Sita is instructed by her husband, Rama, to remain behind a strict cordon. In transgressing this boundary, she allows herself to be kidnapped by Ravana. Over time, her imprisonment is reinscribed as seduction, and thus once rescued she has to undergo an *agnipariksha,* or test by fire, to prove her virtue. Here again is Sita's father:

> Sita? She is like the mythological Sita. Who will care if she was kidnapped? That we filed countless reports with the police? What will matter is that she was in a stranger's house for all this time. Will her reputation survive this? I don't know. Only an *agnipariksha* will tell.

The Masculinization of Politics

The question of peasants in the city has most often been theorized as grounded in a political economy of capitalism, be it in formulations of dependent development (Frank 1979) or in modernization narratives of migration (Lenin 1899; Lewis 1954). But, as the feminization of work is not a generic phenomenon with universal patterns, so there are multiple trajectories of urban change and development. And as the feminization of work points to the contested processes through which the global is localized, so the multiplicity of urban transitions requires a close look at the historicized specificity of how peasants come to be in the city. The specificity of Calcutta, for example, has always been at odds with the urban-theoretic models. Thus, Dasgupta's (1992) neo-Marxist interpretation of the city as a dependent mode of production propped up by a reserve army of cheap labor is not easily reconciled with the heterogeneity of the informal sector that her own research reveals. And the round peg of circular migration does not easily fit the square hole of migration as proletarianization (de Haan 1997).

Rather than seeing Calcutta's rural-urban interface as an anomaly, I am interested in understanding the basis of its constitution. In doing so, I argue that it is not enough to look at the political economy of production. A sturdy analysis has to take into account the "forms of regulation" (Roberts 1995) that mark the presence of peasants in the city, the politics of social reproduction in and through which the "urban question" is negotiated (Castells 1977). If, as Breman (1985) has noted, migration is a differentiated process regulated through intricate systems of personalized control, then I am concerned with how and why such regulation takes place not only in the sphere of production but equally in the social realm of "collective consumption" (Castells 1983). Here, housing is a particularly important analytical arena for it reveals the spatialization of forms of regulation (Cooper 1983) and the ways in which such spatialized techniques link home and community, work and identity, family and nation.

The growing body of research on rural West Bengal has shown that the village *panchayats* are a key site at which the politics of the countryside is articulated. It is in the *panchayats* that the agrarianism of the Left finds its condensed expression, and it is here that the dispensation of state largesse occurs. In the following chapter I will argue that in Calcutta the geography of patronage reveals a network of clubs and party offices in and through which the populist mobilization of the rural-urban poor takes place. Such institutions emerged in the crucible of nationalist struggle, as did a Bengali urban intelligentsia that sought to maneuver control over key municipal functions. In other words, the territory of the city became the apparatus of the party and state. These trends have continued in the postindependence period, gaining a distinctive volatility in the era of liberalization. Here, I am concerned with the nature of these institutions, with their historicized modes of regulation, and their significance for an understanding of the politics of poverty. I take on a relatively simple question: how and why do poor men participate in patronage? If migration histories are narrated as male stories, then how is the patronage of urban shelter described? If urban settlement is presented in the masculinized idiom of personal struggle, then how is the realm of the public imagined?

The answer to such questions, I argue, rests in the masculinization of politics that characterizes the practices of patronage and mobilization in Calcutta. I present the idea of masculinized politics through the narrative of my encounters with two men in two different settlements: Chetla and Patuli.[7] I also relate an account of political mobilization of women in Patuli to show how poor women are positioned in Calcutta politics, an arena that Ray (1999, 10) designates as "a hegemonic political field."[8] Further, building on a growing body of research that attempts to sort through the cultural genealogies of the Left Front (Chatterjee 1990a; Basu 1992), I historicize the contested construction of masculinist identities. In doing so, my intention is to emphasize that masculinist power implies much more than simply the power exercised by men; instead, it indicates the construction of a normalized subject-citizen, a regulatory fiction whose presence delimits the field and agenda of politics.

Sudarshan: *Bekar* and Proud of It

I had first met Sudarshan when he had interrupted my conversation with his wife, Purnima, in their shack in Chetla, an encounter described in the previous chapter. Sudarshan had, on that day, proudly declared that he was *bekar,* or unemployed. But he had also asserted that he provided for his family. Over the course of the next few months, it became apparent what he meant.

> When I moved here fourteen years ago, the settlement faced constant demolitions and evictions by the port authority. Strongmen would come and loot our belongings. The police would come and beat us up. We would live cowering in our shack. But then I along with the others repeatedly asked the CPM party office for help. The local councillor, Moni Sanyal, was a great man. He protected us. He promised us water. He turned the police into our friend . . .
>
> I remember those days clearly. I would spend all afternoon and evening at the party office. I would go to every single meeting and rally. It wasn't easy. At times we had fights with boys from other settlements. At times, with boys from other parties.

During our first meeting, Sudarshan had made it seem that he was a staunch CPM supporter. On our second meeting, I asked him how he felt about the Congress sweeping the settlement five years ago and with the local councillor being a Congress representative. He surprised me.

> Well, I have to admit that five years ago, I too voted for the Congress. The CPM wasn't doing much. But I will never vote for the Congress again. The councillor, Ruby Datta, just made a lot of empty promises. He never even comes to the settlement. I am a CPM supporter once again. I work for them.

When asked to clarify this concept of "work," he explained:

> The party does not pay me. But I mobilize people. During rallies and brigades, I gather them up and ensure high attendance. When the leaders come to the settlement, I organize meetings. And I maintain the club. Do you think that this is any easy task? Running the club is like running a *panchayat*.

Sudarshan was talking about the local club, Saradamai Sporting Club, the chief club of the Chetla settlement, which had been established eight years ago. When asked if any one party dominated the club, he proudly stated that three major parties, the CPM, Congress, and BJP, each had a presence within the club. But his most detailed accounts were of the everyday work of the club.

> We keep the neighborhood peace. We maintain unity. We don't let women attend our meetings. They would only create trouble. Just like my wife. She is always complaining. But we call them in if they are a part of some conflict. Just the other day, some of the young girls of our settlement were becoming too friendly with boys from the club near Durgapur Bridge. We called them in and warned them. And as for the boys, we caught two of them and gave them a good beating . . .
>   We raise money on a regular basis—whatever people can afford—to organize celebrations and festivals. May Day. *Durga puja.* This is the soul of our community. We keep everyone together in this way. If it weren't for the club, this whole place would fall apart . . .
>   You are categorizing me as *bekar,* unemployed, huh? Well I am *bekar,* and proud of it. All of the men who work and earn a few pennies. They would not be able to live here without men like me.

To understand the significance of Sudarshan's narrative, it is crucial to pay attention to silences and disjunctures. The persistent silence is his repeated unwillingness to address issues of family, the complete separation between his life at the club and his role as husband and father. Such a discursive separation can be interpreted as his legitimation of being *bekar*— his disdain for working men and his reinscription of politics as work.

But what is also striking are the disjunctures between the life history and the sociopolitical history of the context, between Sudarshan's words and the realities of the club and settlement. For example, the Saradamai Sporting Club did very little to maintain the Chetla settlement. During the year of my fieldwork, mid-ranking CPM party cadres came only twice to the settlement, including an occasion of festivities. The real activity took place in the

CPM party office seven blocks away. Having conducted ethnographies in both the Saradamai club as well as the CPM party office, I found important differences between the two settings. The club was for the most part a site for the men of the settlement to spend their time. Every few weeks it would erupt in violence, usually because of petty fights between competing political parties and factions. But for the most part, and unlike Sudarshan's breathless accounts of its activities, its pace was lethargic. This disjuncture was perhaps best expressed by Jamuna, Sudarshan's feisty three-year-old daughter who, at the end of his long monologue on another day of keeping the neighborhood peace, simply stated, *"Baba tumi to okhane khali tash khelo* [But Father, you only play cards there all day long]."

In contrast, the party office was a site of endless negotiations, a hyperpoliticization. Here, cadres resolved marriage and property disputes, promised to find jobs for middle-class youths, and maintained "election-readiness" by constantly formulating electoral strategies. The chief link between this party office and the Chetla club was a stream of young men who would be asked to run errands by cadres. Some of these errands were as innocent as taking me to meet different cadres. Others involved more complex and often violent tasks, "paying dues," as one cadre put it. These latter negotiations were rarely revealed to me. However, the complete subordination of the club to the party office was evident.

But perhaps the starkest disjuncture was between Sudarshan's account of political self-organization and the reality of the settlement. Chetla was a

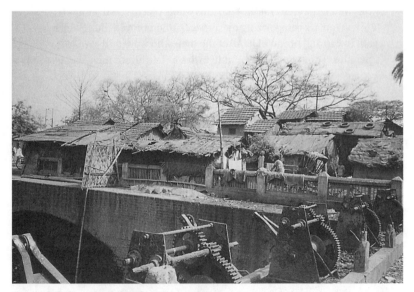

Figure 3.7. The Chetla settlement bordering a sewage-fed canal.

miserable place. The shanties were tightly sandwiched between a putrid canal and a busy road. Within the settlement, amidst the maze of walkways, often only a few feet wide, it was hard to tell whether it was day or night. The only open space was a concrete platform along the canal, where bloated bodies of dead animals frequently washed ashore. Vultures circled overhead while the settlement's children played amidst the rotting carcasses. During my first few visits to Chetla, I had to muster up every strength in my body to stop myself from throwing up. It was a nausea that was as Sartrean as it was physical: an unbearable sense of my existence.

This was the everyday reality of Chetla. While the settlement did not face any immediate threat of evictions, it also had no infrastructure. Purnima, Sudarshan's wife, complained every time I met her of the back-breaking burden of carrying water from almost a mile away twice a day. The corporation tap, which had water for only two hours every morning, served three hundred households. Jamuna, the three-year-old daughter, developed nasty scabs from the canal water. Like the other children of the settlement, she was never treated for them.

At the CPM party office, cadres officially blamed the port trust authority, the public agency that owned the land, for the lack of infrastructure. In private conversations, they told me that they weren't willing to invest in the settlement since it had turned Congress. Congress party officers ironically gave the same explanation, arguing that while the settlement had supported the party it seemed to be wavering in its support. This stalemate was evident in the Saradamai club, where fights would often break out among different political groups. Sudarshan's claim of neighborhood unity was a fiction. And so too was his sense of the club as a *panchayat*. Saradamai had no resources to spend other than the money that it often bullied out of the residents of the settlement. The economic and political resources were in the party offices of the CPM and the Congress and neither was interested in making improvements in Chetla. After all, they had managed to get by for so long with the support of men like Sudarshan.

Perhaps the most poignant evidence of the tremendous limitations of Saradamai club and its stalwarts like Sudarshan was Purnima's frantic complaints that Jamuna did not have a birth certificate:

> I don't know whether she will ever need it. But I know that it is important. Can you help me get one for her? I have been asking Sudarshan ever since she was born. He tells me that he runs the club. His daughter can get a birth certificate any time that she wants to. But it's been three years now. Just don't tell him that I asked you for help.

Figure 3.8. Washing up at the Chetla settlement.

Sridham: King of All He Surveys

I had already conducted five months of fieldwork in the Patuli settlement before I came to know the residents of Block N. The block, like the others, comprised an eclectic collection of one-room quarters taken over by squatters, some extended through *kujis,* punctuated by a few two- or three-story allottee houses. Block N residents were talking about the possible regularization of the settlement. Over and over, they asked me to talk to the leader of their block, Sridham.

A few weeks later I set out to meet Sridham. Block N residents were eager to point me toward his two-roomed quarter. That afternoon, his wife and daughter were home. The remains of an empty whisky carton littered the floor. Amidst it, his six-month-old granddaughter slept peacefully. In one corner of the room was a ramshackle desk and chair with piles of yellowed paper. On the wall was a certificate from the local office of the Congress party recognizing him as a member. It was framed and displayed as it if was a certificate of valor. While I waited, the women talked to me about their work as domestic servants in the nearby houses, the details of their shifts, and the low pay.

Sridham, who turned out to be a middle-aged burly man, finally returned from an afternoon swim, carrying a ten-pound fish. He wasn't expecting visitors and he impatiently beckoned to his wife to store the fish. "I caught it in the pond while I was bathing so I guess it is mine," he said to

Figure 3.9. "Come to the Brigade"—slogan on Patuli Block N core unit.

me, half sheepishly and half defiantly. His eyes were bloodshot and his breath reeked of alcohol. I started by catching him off-guard. I asked him where he was employed. He replied angrily:

> I have been too ill to work for the last ten years. Didn't my wife tell you how ill I have been? She needs a tight slap once in a while to remind her of things.

He quickly turned the conversation to the issue of regularization:

> I have been a loyal follower of the Pradesh Congress. I single-handedly got them hundreds of votes from this settlement. Every man and woman in Block N votes as I tell them to vote. Gobinda Naskar[9] is personally grateful to me. We filed a case together. But those traitors from the Youth Congress stabbed us in the back. They filed a second case. And that's why we lost the first case. I keep telling my people. Believe. Believe in me.
>
> Come and spend time in the Block N club and I will show you how I maintain loyalty.

Just at that time, shouting broke out near the quarter. A group of men and women rushed over:

> Sridham, come quick! He is going to kill her—he has thrown her to the ground and she is bleeding. Come quickly.

Sridham heaved himself out of his chair:

> It is a domestic dispute. He is beating his wife because she has been nagging him about his second wife. You see, I don't have a moment's peace. I have to go and break up the fight. Tonight, I will call a meeting in the club to discipline them. I am so ill and yet I put my body at risk by working so hard for these unfortunate people. What can I do? It is my calling.

In Block N it was easy to come to the conclusion that Sridham was the boss of the block, the chief mediator between the Pradesh Congress and loyal block residents. But as I spent more and more time in and outside of Block N it became apparent that all was not well in this self-proclaimed kingdom. Gobinda Naskar, the Pradesh Congress leader, was completely dismissive of Sridham: "Oh, you met him. Well, he is useful at times and so we put up with his nonsense."

But more important, Block N itself was no longer completely controlled by the Pradesh Congress. During my first round of interviews, almost all of the residents had insisted on letting me know their allegiance to the Pradesh Congress and to Sridham. But as I started spending more time in the block, it became clear that many of the residents were also negotiating with the rival Youth Congress. From time to time, fighting would break out between clashing groups. Sridham had prepared a list of beneficiaries in anticipation of regularization. But Youth Congress leaders, from S block, had also listed some Block N residents on their tallies. It is precisely the proliferation of such multiple claims in the face of growing factionalism that led to the breakdown of all regularization negotiations. In the stalemate that resulted, the CPM, the ally of the middle-class allottees, moved in to reclaim the settlement through brutal demolitions. Every squatter household in Block N, including Sridham's, was evicted, their homes reduced to rubble.

Locating Marginalized Masculinities

How are the stories of Sudarshan and Sridham to be understood? How is the stark disjuncture between their narratives and the sad realities of their settlements to be interpreted? And how does this speak to the issue of persistent urban poverty?

It is important to bear in mind that squatter men like Sudarshan and Sridham have roots in an agrarian hierarchy. Their rural landlessness is not incidental but rather fundamental. For it is this that denied them access to local political institutions in the villages, that made the *panchayats* impenetrable. In the city, these political boundaries, mediated through class differences, become permeable as migrants gain access to party patronage and young men are initiated into parties.

Following Connell (1995), I designate this reworked identity as "marginalized masculinity," an ensemble of practices and discourses through which poor men locate themselves in class and gender hierarchies.[10] What is crucial is that this location is articulated and negotiated in relation to both a gender and a class binary. In fact, marginalized masculinity can be understood only through its connections with hegemonic masculinity: "the configuration of gender practice which embodies the currently accepted answer to the problem of the legitimacy of patriarchy, which guarantees (or is taken to guarantee) the dominant position of men and the subordination of women" (Connell 1995, 77).

Accordingly, I interpret masculinist patronage as what Bourdieu (1987) calls a "field": a structure of relations between positions occupied by agents or institutions competing for the legitimate form of specific authority or capital. What is interesting about such fields of patronage is that the specific authority at stake is not only power in the political community but also power within the home. Bourdieu (Bourdieu and Wacquant 1992, 104–5) emphasizes that the field of positions is methodologically and analytically inseparable from the field of position-takings. In this case, position-taking in the political arena is inextricably linked to position-taking within the household. Nowhere is this more apparent than in the clubs of squatter settlements.

If the clubs have little power, if they are unable to procure infrastructure or stop evictions, then how and why are they important? The narratives of Sudarshan and Sridham highlight a key aspect of the clubs: their disciplinary function. The maintenance of neighborhood peace, of family values, checking the waywardness of rowdy women, all become important functions. And through this work, squatter men are able to claim a semblance of power. It is thus that Sudarshan declares himself *bekar* and proud of it, and Sridham claims to be ill. Such invocations of unemployment and failed bodies constitute a crucial idiom in the precarious construction of masculinities. By declaring himself *bekar,* Sudarshan simultaneously maintains the masculinist privileges of head of household and lodges a critique of a hegemonic masculinity predicated on economic and political dominance. Claiming to be ill allows Sridham to shrug off normatively constructed responsibilities within the household and to reconcile the illusions of political power with the constrained realities of his everyday existence.

Equally important is the idiom of violence through which Sridham disciplines his wife but also secures a position within patronage relations. In fact, for squatter men, this violence, despite its manipulations by party cadres, is a powerful means of asserting territory and confronting the state. The overwhelming majority of squatter men describe the state apparatus as an ensemble of oppressions, bearing down on their lives without mercy. They see their own practices of violence as subversive of this mammoth force, critical disruptions of hegemony. Indeed, the term *bekar* thereby shifts from meaning unemployment to indicating that these men can invest bodily strength and violence in ensuring access to shelter.

I do not mean to imply that squatter men and women simply enact pre-given and stable gender roles and identities according to an inherited script. In fact, I have found it extremely discomforting to locate the persistence of poverty in this suturing of family and regime. I have feared that the idea of masculinist patronage could be the beginning of a slippery slide into "culture of poverty" arguments. I do not see the ideal of domesticity as a functionalist device that neatly links capitalism with patriarchy but rather as what Williams (1977, 108–9) calls the "lived practices of domination and subordination."

It is in this sense that masculinist patronage can be interpreted in Mouffe's (1988, 95) sense of a "contradictory interpellation": a provisionally fixed ensemble of subordinate and dominant subject-positions that indicates the multiplicity of social relations through which social agents are constituted. Squatter men participate in club politics, transforming their once subordinate role as landless peasants into the possibilities of being an urban voter. And yet it is clear that this newfound power rests not in urban citizenship—a status that continues to elude them—but instead in a sense of manhood. They participate in patronage politics as men, as patriarchal heads of households. It is through the paradoxes of this contradictory interpellation that squatter men frame their political participation as acts of resistance, an exercise of choice where menial wage-earning work is rejected in favor of party work.

Such interpretations are inspired by Willis's (1977) analysis of the social reproduction of the working class in England. By paying attention to "culture" as "collective human praxis" (p. 3), Willis shows how class differences are negotiated in a gendered idiom, with working-class boys choosing to engage in manual work as a rebellious expression of their masculinist identities. But, as Willis so perceptively points out, these seeming acts of resistance constitute the basis of self-damnation:

> There is a moment—and it only needs to be this for the gates
> to shut on the future—in working class culture when the manual
> giving of labor power represents both a freedom, election, and
> transcendence, and a precise insertion into a system of exploita-
> tion and oppression for working class people (120).

It is thus that Calcutta's squatters "freely" participate in the conditions of their own oppression, ascribing resistance and choice to the very moment of their oppression. If patronage is what Scott (1985), following Bourdieu, calls the "euphemization" of power, then gendered practices and meanings make this euphemization possible. And if masculinist patronage is what allows access to shelter, then it is also what damns the rural-urban poor to unceasing dependence on fickle-minded political parties, a vulnerability starkly evident in the disjuncture between the proud masculinism of club stories and the miserable reality of squatting.

Such hegemonic formations, however, are always incomplete, subject to disruptions, an issue I take up in chapter 5. But let me provide a glimpse of these cracks and fissures. If squatter men invoke the "body"—usually failed or violent bodies—to articulate a marginalized masculinity, then squatter women often rework this theme to develop subtle critiques of male irresponsibility. One of the forms that this critique takes is to constitute husbands as fragile and ill and therefore unable to work. Through it, women gently and politely legitimize their participation in urban labor markets. Thus, Sridham's insistence: "Did my wife not tell you that I am sick?"

But in another form, the theme of the body is reinscribed. If squatter men like Sudarshan declare that they are *bekar* and proud of it, then in gendered critiques such terms are given new meaning. Violence, or *goondagiri*, for example, is stripped of its power and reinterpreted as a mechanism of political obedience. Thus, fiery-eyed Jyotsna said to me one afternoon as she boarded the southbound train to Joynagar, "In order to win the favors of the party, our husbands have to be *goondas*. But many of them are too weak to do even that. They are too lazy to even grovel."

That Jyotsna was a commuter woman rather than a resident of a squatter settlement is significant, a point I will return to later in this book. Her words render meaningless the one "asset" that Jackson (1999) argues men of the rural working poor own: their bodies. And it undermines the sense of the body that is implicated in the construction of masculinities (Connell 1995). Masculinist patronage as a hegemonic process seeks to transcend such disruptions, to domesticate such critiques. In the following section, I argue that this takes place not only through the incorporation of poor men into systems of patronage but also through the mobilization of women around the normative identity of motherhood.

The Mobilization of Mothers

The club stories indicate that politics in the informal settlements is constituted as a male and masculinist arena. This is not to say that squatter women do not participate in the institutionalized practices of party and polity. In fact, women in squatter settlements regularly attend party meetings and rallies and vote in high numbers. In the resettlement colonies, which have *mahila samitis*, or women's committees, such organizations remain completely subordinate to party offices but nevertheless ensure the political participation of women. My concern is not with the fact of participation but rather with the terms of participation. Squatter women are mobilized as mothers and wives, and in the process a whole set of issues—domestic work, infrastructure, health care—is rendered irrelevant to the political agenda. Here, I briefly describe one instance of political mobilization in the Patuli settlement to indicate the ways in which women and women's issues are constructed in the field of masculinized politics.

I introduced Sakila and her clan in the preceding chapter. Over the months, Sakila had related to me how she actively participated in party rallies and voted at every election: "We have to vote to stay here—we have to help those on whose land we live." She also explained that while the settlement did not have any permanent women's committees, during the elections the clubs would establish ad hoc committees to mobilize women. When asked if she participated in politics in any other way, she gave this very interesting answer: "I work with Sachin Mukherjee, the Youth Congress leader. I help him take care of the settlement."

Her answer had echoes of Sudarshan and Sridham's concept of "work" and so I set out to find out what she meant, specifically through an ethnographic study of Youth Congress organizing in the settlement. On each visit, Mukherjee spent much of his time meeting with women, handing out medicines for pre- and postnatal care, and naming newborn babies. He repeatedly chastised the men for their "animal-like" behavior and said that only their wives and mothers, "pure" women, could save them.

But if this attention to women is unusual, then Patuli is the exception that proves the rule. Mukherjee was incredibly patronizing. His idea of political mobilization was to tour the settlement, followed by a small entourage. Some of them, like Sakila, defined this as "work." And while he referred to the women as *ma*, or mother, it was quite clear that he was the boss. In fact, such socially constructed meanings—of womanhood and motherhood—are an integral part of the political and social regulation that marks masculinist politics. In the squatter settlements, male and middle-class party leaders banded together hard-working women to present them to the community as symbols of altruism and moralism. Mukherjee thundered, "You lazy men must learn from these mothers. Kneel to the mother, to the mother-goddess." Obviously, the mobilization of women has been advantageous for electoral success, for, away from the settlement, Mukherjee said, "Before the women joined, our organization was weak. The men are lazy. The women work hard. And now we are much stronger than our rivals."

Perhaps one incident above all surprised me during one of these visits to Patuli. Mukherjee was doing his usual round of houses, followed by a small contingent of loyal women and a handful of bored men. At one point, he stopped at the house of a young squatter woman, Soma. Soma and her husband have been married for three years and are childless. Mukherjee quickly scribbled a note on party letterhead to the local councillor asking for Soma to be taken to a fertility clinic: "Be patient," he told her husband. "Follow my instructions and you will be a father soon."

What I found astounding about this incident was not Mukherjee's interest in being a lifegiver but instead the publicness of the exchange. During the discussion of their fertility dilemma, a small crowd of men and women surrounded Soma and her husband. In fact, Mukherjee's resolution of this fertility issue is part of a broader pattern of hyperpoliticization in West Bengal where political parties intervene in "private" realms through an idiom of personalized politics. At party offices of both the Congress and CPM, I observed that everything, from property settlements to fertility, was negotiable. In fact, party cadres reported spending a great deal of time and energy sorting out domestic disputes. These interventions possibly provide poor women with a valuable source of support against philandering, polygamous, and abusive husbands. As one high-ranking CPM party officer put it:

> We seem to be fighting a losing battle against polygamy. No one cares about the Hindu Marriage Act anymore. The least we can do is to ensure that abandoned wives get their fair share of property and money.

But despite this concern for women, such political interventions perpetuate the larger structure of masculinized politics and the ideologies of domesticity. Cadres, regardless of party affiliations, ultimately defined cases of domestic dispute as "private" and therefore feminized. While they are not in the least hesitant to exercise authority in such private realms, they do so as an extension of male authority.

In this way, the field of politics has been defined, with a whole set of issues falling outside the boundaries of "women's concerns." For example, as in the larger context of West Bengal (Agarwal 1998, A7; Basu 1992, 63), landownership has remained a male issue, with all land titles being distributed to male heads of household. The question of women's wage-earning work has remained off the agenda of squatter politics, a cruel irony in settings where women are the primary earners. Unlike Ray's (1999) findings of how the women's wing of the Left Front, as well as autonomous women's groups, organize around issues of employment, in squatter settlements I found that such women's committees and groups rarely make an appearance.

But the key to understanding the particular masculinist idiom of Patuli politics lies not in my ethnographic observations of Mukherjee's mobilizing efforts but instead in the disjuncture between these ethnographies and my conversations with Mukherjee in his office. Away from Patuli and its political performances, Mukherjee reinscribed the "pure" wives and mothers as promiscuous, worthy only of patronizing protection:

> These were once innocent, rural women who would not even lift their heads and look at other men; today, for a *sari* they are willing to sell their bodies. The women of our villages who would cover

their heads and pray at the *tulsi* tree every evening, who walk so
gracefully with their water pots on their hips, they have been reduced to this. The pet cat that was once used to being fed at home
has now learnt to roam the city in search of food. We must end this
roaming.

Mukherjee's words eerily resonate with those of Gopal, the commuter, and with the ambivalences of Noyon's father. The slippages in meaning between his greeting Patuli women as chaste mothers and later constructing them as sexual tramps point to a particular idiom of political
mobilization. It is this that Basu (1992, 22–24) designates as *bhadralok*—
male and middle-class—concerned with the ideals of home and family.
Her argument resonates with village-level studies that pinpoint how a crucial component of party mobilizations is cultural upliftment, a project of
Sanskritization where the poor are encouraged to emulate the Bengali
bhadralok (Ruud 1995; Bhattacharya 1993). The conservatizing tendencies
of patronage are thus amply evident.

I want to emphasize that such processes of hegemony must be crucially located in the regime. In other words, the question of subject-formation cannot be separated out from the question of state-formation. Here, I
am indebted to the work of feminist researchers like Radcliffe (1993) who
have shown how informal settlements can be a crucial site for the deployment of state-produced femininities, how different state regimes are also
regimes of gender.[11] This means that political mobilization might reinforce
rather than challenge gender ideologies, domesticating the issue of community involvement and development (Craske 1993).[12] Put another way,
the "urban question" becomes the "woman question," defining and regulating a normative subject-citizen through models of domesticity. The
"woman question" is of course also the "national question," where the regulation of the female body is in fact a project of regulating the body politic
(see also Ong 1990).

In the case of Calcutta, this implies a particular class logic to the practices of populist mobilization. What is created through the discourse of
motherhood is, in fact, what Fernandes (1997, 124–25), in the context of
factory work and housing, has described as a "bourgeois public sphere"
shaped by distinctive notions of social order and morality. But a historicized interpretation of the tropes of this bourgeois order, such as of the
theme of mother-goddess, indicates that there are other cultural dimensions to this hegemonic project. The *bhadralok* ideal, as Chatterjee (1990a)
reminds us, has roots in the nationalist imaginary of motherland. It is in the

gendered project of citizenship, in the impossibility of that citizenship, that another project is inaugurated: that of a bourgeois, Hindu nation.

Historicizing Masculinities

In seeking to uncover the historicocultural roots of the gendered subject-citizen, I do not mean to imply that this culture or this history has a single model of gender. Instead, as Moore (1994, 55) notes, if in fact there is a multiplicity of discourses on gender, then it becomes imperative to note the conditions under which one particular set of symbols becomes hegemonic.

The complex oppositionalities that undergird the social construction of class and gender in contemporary West Bengal have roots in a nineteenth-century discursive formation that, following Chakrabarty (1994), I will call "Bengali modern." At the core of this cultural narrative is the issue of domesticity—the ways in which the domestication of women came to be irrevocably linked to domestic/nationalist interests. In the imagination of a burgeoning nationalism, it was the deployment of an image of virtuous womanhood that made possible the inscription of the country as "motherland." This endeavor became an integral part of the cultural project of the Bengali urban middle class, the *bhadralok,* with expressions in a "modern vernacular" marked by important historical continuities (Chatterjee 1992).

Not surprisingly, the public discourses of the *bhadralok* in the late nineteenth century borrowed heavily from Western traditions of liberalism. This was after all a class constituted in the crucible of colonial education and service. But what distinguished this period from the previous social reform era, also known as the Bengal renaissance, is the rise of a nationalist passion that evoked the cultural symbols of Hindu mythology and Bengali folk practices. The new ideal of domesticity was then a hybrid incorporating elements of Victorian womanhood as well as of the mother-cult traditions of the region (Bagchi 1990; Grewal 1996, 25). Such borrowings tamed "traditional" concepts of womanhood that, in Hindu mythology and Bengali folklore, have manifestations in images of unparalleled strength and power, or *Shakti.* In the nationalist discourse the *grihalakshmi,* or goddess of the house, was stripped of her powers. Situated ineluctably in a colonial field of power, the *bhadralok* could in this way make the claim of being "different but modern": "It was the voice of the colonial modern looking to orient domesticity to the requirements of the civil-political" (Chakrabarty 1994, 77).

What were these articulations of difference? The British colonizers had constituted the Bengali *bhadralok* as *babus*—effeminate and lazy (Chatterjee 1992)—and, indeed, the colonized Orient as feminized and sexualized (Grewal 1996). In the discourses of the late nineteenth century, this feminization was appropriated by Bengali nationalists and reconstructed as a set of oppositional femininities. On the one hand stood the image of the *memsahib*, the Englishwoman—idle, sexually promiscuous, and immodest (Chakrabarty 1992; Sarkar 1987). On the other hand stood the image of Bengali/Indian housewife, the *grihalakshmi*, constructed as the moral and spiritual opposite of the *memsahib*, a repository of domestic/homemaking values and domestic/indigenous traditions. The disciplinary power of this oppositionality is undeniable. It made possible the use of the *memsahib* stereotype as an idiom of regulation, setting real and discursive limits on the freedom of Bengali/Indian women—what Banerjee (1990) calls the "*bhadralok* offensive."

At the same time, the discursive construction of the *memsahib/grihalaksmi* binary allowed the *bhadralok* to articulate a critique of colonial power, an assertion of cultural and moral superiority in the face of imperial conquest. The *antapur*, or inner sanctum, was to be sealed off from encroachments by the colonizer and the material temptations of colonialism. In the public world, the *bhadralok* would be rationalist and modern; at home, he would lead a life of spiritual detachment, "as a maidservant in a master's house" (Chatterjee 1990a). Such purity would be ensured by regulating the passions of women: "the figure of woman as temptress turned into the safe, comforting figure of the mother, erased of sexuality" (Chatterjee 1992, 58; see also Bose 1995).

It is this architecture of oppositions that makes possible the ultimate ideal of domesticity: the nationalist imaginary of an independent "motherland." As is the case of the *memsahib/grihalakshmi* binary, the motherland icon and fiction contains subversive possibilities: it could be the image of *Shakti* wreaking destructive havoc, exacting blood from her martyred sons. But it is instead constituted as *Bharatmata*, or motherland—often portrayed as pale, tearful, and frail, an innocent mother figure deserving protection (Sarkar 1987).

The discursive formation of Bengali nationalism, specific in its gender and class oppositionalities, constitutes the scaffolding of what I have earlier referred to as hegemonic masculinity. My case for historical resonance rests on two key issues. First, the Bengali urban middle class, or *bhadralok*, continues to be the region's political elite, dominating the machinery of regional parties and the state apparatus (Basu 1992; Chatterjee 1997). While the struggle against British colonization is clearly over, the nationalist moment leaves its daily imprint on the cultural politics of the region.

Second, the gender discourses of the nationalist period are congruent with contemporary articulations of hegemonic masculinity and the complicities of marginalized masculinity. In making the case for congruence, I am not arguing that these discursive constructions are synonymous. They instead resonate because they constitute class and gender differences in a similar cultural idiom, an idiom that was in fact first developed in the crucible of nationalism. What is important here, then, is how "history figures as a participant in the production of knowledge about sexual differences . . . that history's representations of the past help construct gender for the present" (Scott 1988, 2).

While I interpret masculinist patronage as a field of power, I do not invoke Bourdieu's attendant idea of "habitus," a set of historical relations deposited within individuals in the form of mental or conceptual schemata (Bourdieu and Wacquant 1992, 16–17). As Smith (1994, 84–85) notes, the concept of habitus is quite static and assumes conformity. Instead, I use the idea of culture as it emerges in post-Marxist interpretations of hegemony. Perhaps the most appropriate concept here is that of Williams's (1977, 132) "structures of feeling"—"actively lived and felt meanings and values." It is thus that I talk about the everyday enactment of cultural symbols.

There are interesting aspects to the historical congruence, to the interweaving of class and gender hierarchies. In the nineteenth century, colonial administrators defined the colonized—in this case, the Bengali *bhadralok*— as effeminate creatures, weak and lazy. The Empire, in contrast, was described in male terms (Sarkar 1987). The nationalist imaginary appropriated and deified this feminization as the image of the motherland. The act of reconstruction set up a field of oppositions where the *bhadralok* was constituted as a "subaltern elite," subordinate to a colonial elite but dominant in relation to a whole range of other subalterns, including poor men and all women (Chatterjee 1990a). In the postcolonial period, as the *bhadralok* assumed positions of power, its discourses became universally hegemonic, albeit contested. As party bosses and state administrators, *bhadralok* men now constitute poor men as effeminate, weak, and lazy, dismissing them as irresponsible alcoholics. A good example of this is Mukherjee's pattern of political mobilization in the Patuli settlement described earlier. What is at work here is a hegemonic masculinity asserting its normative standards vis-à-vis the marginalized masculinity of poor men. A crucial part of these power dynamics is the way in which gender difference is inscribed onto the difference between multiple masculinities within the same social setting (Moore 1994).

Another dimension of historical congruence is the disciplining of women, especially poor women. Poor women could not be contained within the public/private binary and were thus seen as dangerous threats to the ideal of domesticity (Banerjee 1990). Similarly, in contemporary Calcutta, the public presence of poor, working women is repaired by seeing their work as simply an extension of private realms, thereby depoliticizing, domesticating if you will, their economic and political claims.

But there are cases when such domestication is not possible, when poor women rather obviously occupy "public" space. The commuters are a case in point. Their constant travels, their collective presence on trains and in the city, threaten elite women and elite and poor men, disrupting oppositional femininities and masculinities. I would argue that such disruptions are especially acute because of their presence in urban spaces, rendering unstable not only the public/private binary but also the rural/urban binary.

In the nationalist mapping of world and home, the rural often came to be seen as home, a refuge from a city permeated by money and power (Sarkar 1987). This pastoral vision was also a feminized one, endowing fertile rural lands with motherly virtues (Bagchi 1990). Such oppositional constructions of city and countryside echo with those in the English literary tradition as documented by Williams (1973). At the turn of the century, this oppositionality became particularly acute, taking on a "neo-urban" imagery—a wasteland of desires, hollow men, a mass undone by death—that evokes the loss of rural innocence and spirituality. Looming large in these images is the figure of the prostitute, beckoning a young man in labyrinthine alleys (Joyce 1916), twisting a paper rose that smells of dust and eau de cologne (Eliot 1917). The city becomes the site of fallen womanhood (Wilson 1991).

It is hard to trace the complex ways in which the *bhadralok* might have drawn on this Anglo-American imaginary. Grewal's (1996) work suggests that they did. But what I wish to emphasize is the manner in which the urban experience becomes sexualized, and how this sexualization is interpreted in gendered terms. Male commuters constitute themselves as Baudelairean flaneurs, "bathing in the crowds of the city" (Baudelaire 1869), explicitly talking about the sexual freedoms of the city. Female commuters define themselves as the working poor. But they are instead reinscribed as "public" women, corrupt and corruptible, displaced from the anchors of domestic virtue, motherhood, and village, their rowdiness a sign of sexual promiscuity, of their failure as *grihalaksmis*.

In his discussion of the discursive formation of the Bengali modern, Chakrabarty (1994) argues that while the construct of *grihalakshmi* is disciplinary, it also contains an excess that cannot be contained within the "straightforward bourgeois project of domesticating women." For Chakrabarty, this excess is made possible by the mythicoreligious component of the construct, a repository of culturally available symbols outside of the regulatory constraints of the nationalist project. Banerjee (1990) sees this excess as almost exclusively the realm of poor women—a folk culture parallel to the masculinities and femininities of the Bengali modern. He describes the discourses of these women—domestic servants, fruitsellers, folk performers—as "tough, sensuous, and bawdy," formulating powerful critiques of male irresponsibility: *"Bhaat debar naam nei, kil marar Gonshai.* He can't provide me with rice, and yet is quite a mighty one in beating me with his fists" (132–35).

Conclusion: Encounters with a Man-Boy

The ethnography of squatting and commuting reveals an ensemble of vulnerabilities that I have designated as the logic of double gendering, the articulation of feminized livelihoods with masculinized politics. I wish to end this discussion by drawing attention to how this ethnography inevitably meant negotiating a field of gendered meanings. In other words, I was not simply investigating the construction, legitimation, and reworking of class and gender hierarchies. Instead, I was thoroughly implicated in such hierarchies. Nowhere perhaps was this more apparent than in the ways in which I had to negotiate access to the squatter clubs. In party offices, I was often taken at my word, seen as an American researcher who had to be convinced of the merits of the party. In squatter households and at commuter stations, I could often build relations of trust. But the clubs remained a site of antagonistic encounters, one of which I describe below. I first interpreted such antagonisms as anomalies in my relatively smooth negotiation of the field. But I eventually came to see them as much more significant, raising key questions about my politics of location.

I had already conducted four months of fieldwork in the Jamunanagar settlement before I approached the club. Given that it was a resettlement colony, the details of which I present in the following chapter, the club was the undisputed territory of the CPM. During the course of fieldwork, I had taken great care to avoid drawing the attention of the club, mainly to maintain the independent routines of my research. I had taken equal care to avoid access through NGOs or government agencies. When at times confronted by neighborhood youths, I had managed to slip by on the pretext of "talking to women."

By the time I sought access to the Jamunanagar club, I had already started research on the urban transformation of Calcutta's southeastern fringes, and this had brought me in ethnographic contact with party offices and state bureaucracies. I was thus referred to the club by a high-ranking CPM cadre of the district office.

The Jamunanagar club was a one-room concrete structure nestled in the heart of the settlement. It was early afternoon when I walked into the room to find a desk and three benches, on one of which were sprawled two bare-torsoed teenage boys, their fake Timex watches glinting in the sunshine. They barely moved as I sat down but when I mentioned my contact, one of the boys, Nirmal, got up and said that he was in charge. "I can't let you just enter the colony like this," he said. "You have to be cleared by the party bosses."

I was curious to see how far Nirmal would go with his gatekeeping mission, and so I insisted that the district office had promised me that I could have immediate access to the colony. But Nirmal would not budge. I wondered what he would do if I simply walked out and started talking to residents of the colony, something I had been doing for four months now! After a few minutes of silence, he pointed to a set of faded photographs on the wall. They seemed to be of a club event. He wanted me to identify the cadre who had referred me to the club. When I did, he still did not change his mind.

I then suggested to him that he perhaps did not have the power to "clear" me, that perhaps this was the party office's prerogative. How is it that the club had no authority over the colony? Nirmal became indignant, shouting, "You want to talk to the people of the colony? They will have to talk to you whenever I command them to do so. I can even pull them out of their homes in the middle of the night and make them talk to you. But you cannot talk to them now. Not today."

This first meeting with Nirmal was one of my many encounters with the man-boys who are guardians of settlement clubs. It was an incident that I interpreted with great sadness, because the disjuncture between Nirmal's claims of gatekeeping and the limits of his power was so stark. But it was also an incident that made me realize the class and gender hierarchies that structure the field of research and require some critical attention. Two issues in particular come to mind.

The first goes to the question of honesty. I clearly misrepresented my research many times to party cadres and club boys. The incident with Nirmal ended with my invocation that I was "talking to women about women's issues." A lie? No. The truth? No. At commuter stations, when I would find myself surrounded by patronizing middle-class men angrily demanding to know why I was talking to poor women, I would grit my teeth and once again invoke the dark mysteries of "woman talk." Since I always explained the intent of my study to my subjects, did this matter?

The second is my particular politics of location. I negotiated the field

Figure 3.10. Nirmal, man-boy, in his Jamunanagar home with his mural of Bollywood images.

marked by a specific oppositionality. I was simultaneously insider and outsider (Zavella 1992), intimately familiar to my subjects in my Bengali womanhood but drastically unfamiliar in my middle-class status. Or was this middle-class status all too familiar? Perhaps I was most known to my subjects in my class incarnation—in the last instance, simply another *babu*. Class and gender encounters are especially thorny in the arena of domestic work. During my presentation of findings to the Centre for Studies in the Social Sciences in Calcutta, scholars and policy-makers acknowledged their deep discomfort with their personal implication in these hierarchies of class and gender. I could only share with them my own sense of complicity.

But this insider/outsider positionality was not fixed and often took on very different meanings. I was often not *babu*ized precisely because I was seen as a *memsahib,* a foreigner. And how can I separate out these two terms when, in contemporary Bengal, the working poor often use the word *memsahib* to designate not so much a foreign woman as a woman belonging to the metropolitan elite? It is the foreignness embedded in this most intimate of class exchanges that defines the hegemonic project of nationalism.

During the course of research I could violate the boundaries of my Bengali womanhood and the complicities of my middle-class status, because of the privileges of being "American." My subjects repaired the transgressions of my fieldwork by situating me outside the "domestic" imaginary. For me, this inscription was often startling because I had thought that, by recognizing Calcutta as a home, I was confessing to my direct implication in the politics of its poverty. But as in the case of the Patuli incident detailed in the previous chapter, this self-definition had also euphemized my role as researcher, masking the privileges of my foreigner status. Despite my encounters with man-boys, I had access to the settlements perhaps because I was seen as an outsider, little threat to immediate politics. And at party offices I was perhaps treated as another NRI, or Non-Resident Indian. The privileges of travel had allowed me unusual access to various territories (Kaplan 1987; Wolff 1995, 122).

I see this liminal positioning, these slippages in "insider" and "outsider" meanings, as the fifth instance of domestication, my uneasy negotiations of "home" and "field" (Viswesaran 1992). The weight of my inheritances—the "doxa" of my academic and intellectual "fields" (Bourdieu 1977) as well as the irrepressible passions of "home"—have marked this study. I have felt this weight at moments when my configuration of questions, or the turn of a phrase, has disrupted the domestic imperative, taking on an agency I had not intended. As Sartre said, "Words wreak havoc . . . when they find a name for what had up to often been lived namelessly" (quoted in Bourdieu 1977, 170; in turn quoted in Holmes 1989, 197).

Or had I always intended this? I felt this havoc in working daughter Noyon's growing anger at having to confront the issue of her low wages: "Why do you always ask me how much I earn?" Over the months her angry question turned into a brooding interrogation of how much she really earned. I also felt it with the commuters, who in the process of spinning an oppositional language would often ask me to articulate the terms of their demands: "Why don't you tell us how we should organize? How should we demand higher wages? What should we do?"

I was paralyzed by these questions precisely because they pointed to the unbridgeable gap between their lives and mine. I had dared an interpretation but the dissonance between fieldwork and ethnographic product (Stacey 1988) was inevitable. How did I see man-boys like Nirmal? With the smug disdain of a *babu*? Of a *memsahib*? The antagonism in the Jamunanagar club that afternoon was as much a reflection of who I am as it was of the man-boy.

I have chosen to end this long discussion on the lived meanings and practices of poverty with words that are a great deal more intimate than this chapter—random verses that I wrote in parallel to my field notes. Their images return me to the soul of the project, the negotiation of a field of poverty.

But more important, they show that ethnographies are always acts of "translation," what Tsing (1997, 253) calls "faithless" rather than faithful "appropriation." These sidenotes to the official text of fieldwork reveal a particular hierarchy of knowledge and the acts of gazing and writing that structure research projects. I present them neither as evidence of the impossibility of feminist research[13] nor as a claim to feminism. Instead, I see the disjuncture between field journal and academic notes as indication of how feminism has to be earned, how the abyss that gapes between "here" and "elsewhere" has to be crawled over, painfully.

> I meander through these passages
> Lined with aged mud
> Unearthing secrets
> Laying bare this excavated heart
> And its itinerant passions.
> I stumble along dirt paths
> So narrow that I must reflect off words
> And use the smoke as a crutch.
> I see you silhouetted at the end of the light
> Timeless, universal, amorphous
> To be shaped through a question I put to you.

> You bend over your mud stove
> You are only fifteen, silent.
> Unruly eyes.
> The next time you lift your head to look at me
> You are wizened, ancient, spilling forth words
> Tame eyes
> You have cooked a million meals
> For a million clamouring mouths.

> You are precariously steady
> Beads of sweltering heat dotting your life
> Carrying piles of splintering wood
> Chosen by work-weary fingers.
> There are fires that you must light
> But do any burn within you?
> Around you, the hustle of colliding destinies
> But in you, utter stillness.
> You move at the speed of light
> But you are statuesque, statue-like
> More compact than the porous soils of your village
> More resistant than the melting asphalt of my city.

You are an island and to reach you I have to be a circus performer
I find you amidst a riot of Hindi-movie colors
A synthetic image, tattered smile, recycled dreams.
You count your way through countless plastic bags
The city is gathered here at your feet, levelled.

I see you in the margins of my camera vision
You are walking, arms outstretched
On the parapet of an abandoned railway bridge
Suspended over miles of rotting flesh.
This is your playground
And the circling vultures are your companions.
You strain to maintain balance, sanity, life,
A malnutritioned potbelly.
I try not to look into the luminescent eyes that fill your head.
In them, I am afraid to find
All of the reasons why you should not be smiling
And none of the explanations for why you do
With so much grace.

You live in utter and silent darkness.
I cannot hear or see you as you make your way down
Winding village paths, infinite mornings and eternal nights.
At times on the horizon there is the light of a wandering fair
And I wonder if you imagine what carousel of delights await

Beyond

I live on a hill bathed by a thousand points of light
The world shimmers at my doorstep.
But I cannot see the distance
I cannot traverse the distance
You have been to countless galaxies and back
Lain on your back on dewy grass
And traced the lines of clustering stars
I have remained lit by searing light, blinded.

Dreaming of Tombstones

In Ersilia, to establish the relationships that sustain the city's
life, the inhabitants stretch strings from the corners of the houses,
white or black or gray or black-and-white according to whether
they mark a relationship of blood, of trade, authority, agency.
When the strings become so numerous that you can no longer
pass between them, the inhabitants leave: the houses are dis-
mantled; only the strings and their supports remain . . . They re-
build Ersilia elsewhere . . . Thus, when traveling in the territory
of Ersilia, you come upon the ruins of abandoned cities: spider-
webs of intricate relationships seeking a form.

Italo Calvino, *Invisible Cities*

This place, on its surface, seems to be a collage. In reality, in its
depth it is ubiquitous. A piling up of heterogeneous places. Each
one, like a deteriorating page of a book, refers to a different
mode of territorial unity, of socioeconomic distribution, of political
conflicts, and of identifying symbolism.

Michel de Certeau, *The Practice of Everyday Life*

"I dream of a landscape of tombstones," he said, leaning back into his
leather chair, pushing away from the wide expanse of his meticulously tidy
glass-topped desk. He continued:

> You want me to tell you who owns these vast expanses of land on
> the eastern fringes? Well, I can't tell you that. I can tell you that here
> there are squatters and colonies, illegal housing developments and
> legal housing developments; land held hostage and land for which
> blood is being shed. It is all tied to the politics of electoral support,

every inch of it. And it is possible because there is no sure knowledge of who owns which piece of land, and so it is territory up for
grabs. To get rid of this dirty politics we need to mark each piece of
land with a tombstone, clearly identifying its ownership and status.

He then proceeded to explain by using a gendered metaphor:

Think of it as *sindur*.[1] You modern women don't wear such markings, so how can anyone tell if you are married or not? It creates
a great deal of confusion for us men. So is it with land.

My search for an answer to the question of landownership in Calcutta's
fringes had brought me here, to the office of Anil Shah,[2] a Marwari developer,
on a monsoon afternoon in 1997. I had first met Shah at the offices of the
Calcutta Metropolitan Development Authority (CMDA). It was my seventh
visit to the Land Acquisition Cell and I was frustrated at not being able to
locate land records for the southeastern periphery of the city where I had
been conducting fieldwork for many months. This time I had a reference
from a well-respected officer of the state-level Land Acquisition Office and I
was hoping for more cooperation. But the answers weren't quite what I had
expected. At the Land Acquisition Office, staffers had given me the impression that while the processes of land acquisition and compensation were
rather messy, with conflicting legal jurisdictions, there were nevertheless
clear records for each ward. At the CMDA's Land Acquisition Cell I finally
learned that there was no established system of maintaining centralized
and agreed-upon records of land ownership and acquisition for the southeastern fringes. The Senior Land Officer admitted that this had created tremendous ambiguity regarding "vesting," the legal processes through which
agricultural and urban land is acquired by the state, and that the problem
was particularly acute in the open tracts of the eastern periphery: "Yes, no
one really knows which part of which plot is vested. Not even I. There are no
maps or boundaries. We deal with it on a case-by-case basis." He smiled
quietly as his other visitor, Shah, interjected, "This is at the heart of *dadagiri*.[3] This is why anyone, any party, any politician can take over any piece of
land and suddenly declare it vested. Everything is about vesting. We need a
map, I keep telling you that, *dada*,[4] a survey map available to every member
of the public."

A city without maps? Was that possible? The British in Calcutta had
systematically surveyed the city, carefully detailing European areas and
inhabitants. A few Bengali maps had also been drawn up in the late nineteenth century (Dasgupta 1995). But cartography as an instrument of de-

velopmentalism, a tool by which modern states supervise and articulate their territories—this is what seemed to be missing. Early on in my field-work, a top-ranking officer of the CMDA photocopied a page out of her vinyl-bound agenda for me. It was a hand-drawn map of the Calcutta Metropolitan Corporation (CMC) area and its different wards, barely legible in its blurred facsimile copy. I shook my head and said that I needed a map of the entire metropolitan district—of the very territory that she regulated. Why was this so hard?

Toward the end of my stay, I was finally granted the privilege of buying the CMDA's *Land Use and Development Control Plan.* I reproduce the Plan's primary map here in all its illegible glory to indicate the state of mapping—or rather "unmapping"—in Calcutta. The CMDA map also carefully excludes the eastern fringes. By the time I staggered my way through the maze of bureaucracy to the National Atlas Mapping Offices, I was told that aerial maps of the eastern fringes were classified information. Were we at war and I simply did not know it?

Obviously the issue of secrecy is an old one. Chakravorty and Gupta (1996, 425) note that most CMDA planning documents and accompanying maps—from the Mega City Program to the Calcutta 300 Plan—have been classified as top secret, shielding them from all public scrutiny. The Town and Country Planning Act of 1979, which established the CMDA as a statutory body, also mandated the production and circulation of an Outline Development Plan (ODP). Chakravorty and Gupta argue that the CMDA has delayed the production of the ODP precisely to ward off all possible challenges from NGOs regarding the land uses planned for the eastern fringes (p. 425). The CMDA itself is an organization of unprecedented power, "nonelected, politically fortified against the environment, well-funded and high profile, imposed upon a bewildering array of other public agencies and weak local authorities (Harris 1989, 20).

A city of secret maps? I had visions of smoke-filled back rooms and secret dealings in overstuffed chairs. I imagined an urban oligarchy that was selling off the eastern fringes at a hectic pace. One cinematic scene, in particular, haunted me: that from *Chinatown*, with Jack Nicholson in the Land Records office discovering the flurry of land transactions in the San Fernando Valley, the names all a front for the real owner. He steals the page with the latest escrow transactions on it, the plots all marked out, and the names, though *benami*,[5] listed for each plot. This was the kind of paper that I wanted—boundaries and transactions, space and people inextricably linked.

The piece of paper that did eventually prove illuminating was nothing of the kind. It was an article that appeared in the *Telegraph,* an English

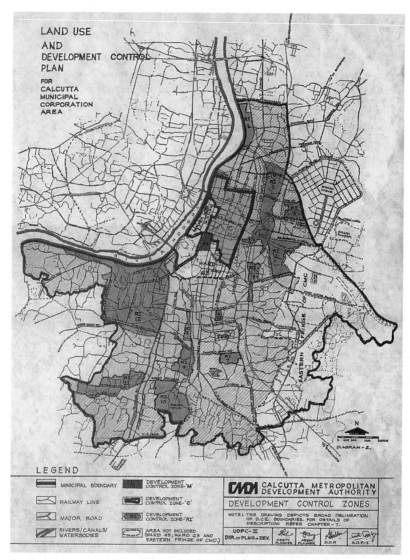

Figure 4.1. The map of the Calcutta Metropolitan Development Authority for its *Land Use and Development Control Plan*, 1996.

daily, on 2 December 1997, "CMC Caught without Master Plan; High Court Demands Copy; Corporation Grapples with 75-Year British Map":

> Unbelievable but true: Calcutta is the only city in the country
> without a master plan. The absence of the master plan supposedly
> came to light during a court case filed by a NGO in the public in-

terest. When the CMC failed to present the court with a master plan, the Chief Justice of Calcutta High Court directed all chief engineers of all major city agencies to appear before him. The only plan they could produce was the CMDA's *Land Use and Development Control Plan* for the CMC. The CMDA said that it had been unable to prepare a master plan because of the lack of reliable data. All that the agencies have in their possession is a 75-year-old survey map prepared by a British expert.

I say that this article was important not because it generated any public outrage in the city. No heads rolled and seemingly no attempt to create a master plan was initiated. It was crucial for me because it sent me back to my field notes and to a massive collection of land-related incidents that I had researched from five different Bengali and English dailies covering a span of two years. I returned to the emphasis of Shah and the CMDA Land Acquisition Officer on fuzzy boundaries and the absence of maps and plans. In the process, I came to focus on how, in the absence or unavailability of such official representations, land is exchanged, acquired, and developed. I set aside my initial questions: How can I find the appropriate map? Who owns this piece of land? How did the government vest this other piece of land? What uses are planned for it? In their place, I asked: What does it mean to have fluid and contested land boundaries? How does this ambiguity regarding status and use shape processes of urban development? How does this establish the possibilities and limits of participating in such land games? I thus came to piece together how the absence of a core of bureaucratic and public knowledge about land imparts a specific character to the urban transformation of Calcutta's fringes. This, then, is a story about the politics of an unmapped city.

I have argued that the dynamics of squatting, specifically the persistence of poverty, need to be understood in light of a logic of double gendering, the linking of feminized livelihoods with masculinized politics. I now seek to situate squatter settlements within the broader urban transformations of Calcutta's southeastern fringes. If, as I have shown, the disjuncture between settlement/male histories and settlement realities indicates the fragile vulnerability of squatters, then this chapter maps the cycles of evictions and resettlements that constitute this stark reality.

In particular, I highlight the ways in which, and the terms on which, squatters negotiate claims to land, how negotiability frames the encounter between the urban poor and the apparatus of the regime. I use the idea of negotiability in Berry's (1993, 13) sense of "law as social process, transactions as subject to multiple meaning, and exchange as open-ended and multi-dimensional rather than single-stranded and definitive."

Negotiability is of course implicit in the idea of informality and thus inevitably accompanies squatting. In previous chapters I have outlined the ways in which gendered subject-formation is a crucial part of the politics of poverty. I now emphasize how these cultural practices are negotiated in and through an ensemble of political institutions whose mode of regulation is urban informality. In the case of Calcutta, the specificity of these norms derives from a context of regulatory ambiguities that allows the state and political parties tremendous flexibility in controlling the poor. But as such forms of negotiability do not guarantee the poor land rights, nor do they secure the regime. Instead, the view from the city's fringes reveals the spatialities of an ongoing and contested process of hegemonic stabilization. Here, and possibly unlike rural West Bengal, the contradictions of the regime become apparent, not least in the form of territorialized factionalism.

This hegemonic consolidation, and its paradoxes, can only be understood by situating squatting within a specific historical moment of the Left Front, a "communism for the new millennium." The New Communism does not signify a shift from agrarian reformism to urban developmentalism. Rather, fueled by internal succession struggles and electoral competition, this moment is a clumsy balancing act between old and new populisms that plays out within Calcutta's suburbanizing fringes. The persistence of poverty is inevitably located in the volatile geographies of this new frontier. In particular, I emphasize that this volatility does not indicate dynamic growth but instead is a stalemate in territorial claims, where neither squatters nor middle-class suburbanites are able to occupy land with any stability or certainty.

Such findings were made possible through a specific set of methodological strategies that, while broadly congruent with the ethnography of squatting and commuting, involved some important breaks. They are worth a closer look. The imperative to study the urban transformation of Calcutta's southeastern fringes came directly from the squatter settlements. Fieldwork nodes such as the Jadavpur settlement led me to the resettlement colonies. They also revealed that there were important connections between these various forms of urban settlement, that they were linked through the differential geography of political patronage.

But this cartography turned out to be a challenge, the details of which I present in this chapter. Not least of the challenges was the absence of land records and maps. If I first interpreted this as my inability as a researcher, and later as bureaucratic recalcitrance, I eventually came to realize that I was encountering a specific regulatory logic that operated precisely through the absence of knowable maps and records. Indeed, I argue that it is this "unmapping" of the city's fringes that has allowed the proliferation of multiple territorial claims.

Such a plethora of claims also meant rethinking the methodological question of evidence. In the case of each plot of land, I was confronted with radically different stories. At first, I turned to newspaper reports, tracking land transactions in the fringes over a period of two years, in order to sort through the competing stories. But the newspaper accounts only further revealed the irreconcilable divergences in claims to this land. Thus, instead of seeking to reconcile the divergences, I came to interpret them as indications of claims. If the context was marked by the negotiability of rules and transactions, I focused on uncovering how contrasting stories are "a crucial component of the process of renegotiation . . . seeking to define and claim resources" (Fortmann 1995, 1054).

The collection and interpretation of these divergent stories brought me face to face with the workings of the regime. The volatile geography of Calcutta's fringes demanded an ethnographic concept of state and party, a focus on this ensemble of everyday and extraordinary practices. To this effect, for the last four months of the project I expanded my ethnographic boundaries to include party offices, state bureaucracies, and settlement clubs. In particular, I focused on how these institutions shape the specific articulation between squatting and the broader transformations of Calcutta's rural-urban edges. The ethnographic negotiation of this context of unlimited negotiability was an unanticipated but invaluable look at the nature of the regime, the fate of the squatters, and the historicized future of Calcutta.

Urban Informality

That political economy gives shape and form to cities is a rather obvious argument. What distinguishes the urban research of the 1970s is the emphasis on informal processes of urban transformation—the ways in which cities are shaped by grassroots action that is often illegal and in violation of formal regulations. Instead of conceptualizing informality as marginal to mainstream economic and political structures, theorists of this genre have shown that informal processes, such as squatting, are inextricably linked to the establishment and consolidation of power (Perlman 1976). Castells (1983, 175), for example, situates squatting within strategies of urban populism, "the process of establishing political legitimacy on the basis of a popular mobilization supported by and aimed at the delivery of land, housing, and public services." Eckstein (1977, 100) emphasizes that these forms of patronage are crucially important mechanisms in the project of democratization: "the transformation of an unreliable citizenry into an accessible public." But the populist project is also conceptualized as disciplinary, one in which mechanisms of regulation and control are of critical importance (Collier 1976). Patronage networks and grassroots mobilization are thus irrevocably linked to a politics of cooptation (Eckstein 1977), and thereby to the subservience of the urban poor (Castells 1983).

What is striking about this theoretical cluster is that the meaning of "informality" shifts and slides such that it is impossible to anticipate or generalize the precise connections between politics and urbanization in any given setting. AlSayyad (1993) emphasizes that much of the first round of research on informal urban development was conducted in the context of Latin America and is not easily transferable to other political settings. I thus draw on the research on informal urban development not as a repository of universalized models but instead as the source of analytical concepts, the precise meanings of which can only be fixed in historically specific contexts.

There are four theoretical markers in particular that I borrow as analytical concepts. The first is the idea of *urban populism* indicating clientelistic strategies of popular mobilization and disciplinary control. I see these populist tactics as increasingly deployed within contexts of commercialization, and thus involving a much wider range of agents and institutions than simply political parties and the urban poor. The second is the concept of *urban developmentalism,* by which I mean the imperatives of late capitalism as well as the institutional context of neoliberal policy-making. In many ways, both urban populism and urban developmentalism are about the establishment and negotiation of claims to urban territory.

Perhaps more than any other concept, the struggle over claims is captured in the idea of informality, my third borrowed concept. I invoke the notion of *informality* to signify not a sphere of unregulated activities but instead a realm of regulation where ownership and user rights are established, maintained, and overturned through elaborate "extralegal systems" (de Soto 1989, 66). While de Soto intends the idea of extralegality to stand in for a Smithian invisible hand of sorts, creating equilibrium in informal markets, I mean it as a technique of discipline and power. What is useful about the concept of extralegality is that it shows how informality is at once an outcome and a process. The significance of this process lies in the inherent ambiguities of the informal, and it is this that creates a dynamics of constant negotiation and negotiability.

The conceptualization of the informal as a site of extralegal discipline implies continuities with formal systems of regulation. I use the idea of a *regime* to signify a specific structure of power that is predicated on the simultaneous deployment of legal and extralegal mechanisms of control and discipline. Judd and Kantor (1992, 66), for example, describe the urban regimes of nineteenth-century American cities as a merging of governmental authority and the building of democratic political systems through party machines, held in place through the dispensing of individualized and selective patronage by political bosses. Indeed, the broader debates on urban regimes (Lauria 1997) and growth machines (Logan and Molotoch 1987) indicate that the very processes of political power can be thus informalized, what Stone (1989) calls "regime informality." It is precisely this seamless structure of state and party that Chatterjee (1997, 154, 160) evokes when analyzing the Left Front's success in West Bengal: "the daily renewal of the legitimacy of power" through "the coupling of a developmental regime with the organized mobilization and reproduction of political support." His conceptualization echoes Gramsci's (1971, 259–64) designation of political parties as organizers of the consent of the governed—the private apparatus of hegemony that is an integral part of the state.

The emphasis on hegemonic alliances consolidated through informality provides what MacLeod and Goodwin (1999) call a "relational account of the state," indicating the "institutional ensemble" through which power is mediated and expressed.[6] In the case of Calcutta, a key aspect of this relationality is patronage, manifested in either urban populism or urban developmentalism. The relationality of patronage evokes Bourdieu's (1987) idea of a "field of power"—that when the regime stabilizes it does so not as a dominant class interest but as an ensemble of social relations and political transactions. If the bulk of the West Bengal studies have been concerned with assessing the static effects of Left Front rule, then the idea of a regime breaks with this emphasis, shifting the inquiry to how the sociopolitical apparatus of the Left is constituted, maintained, and challenged.

Such conceptualizations are particularly useful in thinking through the hegemony of the regime. The Latin American research, by highlighting the myriad mechanisms of populism, brings to light the multiple guises of state power, what Roberts (1995) would designate as "sources of diversity." But the research also reveals that regime mobilizations are inherently unstable, requiring a constant renewal of power. This is in keeping with Cooper's emphasis on social contingency and with the broader post-Marxist interest in processes of hegemony. It is precisely such an analytical shift that attends Castells's (1985, 7) move from *The Urban Question* to *The City and the Grassroots*, from collective consumption to social reproduction, from state politics to a greater emphasis on struggles over "cultural identity and political self-management." In this sense, the regime is the "partial, temporary, and unstable result of embedded social practices rather than the pre-determined outcome of quasi-natural economic laws" (Jessop 1992, quoted in Amin 1994, 7–8).

It is important to emphasize that the idea of instability does not signal an attrition of state power. Nor do I mean to suggest that the Left Front as a regime is a unitary actor, guaranteed in its dominance and homogeneous in its constitution. Rather, I am concerned with the ways in which there is a coagulation of discourses and practices, what Ferguson (1990, 273) describes as a mode of power: "The 'state' not as an actor, but the name of a way of tying together, multiplying, and coordinating power relations, a kind of knotting or congealing of power." Here, as will become evident in this chapter, informality is a technique of unmatched flexibility, reproducing the regime with great disruptions but few challenges. If masculinist patronage is the social basis of informality in Calcutta, then the volatile geography of the New Communism is its spatiality. Together they produce a regime that is coherent in its fragmentation.

An Era of Liberalization

As a backdrop to my discussion of Calcutta's New Communism, it is important to clarify what I see to be the analytical elements of urban informality in an era of liberalization. In doing so, I am for the most part extending and updating the concepts that I have borrowed from the toolkit of Latin American urban research.

Despite the rhetoric of privatization, it has become clear that neoliberal restructuring involves new regimes of regulation. There are two aspects of this moment that I wish to highlight, both of which are captured in Jessop's (1994) concept of a "hollowing out" of the state. The first is a shift in the scale of state action (Swyngedouw 1997; Peck 2001) whereby new geographies of governance are created through the territorial and functional reorganization of state capacity. The urban is a particularly important arena for regime practices and politics at the moment of liberalization (Smith 1992; Harvey 1994), articulating the simultaneous localization and internationalization that Jessop (1994, 263) sees as a key dimension of neoliberal regimes. I will return to this point later in the section.

Second, Jessop's idea of a hollowed-out state does not indicate a loss of dominance. Instead, it signifies a "productivist reordering of social policy" as well as a shift from "government to governance" in which the latter involves "a set of quasi- and non-state actors in a variety of state functions"

(Jessop 1994, 263–64). Such notions not only undermine the idea of liberalization as a linear path toward transparent markets but also shatter the simple duality of state and market. In the context of liberalization, the state itself has become a site of market activity.

There is of course the "entrepreneurialism" that is made possible by the apparatus of the state (Oi 1986), especially through practices that straddle formal and informal sectors. Thus, Amis (1984, 87–88) discusses how, in Nairobi, the development of rental markets within squatter settlements is linked to the informal allocations of land by Kenyan public adminstrators. In Calcutta one of my earliest moments in the field was an attempt to buy postage stamps. I was confronted with a gruff young clerk who growled, "We are out of ten-rupee stamps. You can buy a whole lot of 50 paise stamps." I declined. He soon pulled out a fresh bunch of ten-rupee stamps from his pocket: "The post office is all out. But I would be glad to help you by selling them to you at twelve rupees each." Through the spatial technique of transferring the stamps from the realm of the state (his desk drawer) to the private domain (his shirt pocket), this entrepreneurial clerk was making a decent profit on his governmental position. However, beyond such practices of corruption, I am interested in the ways in which neoliberal restructuring involves an urban developmentalism aimed at capitalizing on state assets such as public land. Not surprisingly, such markets have emerged with particular rapidity in "socialist" regimes where the territory of the public is substantial (Zhu 1999).

This idea of the state as developer is perhaps most evident in the *ejido* reforms of Mexico. At first glance, the reforms seem to indicate a process of privatization, a shift from communal land tenure to private forms of ownership. However, the *ejidos* have long been commodified, with the land being sold to accommodate informal housing (Castells 1983, 188). Such patterns of development ensured the political allegiances of both the *ejidatarios* and informal settlement residents to the ruling PRI (Gilbert and Ward 1985, 90). The liberalization of tenure that took place in 1992 changed the nature of populism, strengthening the market power of the state, particularly its urban components (Jones and Ward 1998, 89). In other words, if the informal sector can itself be seen as a distinctive type of market (Leaf 1993), then neoliberal restructuring has extended such forms of market power to the state. In making this argument, I have, then, once again returned to the ways in which the regime is constituted in and through informality.

The idea of informality as a mode of regulation implies the need to decouple it from poverty. The research on liberalization indicates that instead of seeing informality as coterminous with poverty, it might be more useful to think of it as a site in and through which social hierarchies are re-produced and negotiated. This is most evident in the growing emphasis on the heterogeneity of the informal sector. If the research of the 1970s focused on how the poor gained access to informal housing, then that of the 1980s and 1990s reveals the commercialization of such housing sectors (Amis 1984). At the core of such discussions is the concept of informal sub-divisions. On the one hand, the idea indicates a middle-class market of informal housing (Smart 1986; Angel et al. 1987; Payne 1989). On the other hand, it shows how informal settlements can take the form not only of inva-sions of public land but also of the development of private plots (Roberts 1989, 685).

Indeed, in many different settings, informal subdivisions have become an important mechanism for both introducing land, quickly and cheaply, to the real estate market and providing a route, through regularization, to formally owned but affordable middle-class housing. In such cases, the role of the state is once again crucial. Soliman's (1996) research on Egypt, for example, shows how government bodies encouraged the development of "semi-formal housing areas" and thereby the urbanization of agricultural land through private subdivisions.

The rural-urban interface implicated in the *ejido* reforms, in the in-formal subdivisions of Cairo, and in the fringes of Calcutta, indicates the spatiality of liberalization. If Jessop's notion of a hollowed-out state signi-fies the changing territorial materialization of the regime, and if informality is a key sociospatial technique of regime power, then such practices are sharply obvious in the semiagrarian fringes of quite a few metropolitan re-gions. These are liminal zones that have been created through transnational real-estate investment as well as through the bizarre intersections of rural and urban restructuring that have accompanied liberalization. Here have emerged new and shifting configurations of actors: real-estate developers, global investors, liberalizing government officials, bourgeois urbanites, and peasants with de facto land rights. And here a cacophony of land regula-tions collide and merge, resulting in such ambiguity that the system of land tenure itself is rendered negotiable. Earlier, I wrote about the "urban" as a particularly important site of liberalization—in the classic sense of the Marxist "urban question" and its attention to social reproduction as well as in the idea of a distinctive arena of state practices. This is amply evident in the case of Calcutta, where the urban guise of the restructured state creates subjects and spaces fundamentally different from the countryside. The rural-urban fringe is not simply a space within which to study liberalization: it is *the* space in which a communism for a new millennium has taken hold, in which its paradoxes are most clearly visible.

But I am also arguing that liberalization gnaws at the boundaries of the urban. This is not to say that cities have ever been finite settlements. Not only have they been socially articulated with agrarian economies; they have also been "open" (Kostof 1992, 69), containing at their edges a set of richly varied spaces that mark the interdependence of rural and urban. But there is a way in which liberalization works through and at once transforms the rural-urban interface. In the case of Calcutta, this has taken the form of a simultaneous urbanization and ruralization: the urbanization of the city's agrarian fringes and the ruralization of villages from which migrants and commuters flock to the metropolis. The hegemony of New Communism rests in its ability, in the face of these processes, to perpetuate the myth of a *Sonar Bangla*, a Bengal of fields of gold, and of a *bhadralok* Calcutta, gentlemanly and Bengali.

The Geography of Urban Populism

During the last two decades, the city of Calcutta has only been growing at the somnolent rate of 2 percent per decade. In contrast, the Calcutta Metropolitan District, which includes the rural tracts and townships that ring the city, has been expanding at a decadal rate of over 18 percent (Census of India 1991). Some of the fastest growth is occurring on the eastern fringes of the CMD. This involves state-controlled developments, such as the Salt Lake township and the proposed New Calcutta at Rajarhat, as well as a flurry of private building activities, especially in the sphere of middle-class housing. The most dramatic change, the conversion of agricultural land into residential developments, involves the selling of land by peasants to developers as well as the displacement of quasi-legal sharecroppers by the state. These informal land subdivisions have become a major source of suburban housing, garnering investments from a middle class unable to afford property in the central city.

The eastern fringes also house a set of squatter inhabitants. While I use the broad rubric of "squatting" to indicate an ensemble of informal and tenuous rights as well as extralegal systems of regulation, there are significant differences among the various constituent groups. There are the refugees from Bangladesh who settled here in the postindependence period. Their settlements are well established, commercialized, and often regularized. In comparison, recent migrants from West Bengal villages eke out a more precarious existence in unrecognized settlements and without any guarantees against eviction (Unnayan 1996). But here again, there are two distinct groups. The first inhabits resettlement colonies sponsored by CPM party bosses and serviced by state agencies, often moved here en masse from squatter settlements in the city. These are invisible colonies, tucked away out of sight from the main thoroughfares of the fringes. The second, in contrast, are squatter settlements and claims that entail the invasion of public, and at times, private land. Unlike the colonies, this is not the undisputed territory of any single party, and thus involves bitter and often violent political battles. I will discuss this second type of settlement in the following chapter. For the purposes of my discussion of a territorialized New Communism, I am going to focus on strategies of populism and developmentalism, showing how resettlement colonies and urban development projects are part of the same paradoxical geography of hegemony.

Frontiers

The eastern fringes of Calcutta have long been a site of Left Front mobilization. There have been various moments of populism—from the landgrabs of the 1960s to the "refugee" settlements of the 1970s. In the 1980s, as the Left gained state power, it established a set of "colonies" meant to resettle squatters under conditions of long-term but unregularized tenure. It is hard to tell how many colonies are in existence because they are strategically located in remote sites and are invisible in official documents. During interviews, party workers named as many as ten. Directed by squatters residing in central city locations such as Jadavpur, I conducted research in three: Jamunanagar, Sahid City, and Mukundapur (Figure A.1, in the book's appendix). Indeed, settlements like Jadavpur remain connected to the colonies both through the history of resettlement and through ongoing household and kin networks.

Jamunanagar is a collection of about a thousand huts nestled in shady groves of trees out of sight from VIP Road. It is a rather soothing place, with all the gentle and verdant beauty of rural West Bengal. Unlike central city squatter settlements, it is clean, with wide brick roads, well-spaced huts, and a decent infrastructure in the form of electric lines, water taps, and freestanding toilets.

The settlement is composed of families who were moved here from a multitude of locations. I was particularly interested in those that had been resettled from Jadavpur and soon realized that these 160 households or so were all clustered together to form a large neighborhood within the colony. Without exception, the households were landless migrants from South 24-Parganas villages who had been squatting near the Jadavpur railway station. During the construction of the Sukanta bridge ten years ago, they were

Figure 4.2. The verdant setting of the Mukundapur colony.

Figure 4.3. A plot in the Jamunanagar colony, complete with CMDA toilet and self-built mud homes.

evicted but resettled here by Kanti Ganguly, a prominent CPM leader. "We pleaded with the party every day," said Anila, a middle-aged widow, as she meticulously sliced the vegetables for the evening meal. Her hut was at the western edge of the settlement. Beyond it stretched green meadows glistening in the hot afternoon sun. She continued: "We would go to the party office in Santoshpur and wait there all night. Finally, Kanti*babu* told us to demolish our own shacks. Within two months, he brought us here. He himself supervised the lorries being loaded with our possessions."

Each of the resettled families were given 1.25 *kathas*[7] of land on which they were allowed to build their own hut. What was most striking about these narratives was that, unlike other squatter stories, the descriptions of settling at Jamunanagar involved few instances of struggle for land. Instead, I was treated to a host of what I came to call "frontier stories," detailed portrayals of how the families tamed the land and made it habitable. Ranen, a man in his thirties who works *jogar*, described the state of the settlement ten years ago:

> We were brought here by Kanti*babu*. But the area was jungle. It was crawling with snakes. And it was all wetland. We had to dig for months, filling the marshes with earth, before we could even begin to build our huts. All of this time, we slept in tents. This infrastructure that we now have—these roads, corporation taps, tubewells, electricity—none of this was there. All of this was only provided to us last year. We lived all of this time without anything.

Like Jamunanagar, the other two colonies I studied, Sahid City and Mukundapur, were also established by Kanti Ganguly in the early 1980s through the resettlement of central city squatters, most of whom were originally landless migrants from South 24-Parganas district. In Mukundapur each household was given a land allotment of between 2 and 2.5 *kathas*. Party cadres confirmed that the residents had no *dalils*, titles of ownership, but that they would not be evicted.

The colonies embody a particular combination of formality and informality, of party and state. This is most apparent in the patronage politics of mid-level CPM leaders such as Kanti Ganguly, who also hold governmental positions, in this case Mayor in Council.[8] On the southeastern fringes, Kanti is omnipresent. One asks which squatters were relocated from Jadavpur to the colonies, and the answer is "Kanti's people." Why is the *bazar* at Jadavpur, at which most of the colony residents are merchants, still standing? And the pat answer: "Kanti." How is it that some families are stretched across multiple colonies and squatter settlements, maintaining claims to all of these plots of land? "Kanti. He has blessed them." This geography of patronage—the barely visible colonies, the gossamer webs that link Jadavpur to Jamunanagar, and one colony to another—is Kanti territory. Kanti Ganguly's patronage politics indicates the coupling of party and state, the combining of informal party tactics of mobilization with the formal state apparatus of infrastructure provision. It is in this sense that region and regime are inextricably linked, each implicated in the other.

Everyday Control

Colony: a group of people who settle in a distant land but remain under the political jurisdiction of their native land; a territory distant from the state having jurisdiction or nominal control over it; colonization—act of colonizing or state of being colonized; also in politics, the fraudulent temporary settlement of a voting district
Webster's New Universal Unabridged Dictionary, 1983

Desh: village, country, countryside, native land

"Do you know that song by Suman[9]?" Kanti Ganguly asked me during an interview. "The one about all those poor and wretched families living in spaces only ten feet by ten feet?" He continued: "Well, the people I took and resettled in the colonies, they did not even have ten feet by ten feet. They were cramped into tiny, claustrophobic holes. They now have both a respectable environment and self-respect."

The party tells an uplifting story about resettlement, one that is also mythologized in resident narratives of generous party leaders. Indeed, residents often refer to the colonies as *desh*, evoking an imaginary space rich with hints of rural nostalgia and unquestioned citizenship.

The term "colony," while English, is of common usage in Bengali mainly in reference to housing settlements. But there is also a provocative, albeit unintended, dimension to such terminology, which signifies the hierarchies of power that structure this particular type of settlement.

The colonies indicate a reterritorialization of political mobilization and control, involving the movement of squatters from scattered urban locations to a single, isolated, and circumscribed space. This spatial journey marks the conversion of poor migrant peasants into an organized and captive urban electorate. If Bhattacharya (1993, 68) is arguing that the political strength of the CPM in the West Bengal countryside lies not in the schema of land reforms but rather in the institutional mode of land distribution, then a similar argument can be made about the colonies. What is distinctive about the colonies is that the relationship of patronage is reproduced on an everyday basis through the operation of party offices that oversee every detail of daily life from clogged toilets to religious rituals.

I have already detailed how masculinist patronage is reproduced in the clubs of squatter settlements, and how the clubs are in turn locked in a territorial warfare between various political parties and factions, all overseen by party offices located outside of the settlements. In the case of the colonies, the institutional level of clubs is rendered moot because a single party, the CPM, dominates. It is the party office that mediates state intervention, as in the provision of infrastructure. It is the party office that establishes rights to the informal use of electricity, drawing lines from electric poles to individual houses. It is the party office that distributes ration cards, creating official identities recognized by the state during elections. And it is the party office that establishes committees to draw and redraw boundaries, regulates the selling of plots with appropriate commissions, and moves families at random from colony to new colony, from settlement to resettlement.

I remember my first visits to some of the party offices in these colonies, the endless stream of clients seeking audience with party bosses. An eviction, an abusive husband, a job for a lazy son, property disputes—it was all up for negotiation. After having spent my first evening on a rickety bench in a party office with mildewed walls, yellowing photographs, and a great deal of loud talk, I wrote in my field journal:

Figure 4.4. One of the numerous CPM party offices that dot the Calcutta fringes.

I have to admit that I am very uncomfortable in party offices. I see them as peculiar cultural artifacts and am thus fascinated by their bizarre decor, the choice of portraits, and so forth. My family has never practiced *para* [neighborhood] politics: in our circle of acquaintances party talk is refined, rarefied, and rare. I do not know whom my parents vote for and would never dream of asking them. For me, democracy in Calcutta has always been a quiet, silent and polite system. This abstraction bears little resemblance to the cacophony and intrusiveness of party politics that I am now suddenly witnessing.

But party offices are not "peculiar cultural artifacts" in the colonies. They constitute a crucial point of social control. Here, whom one votes for is guaranteed, pre-fixed, and it is this surety that ensures access to shelter in an uncertain world. Such mechanisms of patronage—the exchange of favors in return for votes and the assured presence at meetings and rallies—is not new or unique to the CPM. Chatterjee (1997, 183–84) details the wide range of organizations through which the Congress mobilized popular support in the preindependence period, and their continuities in the postindependence period. But what is specific to the Left Front is a campaign machinery that works so effectively because it works in tandem with a regime of development: "Party politics in the West Bengal countryside is not something which arrives along the campaign trail once every five years; it is everyday business and goes hand in hand with government work" (160).

Chatterjee is mainly talking about rural West Bengal, where he sees the everyday politics of the *panchayats* as a cornerstone of this essential link between party and state. The colonies seem to provide just such an institutional space for the Left Front in Calcutta, its weakest electoral base. The Congress threat, especially dire on the fringes of the city, has necessitated a constant search for new voters and new territories of support. For example, in the parliamentary elections of 1996, a breakaway faction of the Congress, the Trinamul, headed by fiery Mamata Banerjee, swept the Jadavpur constituency, which includes the southeastern fringes, undermining the CPM's long-established presence in the area (*Asian Age*, 11 February 1997). Such patterns of uncertainty have made imperative a constant recharging of patronage. Not surprisingly, before each major election the colonies have been treated to infrastructural improvements—one time the provision of quasi-legal electricity; another time the paving of roads, albeit often left unfinished.

But the daily renewal of legitimacy does not create any guarantees for the rural-urban poor. The ambiguities regarding land ownership that make

Figure 4.5. Infrastructure: electricity and semifinished roads at the Sahid City colony.

possible claims to land also make impossible rights to land. The Left Front justifies the absence of regularized tenure through the ideology of housing, arguing that the commodification of shelter runs contrary to the party's principles. If the frontier stories of the party and the colony residents romanticize practices of self-help, then the Left's policies regarding property rights continue such utopian notions, presenting the poor as needing to be protected from bourgeois corruptions. Thus, in the colonies, where the price of property has dramatically increased, and where residents are aware of market rates, the Left Front prevents residents from selling their land except to the colony committee, which in effect is an arm of the party. Indeed, the absence of land titles ensures the party's role as the ultimate proprietor of this land. At one level, such tactics can be interpreted as an ideological resolution of what Herring (1989, 89) poses as a central dilemma of parliamentary communism: the importance of tactical mobilizations in the name of land but the conservatizing influences of actually distributing ownership of land. The politics of squatting in Calcutta seems to present one solution: where a poor electorate is continuously mobilized because land is always promised but never secured.

However, as self-help involves significant amounts of sweat equity, so the ideology of housing mystifies the workings of housing and land markets, and particularly the regime's own role in such transactions. This role entails the "extralegal" regulation of commercialized informality, where everything from the fisheries of the northeastern fringes to the squatter rental markets and informal vending of the city is subject to an intricate system of fees, bribes, and payments. Increasingly, it also means the patronage of real-estate development. In such instances, the volatile geography of the fringes must be read not as a jostling of populist and developmentalist strategies but rather as a territorial expression of an urban developmentalism that is negotiated in a populist idiom. This inherently paradoxical nature of the regime has had serious implications for the fate of the colonies.

Evictions

When I first arrived in Jamunanagar, it was surrounded by a mushroom growth in new houses. All around the settlement, luxuriant paddy fields and grazing meadows were carved out into residential plots.

The developments worried Jamunanagar residents. "I can feel it in the air," said an old and wizened member of the residents' committee, an organization completely subservient to the colony's CPM party office. He continued:

Figure 4.6. Plot lines marking new development just outside of the Jamunanagar colony.

> We pay corporation taxes but we do not have any *dalils*. Last year, the party built new roads, put in new water taps, all before the elections. But these developments cannot be for us. I think that we will be evicted. We will be given a place to stay, but it will be even more remote than this place, further from our livelihoods, isolated from all services. You see, there is an unwritten law here—that the poor like us develop areas, fill in marshes, build homes, struggle to get infrastructure, and are then evicted to make way for the rich who move into a now desirable area.

As housing developments began to dramatically change the landscape of the southeastern fringes, I heard the same insecurities echoed at Sahid City and Mukundapur. All the while CPM party leaders and cadres repeatedly assuaged these fears by promising colony residents that they would never face evictions.

But in December 1997 the resettlement colony at Mukundapur was disbanded to make way for a state-sponsored medical facility. While local party leaders asserted that the colony was a peasant cooperative, the state and high-ranking party leaders said that the residents were squatters, occupying the land in flagrant defiance of the law. Kanti Ganguly, godfather of the colonies, was prominently among the latter. He argued that while this land was *khas*, or vested, having been taken over by peasants in 1967, it was now up to the state to decide what to do with it. He assured the party's peasant wing, the *Krishak Samiti*, that the evictees would be given alternative sites. While controversy brewed over the allocation of new land to the displaced colony residents, particularly in a region where all land was now extremely valuable, the medical facility was billed as a "charitable institution," a cause worthy of evictions (*Bartaman*, 21 December 1997). In effect, the clinic was a Rs 40 crore development project initiated by the Manipal Group, and it had the patronage of key Left Front leaders, including Chief Minister Jyoti Basu and Information and Home Minister Buddhadeb Bhattacharjee.

Across the road from Mukundapur, another development project took shape in 1997. Udayan, the Condoville, bore the promise of "700 condominiums with 65 percent open space":

> More than fine homes and lifestyle, Udayan promises you life. A life outside of your home . . . serene greenery, walkways and jogging tracks, parks for kids to play, a uniquely self-sufficient commercial centre, a club of your dreams. (Udayan advertisement, *Anandabazar Patrika*, 8 March 1997)

The Rs 135 crore Udayan project was launched by the Bengal Ambuja Housing Development Limited, a joint enterprise of the West Bengal Housing Board and Gujarat Ambuja Cements. In November 1997 Chief Minister Basu inaugurated the condoville, praising the public-private venture into "mass

Figure 4.7. Construction begins on the Udayan housing project in the southeastern fringes.

housing" (*Asian Age*, 17 November 1997). That this "mass housing" was in effect a bourgeois landscape of aestheticized gentrification signals the new rhetoric of the Left Front: urban developmentalism. If bourgeois suburban-ites, liberalizing communists, and private speculators seem to make strange bedfellows, such is the vision of communism for the new millennium.

Liberalization has come to Calcutta in the form of new political al-liances between the regime and industrial and commercial investors. There are multiple strands to this urban developmentalism. First, such strategies are aimed at strengthening the Left's electoral position in the Calcutta met-ropolitan area, a political space where the Left has been unable to replicate its agrarian successes. Second, the patronage of development is linked to internal struggles within the regime, which have taken the form of long-standing factionalism and more recent succession struggles in the scramble to nominate an heir to Jyoti Basu. I will return to the territorial implications of such issues later in this chapter.

Third, urban developmentalism is part of a broader state-level New Economic Policy that is in keeping with national trends of liberalization that took hold in the 1990s. Launched in 1994, the West Bengal policy is meant to reverse the state's stand against multinationals and attract foreign and domestic capital to the city, thereby salvaging the region's miserable eco-nomic performance (Mallick 1993; Banerjee 1996). The emphasis in the policy has been on urban development. On the one hand, this involves the rectification of a crisis of infrastructure, an issue that has been a key factor in the economic decline of the region (Mallick 1993). For decades, indus-tries shied away from West Bengal, avoiding a nightmarish power situation, a deplorable transportation network, and the absence of industrial estates similar to those in Maharashtra and other industrial states (Sengupta 1989). Urban development is thus meant to be a spatial catalyst of the Left's pro-ject of economic rejuvenation. On the other hand, there is renewed atten-tion to the tertiary sector, particularly to such components as trade/hotels and real estate. As I have discussed earlier, such arenas have been impor-tant contributors to the state's economic growth, far surpassing the perfor-mance of the formal manufacturing sector.

At the core of the new liberalization policy is a broad range of public-private partnerships in the provision of housing and infrastructure, most notable of which is a plan for a "New Calcutta" on the northeastern fringes of the metropolitan area (Chakravorty and Gupta 1996; Shaw 1997). The reforms also involve a fundamental restructuring of the budgetary alloca-tions of the CMDA. Since 1973 the World Bank has been pouring money into a series of Calcutta Urban Development Programs (CUDP), encom-passing such infrastructure issues as water supply and drainage, as well as slum improvement efforts (Sivaramakrishnan and Green 1986, 156). The CMDA's 1994 Calcutta Mega City Program, however, institutionalized a shift from equity goals to investments in the upper-end housing market, with a keen eye on cost recovery. As analyzed by Chakravorty and Gupta (1996, 426), metropolitan expenditures on housing and new area developments jumped from about 13 percent in CUDP II (1979–82) to 28 percent in the Mega City allocations of the eighth plan (1992–97). During the same period, expenditures on slum improvement dropped from 24 percent to less than 2 percent. Shaw (1997) sees the changes thus:

> The imperatives of economic liberalization and globalization have brought to the forefront a city management model that serves the interests of economic growth. Active supporters and beneficiaries are business and industry and the upper and middle class income groups. If successfully implemented, it will lead to an extension and an improvement of the quality of the formal city.

How indeed is the formal city implemented? How is the project of urban developmentalism inaugurated? And if its primary idiom is a territorialized populism, how do such strategies carve out new spaces amidst a history of claims? On the fringes of Calcutta, the formal titling of the city has been what Krueckeberg (1999, 180) would call a "stripping operation," an "Orwellian doublespeak" that serves to evict informal claimants and assure investors. Yet, as evident from Table 4.1, such formalizations have been constantly challenged.

Table 4.1

Selected list of contested plots of land in the southeastern fringes, 1997

Locality	Proposed use	Rival claimants
Anandapur	Bengal Non-Resident Indian Complex Limited	200 sharecroppers
Dhapa	Stock exchange	150 cultivators
Dhapa	ITC	200 cultivators
Mukundapur	Manipal Heart Clinic	600 squatter households
Nayabad	Housing cooperative	800 squatters
Patuli	Sites and Services project	More than 2,000 squatter households

Source: fieldwork, 1997; newspaper archives.

The story of liberalization in Calcutta cannot be told as simply a re-inscription of localities as their "proposed uses," a linear and straightforward eradication of "rival claimants." Rather, Table 4.1 indicates a system of land tenure, one which is inherently multiple, combining corporate, public, and individual tenures (Krueckeberg 1999, 181). The heterogeneity of this tenure system implies the territorialized flexibility of the regime, and it is this that needs explanation.

The Unmapping of Calcutta

New Communism requires a great deal of spatial creativity on the part of the regime: moving the poor around, forging developmental alliances, in many ways replicating capitalism's own breathless imperative for green-field sites. What accounts for this unceasing negotiability, this territorialized flexibility? The answer, I contend, rests in the regulatory ambiguities that mark the Calcutta context and that are most apparent in contending genealogies of land.

Who owns the land on which the colonies are situated? I asked this question over and over again during the course of my research. Colony residents pointed to the meadows that stretched all around them and said that until recently this was "vested" land farmed by de facto sharecroppers who had been mobilized by the Left Front to invade *benami* land. Mukundapur residents, for example, told a history of the vast holdings of an absentee landlord in the name of his employee, Bihari Mondol, which were eventually invaded by peasants. When this land was in turn taken over by the regime for the establishment of the colonies, the peasants were compensated through smaller plots of land.

A senior member of the residents' committee described the process: "The peasants were illegal but they have power. They each farmed about 1.5 to 2 *bighas*[10] of land. The government took their land but gave them 5 *kathas* each. This was also how the government procured the land for us."

Residents explained that since these five-*katha* plots cannot support agriculture, they are being rapidly sold off to real-estate developers, a process that in many ways has sounded the death knell for the colonies. Kanti Ganguly confirmed these accounts, emphasizing that the colonies were situated on a stretch of 8,000 *bighas* of vested land: "Large, rich landlords owned this land as *benami*. We confiscated this land during the agrarian revolution. This is now prime urban land."

Such narratives are complicated by other accounts. While officials at the state's Land Revenue Office generally agreed that many of these areas were completely vested, officials at the CMDA's Land Acquisition Cell directly contradicted this description, saying that the land was a complex mixture of vested and private land. And both bureaucracies laughed off the party story about robber barons, emphasizing that these are mainly nineteenth-century figures that have been kept alive in the legends of the party. Further, neither bureaucracy could or wanted to explain the jurisdiction and management of vested land. A senior CMDA officer concluded, "Kanti Ganguly is a dynamic man. What he does are party matters. We will never really know the full story."

I am quite deliberately resisting any attempt to reconcile these contradictory stories. The stories, the storytellings, are a crucial part of the ways in which competing claims to resources are staked and negotiated. In order to understand this dynamic, it is necessary to understand what I call the "unmapping" of Calcutta, the mode of regulation in and through which the regime takes hold and takes form.

Informal Vesting

Of the key regulatory devices that have evolved within the historical context of postcolonial India and Left Front–controlled West Bengal, perhaps the most crucial with regard to land is vesting, the means by which the state can expropriate private land. In the case of Calcutta's fringes, there are three ways in which land can come to be vested: the confiscation of agricultural land in excess of the land ceilings set by agrarian reforms; the confiscation of nonagricultural land in excess of urban land ceilings;[11] and the acquisition of land in the "public interest" by "requiring" public agencies. In effect, vesting provides a powerful basis for multiple forms of state intervention in the ownership and use of metropolitan land.

What is important about vesting is the ambiguity that is an inherent part of the regulatory context. Some of these indeterminacies are common to most large Indian metropolises, but others are unique to Calcutta. First, the precise governmental, geographic, and land use jurisdictions of each of the three forms of vesting remain ambiguous. It is not clear, for example, to how much of the urban agglomeration the Urban Land Ceiling Act, which was in effect until recently, applied (Bhargava 1983, 67). Second, the absence of knowable and centralized land records means that it is impossible to ascertain which plots of land, or which portions thereof, are vested. While most Indian cities lack a systematic documentation of urban land holdings (Bhargava 1983, 18), the problem is particularly acute in Calcutta, where, as I discussed earlier, the existing survey map dates to 1910. When use of specific plots becomes contested, the only recourse is often a maze of unending legal cases. Third, in the case of the metropolitan fringes, agricultural land remains a particularly thorny issue. On the one hand, it involves a complex ensemble of de facto rights of sharecroppers and small peasants, established during a history of CPM-led agrarian radicalism (Bhaumik 1993, 44). On the other hand, at the case-by-case discretion of the state, cultivated land remains exempt from urban land ceiling laws. Usually, these exemptions are determined on the basis of land uses laid out in master plans (Bhargava 1983, 29), but in the case of Calcutta, the absence of such a plan gives the state unchecked discretionary powers.

There are two specific aspects, then, to the nature of the regulatory ambiguities that shape Calcutta's fringes: a history of competing claims to land, and a historical technique of "unmapping" that allows for the negotiation but not the resolution of claims. If Appadurai (1996, 132) writes about how the colonial techniques "recuperated the unruly body of the colonial subject through the language of numbers," then, in present-day Calcutta, a new spatial vocabulary of control has been created through the absence of land records and maps. It is hard to trace the genealogy of unmapping, but clearly this logic has been present in the region's institutions for a while. Thus, Bagchi's (1987) evaluation of the Ford Foundation's 1966 *Basic Development Plan* reveals ambiguities about the nature of land use and economic data used in the formulation of the plan.[12] In analyzing the legal disputes over the East Calcutta wetlands, Dembowski's (1999, 49) diagnosis of a "problem of governance" is substantially concerned with the absence of master plans, outline development plans, and maps, a regulatory context that seems to have consolidated the CMDA's unchecked powers.[13]

Such regulatory ambiguities have become even more acute on the eastern fringes, which are not only unmapped but also marked by an unmappable history of territorial populism. In the postindependence period, as refugees rushed in from Bangladesh and squatted on the eastern fringes, the Congress recharged its machinery of popular support, consolidating its territorial power (Chatterjee 1997, 186–87; Ghosh 1981). In the late 1960s the project of mobilization changed hands. The United Front, composed of what is now the Left Front and breakaway factions of the Congress, instigated widespread peasant radicalism, urging the landless and *bargadars,* or sharecroppers, to directly implement agrarian reforms by grabbing excess and *benami* agricultural land. Large stretches of land thus came to be declared as "vested," or *khas,* through "quasi-judicial processes" (Bandyopadhyay 1997, 581). New refugees, pouring in after the Bangladesh war, settled on these lands (Unnayan 1996). Such cycles of land-grabbing and settlement became crucial mechanisms for enlarging party membership (Basu 1982, 58).

But this vesting remained, at best, semiformalized. During United

Front rule, the CPM, as the dominant member in the Home Department, coordinated efforts with its peasant wing, the *Krishak Sabha,* to mobilize landgrabs but also to legitimize land thus acquired (Ghosh 1981). However, such mechanisms of legitimacy often bypassed the legal apparatus of the state. For example, Land and Land Revenue Minister Harekrishna Konar stressed the speedy recovery of *benami* land through special land tribunals rather than the civil courts, which he alleged were plagued with delays (Ghosh 1981, 98–99). And as the United Front fell from power—twice—and the Congress unleashed its machinery of repression, West Bengal entered a phase of tremendous political instability. Between 1967 and 1977 the state had eight different governments, three terms of president's rule, and four elections for the State Assembly (Dasgupta 1992). It is impossible to gauge with any certainty the effects of such political rockiness, but it is my surmise that this instability made informal vesting possible but also made the regularization of these invaded and vested lands impossible. Herein lies the key to the current dynamics of urbanization in this area—informal vesting.

The concept of informal vesting seems to be an oxymoron. Vesting indicates the legal expropriation of land by the state. Informality signifies extralegal, and possibly illegal, mechanisms of regulation. But what makes vesting such a powerful instrument in Calcutta is precisely this convergence of legality and extralegality in the same process. Thus, in the case of the colonies, it is the informal vested status of the land that allowed sharecroppers to establish de facto use rights but also allowed the party to come in and reclaim the plot for the resettlement of squatters. And fifteen years later the fuzziness of land ownership made it possible for the state to evict the resettled squatters, claiming the land for developmental purposes.

Such regulatory ambiguities have far-reaching implications, the most important of which is the coupling of the party and the state through populist strategies of mobilization. As a tool, vesting allows the legal intervention of the state in land transactions and service provision. But as an indeterminate mechanism, vesting makes possible the extralegal intervention of the party to negotiate the ownership and use of land, shielding the state from public scrutiny. The party does what the state cannot do. It encourages land invasions, exacts electoral discipline, and maintains political loyalties. The state does what the party cannot do. It deploys its legal authority to provide infrastructure, to selectively regularize titles, and to evict when necessary. Vesting, then, is not simply a bureaucratic tactic but instead a field of constant and ceaseless negotiation of de facto and de jure rights, formal and informal claims. Here, the role of midlevel leaders like Kanti Ganguly, who have one foot in the party and the other in the state, is key. It makes for a regime politics where informal party tactics of mobilization are combined with the formal state apparatus of infrastructure provision. To put it bluntly, the colonies represent a distinctive form of informal subdivisions, founded on the basis of quasi-legal land rights, where the party itself acts as developer, with unique negotiability vis-à-vis the state for infrastructure, and thus with the later possibility of both party and state capitalizing on the upgraded settlement through evictions of the poor.

Such regime strategies also provide a crucial link between the CPM's rural and urban tactics. The transactions of land appropriation, assignment, and compensation that are involved in informal vesting have established key constituencies for the party: the sharecroppers who were first granted informal rights to agricultural land and then compensated during the process of urbanization; migrant peasants who were first inner-city squatters and were then transformed into colony residents. Both these groups can be seen as politically situated at the rural-urban interface, with important electoral links to South 24-Parganas villages and crucial organizational connections with the peasant wing of the party. For CPM leaders such as Kanti Ganguly who have sought to run for Assembly seats from rural constituencies in South 24-Parganas, such connections are vital.[14] In fact, the ambiguous status of vast stretches of land on Calcutta's fringes has provided an unprecedented window of opportunity to the party, allowing it to distribute use rights to land in a manner unmatched in many rural settings.

Finally, informal vesting is an invaluable mechanism of patronage politics because of its inherent ambiguities. As squatters and sharecroppers have staked claim to this unmapped land, so have their claims been rendered ambiguous. In the colonies, residents talked about the possibility of acquiring legal titles to the land, but this remained a desperate hope. They paid nominal corporation taxes and held on to these receipts as proof of legal ownership. CPM party leaders and workers said that as soon as the land was valued the residents would get the titles, but in some cases twenty years had passed without any final valuation. It is this uncertainty—the constant fear of evictions—that articulates the relation of dependency between colony residents and the party. As a young resident of Mukundapur cynically described: "They will never give us *pattas* [land titles]. If they did, we would no longer have to depend on them for everything, every single day. If they gave us *pattas*, the game would be over. Whose lives would they play with then?"

Informal vesting has thus become the mechanism par excellence for the implementation of a territorially flexible urban developmentalism. In Calcutta the moment of liberalization has manifested itself at the level of the urban—in what Harvey (1994) designates as an "entrepreneurial" urban regime seeking to recreate the city as spectacle. But it has taken root in particular, historicized interstices within the urban, such as the eastern fringes, and through historically perfected techniques of regulation, such as informal vesting.

Urban Development and Its Impasse

By now it is obvious that the present history of liberalization is a moment at which the interface of city and countryside is being reworked. The colonies, and their restless geography, indicate one way in which this is being accomplished. A related process is a series of middle-class informal subdivisions being created through a tripartite relationship among housing consumers, peasants with de facto rights to agricultural land, and private developers.

I was first introduced to the process by Jamunanagar residents who pointed out that while the Left Front had displaced quasi-legal sharecroppers to establish the colonies, they had also compensated them through smaller plots. The sharecroppers were now selling off these plots to developers, thereby creating a massive boom in housing construction. Such informal subdivisions have become an increasingly important mechanism for bypassing the tangle of agrarian reform laws and urban land ceilings, and for quickly introducing land to the real-estate market. The continued cultivation of the plot acts as a shield from scrutiny, while sudden and rapid construction establishes claims, albeit quasi-legal, to the land.

While at first glance these processes seem to parallel rather than replicate regime strategies of urban developmentalism, they are in fact part of the same extralegal system of regulation. The informal subdivisions are made possible through the mediation of the party, which acts as a middleman in the real-estate deals. The peasants are made to sign documents stating that they have no claims to the property; they receive a nominal sum from the promoters, who, with the help of CPM cadres, sell the land at ten times the cost to upper- and middle-class suburbanites. No titles to the land are exchanged but the final buyers treat the "no-claims" document as a sign of ownership (*Bartaman*, 12 March 1997). At the very least, the regime participates by withholding participation. For example, during interviews and visits with local developers, I would witness numerous visits by cadres. Each visit involved a hefty payment in relation to specific land deals. On one such occasion, I asked Shah why he was paying off the party. "To do nothing. I am paying them to do nothing," he replied.

Such transactions are blatantly illegal, violating the state's declared zoning codes and plans for the rural-urban fringes. Yet they are in keeping with the imperatives of urban developmentalism. In other words, once again informality acts as the site at which the state can deploy the party apparatus with great flexibility and little accountability toward ends that it itself has outlawed but wishes to achieve. A senior officer of the CMDA Land Acquisition Cell said of the rapid increase in informal subdivisions, "It does not really matter. There are laws against the conversion of agricultural land, the filling up of marshes, but all of this is urbanizable land. Urbanization is inevitable here."

However, the territorialized flexibility of the regime generates its own contradictions, most evident in an impasse in development. One aspect of this impasse is already apparent in the examples I have outlined: the deepening vulnerability of the rural-urban poor at this historical moment of New Communism. But there is also a broader impasse in all forms of developmental projects, a paralysis created by the very techniques of the regime. Let me briefly explain by describing two spatialized moments of the eastern fringes.

The Urban Dream

As part of its celebration of twenty years in power, the Left Front took out an advertising supplement in the *Asian Age* (20 June 1997). "In West Bengal, the CMDA has made the urban dream come true," read one of the faux

Figure 4.8. Informal subdivisions emerge after the last paddy crop in the southeastern fringes.

headlines. The piece claimed that the CMDA has encouraged urban development through investment planning and project implementation. What is this urban dream and to whom does it belong?

A few years ago a series of letters was written to the editor of the Bengali daily, *Anandabazar Patrika* (10 September 1996), by members of a housing cooperative. In their letters the members wrote that they had bought ten *bighas* of land in Nayabad, on the southeastern fringes of the city. The land settlement officer had assured them that the land was not vested. Nor were there any sharecropper claims on the plots. The cooperative members, middle-class clerical workers at a small bank, described how they had each poured their life savings into the plots, hoping one day to retire there. But within a few years the land was suddenly taken over by hundreds of squatters who, supported by local CPM leaders, built rows upon rows of shanties. The CPM local committee declared that the land was *khas*, or vested, and that it was the party's political practice to encourage squatting on such pieces of land. The cooperative members, desperate and frantic, wrote:

> How can this land suddenly be *khas*? And even it if is *khas*, how
> can the CPM exert such control over it? How can they distribute
> this land among the members of their *Krishak Sabha*? We had once
> cherished a dream of having a small home in one tiny corner of
> the world, but I had forgotten that West Bengal is *moger mulluk*—
> a place where anything goes (*Bartaman*, 12 March 1997).

The urban dream? It is evident from the Left's investments in middle-class housing that the regime supports the bourgeois dream of comfortable suburban living. Was Nayabad then simply a case of wayward cadres defying the upper echelons of the party? Nayabad was no aberrant instance of unruly local committees. Instead, it reveals the volatility of an unmapped city, where the search for new sites of patronage is fueled by regulatory ambiguity but can only yield quasi-claims to land. In the absence of centralized and knowable land records, the status of Nayabad remains open-ended. The state's Land Records Office argues that the entire area is vested; the CMDA's Land Acquisition Cell insists that the land in question is only partially vested.

Thus, while the fringes have seen a flurry of middle-class informal subdivisions, such housing production is itself subject to tremendous uncertainty. In the last few years, like Nayabad, many of these informal subdivisions have been suddenly invaded by mobilized groups of squatters and declared "vested." In other words, while informal subdivisions constitute a major source of affordable suburban housing for Calcutta's middle class, they are also damned by the very regulatory ambiguity that made possible their existence in the first place.

The Congress Challenge

As the eastern fringes have been transformed through urban developmentalism, so some of its peasants have entered into commercialized transactions with developers brokered by CPM cadres. But with the Left's repeated attempts to revoke de facto cultivation rights, many sharecroppers have also turned to opposition parties, specifically the Congress, for help.

In 1995 and 1996 the Calcutta Municipal Corporation (CMC) sold eight acres of land on the eastern fringes of the city to the Indian Tobacco Company (ITC), also a developer of luxury hotels, and an adjacent ten acres to the Indian Stock Exchange. The sales came with hefty checks but with the condition that the buyers would be able to get the land within a month or the corporation would have to pay 12 percent interest on the money (*Bartaman,* 13 November 1996). For years following the sales, the CMC remained unable to hand over the land and cash the checks because of ownership claims filed by peasants with the High Court. Led by Mamata Banerjee, then Youth Congress[15] leader and Member of Parliament, the farmers broke fences and tore down the barbed wire that enclosed the sold plots. On 17 September 1996, as a police camp was set up to protect the plot, a couple hundred angry peasants set the fences on fire. Mamata's presence prevented the police from taking any action against the peasants. Before leaving the site, Mamata told the gathered crowds to keep farming (*Bartaman,* 18 September 1996).

There are multiple claims to these contested plots of land. As was common practice in colonial Calcutta, in 1889 the land was leased to a private party for garbage disposal. The lease ended in 1966. During the revised settlement many municipal employees wrote the land titles in their own names (*Anandabazar Patrika,* 18 February 1997). At the same time, sharecroppers, mainly CPM supporters, began to farm this land (*Bartaman,* 20 September 1996). It seems that the ambiguous status of the land allowed the establishment and consolidation of peasant claims. But since these claims are predicated on another set of informal ownership claims, they proved to be vulnerable. The Municipal Commissioner argued that a complex set of transactions between corrupt municipal employees and sharecroppers had allowed many of the peasants to procure titles to the land (*Anandabazar Patrika,* 18 February 1997). In response to the eighteen separate cases that were filed with the High Court regarding these plots of land, the Court ruled that the land belonged to the CMC (*Asian Age,* 18 February 1997). The CMC once again erected fences around the plot, but farming, supported by Mamata, continues.

Here, then, is a political warfare that has taken on the cumbersome territorial tactics of holding land hostage. This was repeated on 19 July 1997, on an agricultural plot of land, 570 *bighas* in size, in Ananadapur, also in the eastern fringes. A large group of peasants fought vigorously against the police and land records officers. The peasants were being evicted to make way for a public-private partnership, the "Bengal Non Resident Indian Complex Limited," which was to build a middle-class housing complex. They claimed that they had been given cultivating rights by the district administration in 1984 and that they had the necessary sharecropper documents as proof. The district administration and the Minister of Police argued that the land was vested and that the sharecroppers did not therefore have ownership rights. The peasants were mobilized by the Youth Congress, with Mamata Banerjee insisting that all evictions had to halt. (*Telegraph,* 20 July 1997; *Bartaman,* 20 July 1997). The district administration announced that two hundred sharecroppers were on the official list and would be adequately compensated, but the struggle over the extent and nature of claims continues (*Bartaman,* 23 July 1997).

It is perhaps ironic that a regime founded on agrarian populism is actively involved in rejecting peasant claims and in converting agricultural land to urban uses. It is equally ironic that the Congress, which has had little success in mobilizing popular support in the West Bengal countryside, is the agent of peasant activism on the margins of Calcutta. This, of course, has to do with the complex electoral politics of the city where, unlike rural West Bengal, the Left Front has had to juggle multiple and contending alliances. Thus, the regime's new efforts to woo developers and middle-class suburbanites place it at odds with sharecroppers and migrant peasants. Such strategies have a peculiar contradiction in that while they are partly a response to electoral losses in Calcutta, they have also expanded the political space for opposition parties like the Congress to develop constituencies among the urban poor. The Congress, particularly Mamata Banerjee's faction—first as the Youth Congress and later as the Trinamul—has made it a business of defending sharecropper rights to rapidly disappearing agricultural land in the metropolitan area, even filing a slew of cases in the High Court. And, of course, it is precisely the ambiguities afforded by "informal vesting" that make possible such Congress strategies.

Needless to say, the paralysis is not looked upon kindly by investors. The double-edged failure of urban developmentalism—the sacrificing of mobilizational alliances without delivering on developmental projects—has made the political footing of the Left even more unstable on the fringes. In the various elections of 1998 the Left Front maintained its grip over the three-tier *panchayat* structure but lost key parliamentary seats in and around Calcutta to the Trinamul Congress allied with the BJP (*Telegraph*, 31 May 1998). With each loss, the dynamo of populism and developmentalism has to be recharged, necessitating a new search for sites of regime consolidation.

Such trends can be summarized as an impasse in suburban development, the most obvious spatial manifestation of which is an "uncontrolled undersprawl of an unprecedented magnitude along the entire metropolitan fringe area—a disorganized, haphazard subdivision pattern" (Ghosh 1991, 69). This is indeed a far cry from the orderly satellite townships envisioned by the 1966 Basic Development Plan and subsequently by the CMDA. Despite wide-ranging regulatory powers, including the power to expropriate land with minimal compensation, both city and state governments remain unable to direct urban development with any vision or surety.

The simultaneity of evictions and rehabilitation speaks, then, not so much to the spatial annihilation of the informal sector as to a microgeography of patronage, paradoxical in its imperatives. This is a chilling impasse, generated through unceasing movement and noise.

Communism for a New Millennium

I have told the story of a Calcutta on the edges of a whirlwind of NRI capitalism, barely holding on by the skin of its teeth. I have told the story of a communist party reinventing itself in light of global imperatives. I have told these stories at the rural-urban interface because I believe that it is within this territoriality that the paradoxes of the moment are most apparent.

One way of interpreting my narrative would be as the tale of a marginalized city on the periphery of the world-system. This is what the epithet of the "dying city" is meant to signal—an exile to the Fourth World, from which there is no easy return. Here, Calcutta could be recovered as the quintessential symbol of a "warped modernism of underdevelopment" (Berman 1982)—of a chaotic and semifeudal *pablik* that violates the Western ideal-type of a liberal public.

Another interpretation would be to see this as the "present history" of a distinctive "Bengali modern"—the experiences of development and modernity refracted through the practices of place. Here, the party and its particular bourgeois elite can be seen to constitute a particular localization of

the global, with a distinctive sociocultural idiom that they make and re-
make in the crucible of post/coloniality.

Indeed, global symbols are not new to the Left Front. CPM leaders
like Jyoti Basu forged their radicalism on the front lines of a nationalist
struggle, informed by stints at Oxford or Cambridge. In the 1920s the vanguard of the original party worked within the Comintern, furthering the
Soviet agenda of fostering a global socialist movement and launching a
Soviet discipline of Oriental studies (Vasudevan 1997). After independence
the party split, with the CPI (Communist Party of India) maintaining its
Soviet ties while the CPM began to look toward Maoist China for inspiration
to interpret the project of Marxism-Leninism in a non-Western context.
The trademark red of the CPM, its sickle and hammer, then, are all symbols
that indicate the party's location within international communist movements. The now-Bengalized term *comrade* is a borrowed one, as is the ideology it connotes.

But the Left's claim to the legacies of Bolshevism and Maoism has
often been rather shaky. Soviet disenchantment with Indian socialists intensified during partition and independence and rendered ties with the CPI
tenuous (Vasudevan 1997). The CPM's faith in China was shaken during the
border disputes with India, and in 1967 an extremist faction, the CPM-L,
broke off to continue a Chinese-inspired struggle through armed peasant
revolution (Basu 1982). The CPM, already shorn of links with the Soviet
regime, was now declared as "neorevisionist" by Mao, relegated to the margins of international communism, and left to be content with its "fiefdom"
in Bengal (Lal 1997).

In the 1990s the isolation of the Left Front ended. Perestroika has
come to Calcutta, but as a project inspired by Deng Xiaoping rather than a
collapsing Russia. CPM delegates regularly visit China and Vietnam, pre-
sumably to learn about market socialism (Lal 1997). And Jyoti Basu has
clearly expressed his aspirations to be prime minister of a bourgeois nation
aspiring to unfettered capitalism. These hopes dashed, he and his col-
leagues within the Front are enthusiastically looking toward Western multinationals for investment in West Bengal. Even Anil Biswas, CPM old guard
and editor of the party's newspaper, *Ganashakti*, emphasized in a recent
interview that the party could no longer afford to ignore companies with
enormous financial capital. "If Kentucky Fried Chicken or the McDonalds
are here in the city," he said, "we would certainly love to have their adver-
tisements splashed on our pages" (*Telegraph,* 1 May 1997). The CPM's new
position is perhaps best summed up in the title of Jyoti Basu's lead piece in

the *Red Star* (20 June 1998), a publication commemorating the Left's "historic achievement"—the right track is "left of centre."

Not surprisingly, the main rhetoric of the New Communism has been urban developmentalism. Prominent CPM leaders have sought to recast the "dying city" as the site of energetic entrepreneurship. For example, in his Dum Dum constituency on the northeastern fringes of the city, Transport Minister Subhas Chakravarty has been busy forging electoral alliances with promoters. During the same time that he was leading Operation Sunshine in order to evict "bourgeois" hawkers, he was lauding promoters for their contributions to the urban economy: "Of course, promoters make profit. But directly and indirectly, promoters are serving society. A few promoters might be corrupt but that does not make all of them evil" (*Anandabazar Patrika,* 8 March 1997).

Subhas was fighting a governmental initiative to broaden VIP Road, the key link between the city and the airport, by demolishing all houses illegally constructed within five hundred meters of the road (*Telegraph,* 17 June 1997). In the final Public Works Department survey, the buildings constructed by Subhas-supported promoters survived, marking a key victory for the new alliances between the CPM and private real-estate interests (*Telegraph,* 30 July 1997). In fact, none of the municipalities possesses clear land records, making the task of identifying illegal building actions by promoters an impossibility and cementing the protection afforded to promoters by CPM leaders (*Telegraph,* 6 June 1997).

It would be too easy to read the simultaneity of Operation Sunshine and such developmental alliances as the assertion of a formal city preceded by spatial evictions, a wholesale gentrification of sorts. On the ground, the reformism of the Left has taken the form of intricate territorial strategies that are best understood not at the level of ideological change but rather as localized struggles over resources and meanings. The CPM's formidable battalion of cadres is unmatched in exacting political discipline, and the party's vanguard carefully walks the tightrope, balancing communist ideologies with parliamentary democracy. But mid-ranking leaders like Kanti Ganguly, Amal Mazumdar, even Subhas Chakravarty are vital because they mediate between these two levels of everyday regulation and regime imperatives. It is they who give shape and form to metropolitan Calcutta by fixing the precise locations of populist projects and developmentalist sweeps. It is they who have used the dual functions of party and state, effectively deploying regulatory mechanisms such as "vesting" to align and realign the regime's territorial base and ward off opposition from contending parties. If the CPM is indeed a party that "runs with the semi-starved hare even as it hunts with the well-fed hounds" (Lal 1997), then nowhere is this more evident than in the restless geography of mobilization and control that marks Calcutta's fringes. Here, with great agility, and sometimes with a tinge of megalomania, the regime's pragmatic visionaries direct a complex orchestra of demolitions and resettlement colonies, peasant rights and middle-class suburbanites.

Quite a few of these struggles are being waged over the largesse of the party itself. There are two aspects to this scramble; the first has to do with the materialization of the regime, inevitably spatial, where the party apparatus itself has become the mechanism of rent-seeking practices. Second, as the Left has matured as a ruling party, it has been marked by succession struggles, a factionalism that has taken on a deeply territorialized form. The regulatory ambiguities and development possibilities of the metropolitan fringes have created an unprecedented space for both political projects.

To the north, the fisheries, popularly known as *bheris*, have become a regular source of income for the party's local committee. Here, cadres have been levying an informal 10 percent tax on *bheri* transactions and supervising the assignment and renewal of leases. District-level party offices charge that this money is siphoned off at the local level and never makes it into party coffers (*Anandabazar Patrika*, 3 March 1997). If in the late nineteenth century the fisheries had made possible lucrative leases (Furedy 1987), at the end of the twentieth century they were still making possible the collection of multiple fees, dues, bribes, and payments. Indeed, the bitter struggle for *bheri* money led the party to launch internal disciplinary investigations, a "rectification" program involving 13,000 party workers (*Telegraph*, 16 November 1997). In 1997, during its twenty-year celebrations, the CPM published a list of corrupt party functionaries (*Telegraph*, 16 July 1997), going on to purge 156 members (*Bartaman*, 5 August 1997). Such trends are a far cry from Kohli's (1997) reading of the Left's sturdy governability. Increasingly, unruly cadres are capitalizing on the dynamics of informality, and sanctions have proved ineffective in containing such commercializations of the party apparatus.

But there is more to the party purges and rectification than simply the disciplining of wayward cadres. Party leaders have been cracking the Leninist whip of democratic centralism, seeking to check the growing wealth of cadres. But the bourgeoisification of the party is well under way. Party workers complain that they are being singled out while top-ranking leaders are leading extravagant lifestyles and while the party itself has amassed a great deal of property (*Telegraph*, 9 March 1997). Nowhere perhaps is this ostentation more apparent than in the swanky new offices of the *Ganashakti*, the CPM's Bengali daily. On my first visit to Ganashakti Bhavan, I was overwhelmed by this structure, wrapped in marble and granite, its postmodern furniture and monogrammed ashtrays, central air-conditioning, shiny new elevators staffed with uniformed guards. It was a long way from the decrepit and musty party offices that I was accustomed to visiting. No wonder that the building has come to be seen as "a towering exhibit of the rich cash flow into the party" (*Telegraph*, 1 May 1997). Why, then, the sudden exertion of disciplinary control? Why the consuming concern with the income of lowly cadres? Such strategies can only be understood in the context of succession struggles within the party, the struggle to choose an heir to Jyoti Basu's uninterrupted twenty-year reign as chief and Chief Minister.[16] The purges of 4 August 1997 were thus inextricably linked to the anticipated battles of the party's 12 August organization polls (*Bartaman*, 5 August 1997). The threats of discipline and expulsion were meant to mobilize and control factions of support.

The rift line that currently runs through the CPM first yawned wide open in 1996 when the newly elected national coalition of parties, the United Front, invited Jyoti Basu to be Prime Minister of India. Basu was extremely keen to accept the nomination but was prevented from doing so by the CPM Central Commitee. The opposition came from the old guard, many of them like Biman Bose and Anil Biswas, who are key players in West Bengal politics. Basu's supporters were a younger group, many of them members of Basu's cabinet, including Subhas Chakravarty, Gautam Deb, and Buddhadeb Bhattacharjee (*Telegraph*, 16 November 1997). Basu termed the decision a "historic blunder," setting the tone for an ideological battle regarding the appropriate role of the party within the Indian nation-state (*Asian Age*, 18 March 1997).

Such jockeying for power within the party has given new importance to the territorial battles between factions. Operation Sunshine, for example, was conducted without the approval of the Calcutta Committee, particularly that of Mayor Prasanta Chatterjee. When the Committee expressed its displeasure, it was sharply rebuked by the state leadership (*Bartaman*, 3 December 1996). During the 1997 *pujas*, the busiest selling season of the year, Anil Biswas announced that hawkers would be allowed to make a temporary comeback. He was immediately contradicted by Home Minister Buddhadeb Bhattacharjee and put in his place by Chief Minister Basu, who emphasized that policy statements can be issued only from Writer's Building, the seat of government, not from Alimuddin Street, party headquarters (*Telegraph*, 28 September 1997).

Similarly, Subhas Chakravarty's impassioned case in favor of promoters in Dum Dum was a showdown between two dominant CPM factions, in this case in the North 24-Parganas district (*Telegraph,* 17 June 1997). Also at stake is the battle for the *bheris.* The Subhas camp was supported by promoters while the rival faction seemed to have established control over most of the *bheris,* thus exerting pressure to preserve the fisheries (*Anandabazar Patrika,* 9 March 1997). In the weeks leading up to the organizational elections, violence erupted repeatedly between the two factions, turning the northeastern fringes of the city into a war zone (*Bartaman,* 30 August 1997).

Such territorialized conflicts have created a new impetus for the mobilization of political constituencies. Nowhere, perhaps, was this more evident than during Operation Sunshine, the eviction of Calcutta's hawkers from the city's sidewalks. At first glance, the drive seems to indicate a battle between old-guard populism and avant-garde developmentalism, an overshadowing of agrarian revolutionary interests by urban reformist ones. But a closer look reveals a complex choreography of populism and developmentalism that is in keeping with the larger volatilities of contemporary Calcutta and its impasse.

In November 1996 officers of the Calcutta Municipal Corporation (CMC), along with huge police forces and CPM party cadres, demolished the sidewalk stalls of thousands of petty traders, which had lined the city's major thoroughfares since the early 1970s. In fact, in 1975 the CMC and CMDA had tried to evict the informal traders. "Operation Hawker" was, however, met by vocal protests, and the traders organized themselves into CPM unions. During the Left Front regime, the hawkers continued to be an important source of political support (Dasgupta 1992, 260–61) and of party revenue extracted through a complex web of police, unions, and cadres (*Anandabazar Patrika,* 22 December 1996).

The Operation Sunshine evictions continued through 1997 and intensified to mark the Operation's first anniversary (*Telegraph,* 13 October 1997). Hawkers staged daily protests, stopping traffic at key intersections. They tried to return with baskets of goods, and Mamata Banerjee joined them to sell their wares on the pavements. (*Telegraph,* 29 September 1997; *Asian Age,* 16 December 1997). The Left Front remained firm in its opposition to the hawkers.

But the story of Operation Sunshine cannot be simply told as a homology between upper-level ideological rifts and lower-level territorial battles. Its micro-geography of patronage was shaped by personalized calculations of local power by regime functionaries. It is thus that Subhas, chief choreographer of Operation Sunshine, who had so energetically directed the movement of bulldozers, preserved encroachments along VIP Road, preventing the construction of a World Bank–funded six-lane expressway. Kanti Ganguly, another key player in Operation Sunshine, argued vehemently against the misuse of public space. But he was also instrumental in establishing rehabilitation locations for evicted hawkers. These rehabilitation projects were always in his zone of control—near the Sukanta Bridge at the Jadavpur railway station, along the Bypass at Rashbehari Connector (*Anandabazar Patrika*, 23 January 1997). And they were always for small groups of hawkers. The new geography of communism, then, is not simply about the evictions of hawkers and squatters; it is instead about the evictions and resettlement of *select* hawkers and squatters.

As in the case of the colonies that Kanti had so carefully engineered, the questions arise: Which hawkers would be rehabilitated? How was this land procured? The selection of a small group of hawkers, the indeterminacies of exclusion and inclusion, ensures political support. And once again vesting is deployed as a mechanism of state intervention and party expropriation. In parallel to the demolition of hawker stalls, Kanti Ganguly supervised the takeover of private plots of land by CPM cadres and CMC employees. In Jodhpur Park, residents vainly crusaded against such a forcible occupation of a five-*bigha* plot (*Asian Age*, 15 July 1997). Kanti declared other private plots invaded by small groups of hawkers as vested, thereby establishing the de facto user rights of the traders (*Anandabazar Patrika*, 27 December 1996). When CPM Secretariat member Anil Biswas suggested

Figure 4.9. Hawker rehabilitation stalls at the Jadavpur station.

that the hawkers be allowed to return to the pavements during the 1997 *pujas*, Kanti protested, arguing that this would undermine the party's credibility with the hawkers who had accepted rehabilitation in designated zones (*Telegraph*, 22 September 1997).

Through this complex geography, Kanti established unchallenged and unmediated control over these groups. He transformed the hawkers from a massive electoral possibility into small bands of personal followers, subject to discipline and regulation. In the case of Mukundapur, by evicting his own settlers he facilitated the construction of a development project but also continued to guarantee the support of his poor constituents by resettling them in a new location. If Kanti is indeed the mysterious "mid-level CPM leader with strong grassroots involvement" who is dreaming of a "Second Calcutta" in the eastern wetlands (Chakravorty and Gupta 1996, 428), my interviews indicate that he intends to carefully combine his developmentalism with urban populism. In his words, "If the poor don't live close by, who will work in the houses of the upper and middle classes? No township can exist without cheap and readily available servants."

Histories

"In what will the history of a party consist?" asks Gramsci:

> Will it be a simple narrative of the internal life of a political organization? . . . The history of a party, in other words, can only be the history of a particular social group. But this group is not isolated . . . The history of any given party can only emerge from the complex portrayal of the totality of society and state. (1971, 150)

In what will the history of the Left Front consist? There are two historical elements that I think are of importance in analyzing the paradoxical totality of New Communism: populism as the agenda and technique of the regime, and the material basis of such populism in the sociocultural identity of the Left.

In a recent piece on current variants on populism, Brass (1997, PE28) delineates some of the differences between Marxism and populism: that Marxism claims as its historical subject the proletariat, while populism claims the peasantry; that Marxism claims a political identity of class, populism that of ethnicity; that Marxism promotes internationalism, populism advocates nationalism. I invoke these differences, albeit exaggerated and essentialized, to help situate the Left Front. It is not that the regime fits easily into one set of dualisms rather than the other, but rather that its discourses and practices slip and slide between Marxism and populism. Much of the West Bengal debates have evaluated the Left Front as a moderately reformist Marxist state government (Kohli 1987; Nossiter 1988; Herring 1989). And yet an ethnography of the state, whether in the village-level studies or in my account of the rural-urban interface, shows that the Left more often stabilizes around populist strategies. The workings of institutions such as the *panchayat* are thus crucial, for they make sense of and sort through the dissonance between Marxist ideologies and populist hegemonies.

Agrarian Myths

In distinguishing between Marxist and populist discourses, Brass (1997, PE 34) argues that the former is concerned with the agrarian question, that is, how peasant economies change, while the latter is concerned with the agrarian myth, that is, how an essentialized, undifferentiated peasant culture remains the same. The Left Front's practices and discourses are marked by precisely such a mythical construction of peasant essentialism, which in turn has underpinned a neopopulist imaginary that pits city against countryside, region against nation.

During the early years of communism in Bengal, when the CPI was still undivided, Maoist-style peasant insurrection was an important strategy, as evidenced in the Tebhaga sharecropper uprisings of 1948. In the 1950s, as the divide within the CPI began to grow, the chief bone of contention was the question of armed peasant struggle. In 1964 the radical elements, unhappy with the constitutional compromises of the mainstream, broke away to form the CPM (Communist Party of India-Marxist). In a 1966 statement the breakaway CPM took the CPI to task for its "deep-rooted reformist understanding," for "distorting the correct concept of all peasant unity in the struggle against feudal landlordism and building that unity based upon the middle and rich peasantry instead of building it around the rural labor" (Roy 1976, 43).

The CPM vowed to "build mass organizations of poor peasants and agricultural laborers" in order to make them "the militant vanguard of the anti-imperialist, anti-feudal revolution" (ibid.). During its two brief stints as junior partner in the coalition United Front governments in 1967 and again in 1969–70, the CPM mobilized a spate of land-grabbing movements. About a million acres of land were vested in the state through "quasi-judicial" processes (Bandyopadhyay 1997, 581). This is precisely how large sections of Calcutta's fringes came to be designated as "vested," with de facto ownership resting with sharecroppers.

But these insurrectionary tactics were short-lived. Despite all the talk of giving priority to the struggles of agricultural laborers, the CPM's peasant wing came to be dominated by middle peasants and even discouraged the formation of a separate agricultural workers' wing (Bhattacharya 1993, 95; Rogaly 1998, 2729). In 1967 a dissatisfied radical wing of the CPM broke away from the party to form a Maoist insurrectionary front: the CPM-L, or the Naxalites. Not surprisingly, the Naxalites took the CPM to task— rendering a scathing critique almost identical to that which the CPM only a year earlier had leveled against the revisionist CPI (Roy 1976, 44). By 1977, when the CPM finally came to power as head of a ruling Leftist coalition, the party had greatly diluted its call for agrarian revolution and had shed its radical elements.

Since 1977, during its twenty-plus years of unbroken rule in West Bengal, the Left Front has carefully constructed a platform of peasant unity. The most striking aspect of its agrarian reforms is the absence of any serious challenge to existing class struggles, sharply evident in its rejection of land-to-the-tiller redistribution, of serious wage-bargaining (Bhattacharya 1993), and of agricultural taxation of landowning peasants (Mallick 1990, 154–55). Indeed, the Left has been able to articulate a party platform that deftly balances all agrarian interests, with the possible exception of large and absentee landlords, whose presence is muted anyway in West Bengal. As Bhattacharya (1993, 82–83) notes, the West Bengal *Krishak Sabha,* the peasant wing of the party, has maintained a strategy of creating a "dialectical peasant unity" to "substitute" for "comprehensive peasant unity," thereby bringing into its fold the middle peasantry, sharecroppers, agricultural laborers, and a nonpeasant middle class.

Like Bhattacharya, other village-level researchers have located this populism in the *panchayats* (Webster 1992; Ruud 1994). During the Left Front regime, the three-tier *panchayat* system has been given substantial resources for local development (Sengupta 1989, 892), but they have also been closely supervised through the party hierarchy. The *panchayats* are thus populist in two ways: they dispense patronage and skillfully manage what Rogaly (1998, 2734) describes as the accommodation of competing claims in the "name of peasant unity."

With class struggle no longer located within the peasantry, the Left has had to construct a new class enemy: urban monopolists. In this new imaginary, the Left has directed its diatribe against a bourgeois, feudal, and imperialist Indian state. Its slogan of "Delhi *Chalo*"[17] has been an indictment of all that it portrays as evil, rallying peasants around the so-called oppressions of an unsympathetic central government. Chief Minister Basu (1983, 19–21) has repeatedly railed against the "conspiracies of the central government," "its collaborations with foreign monopoly capital," and its "corrupt" attempts to "destabilize" the Left Front. In many ways, this tactic is simply the expression of a regional party vying for power. But it is also a cornerstone of the Left's agrarian discourse: the recuperation of a bourgeois/ urban/imperialist threat that allows it to maintain the agrarian myth of peasant unity. Perhaps the most appropriate framework for understanding such discursive constructions is Lipton's (1977) neopopulist idea of urban bias.[18] Following Kitching (1982, 11–12), I refer to the Left's agrarianism as "neopopulist" rather than "populist" because it is a moral defense of the peasantry as well as an economic argument in favor of small-scale enterprise and agriculture.

The bulk of the West Bengal debates have interpreted the Left's state capacity as evidence of class alliances. For example, Mallick (1993) has advanced a "rural bias" thesis—Mitra's (1977) sense of a rural oligarchy outflanking and outmaneuvering the city. This, of course, is a mirror image of the Left's assertion of Liptonian urban bias. Moore's (1984, 21) critique of the rural/ urban bias debates is equally applicable to West Bengal:

> It is an illustration of the weakness of the political analysis in the
> work of Lipton and Mitra that they operate with almost identical
> politico-economic models, and yet by adding different assump-
> tions about political alliances, reach opposite conclusions about
> whether India is characterised by urban bias or rural bias.

I am arguing that there is more to the regime than simply the structural expression of a dominant class. Reading the Left Front not just through its class alliances, but also through the everyday and extraordinary practices through which these alliances are consolidated, produces a very different understanding. If the Left's political economy has most often been seen as the constraints of a parliamentary communism, I have highlighted how an ethnography of the regime reveals its neopopulist logic and mechanisms. Here, I am following de Janvry's (1981, 232) mandate:

> [to be] not so much concerned with an analysis of the internal
> efficiency of a project in achieving stated ends as . . . with under-
> standing the global logic of the project (by identifying its implicit
> objectives) and the contradictions in the implementation of the
> project (by contrasting the implicit objectives to the use of a par-
> ticular set of means).

The nature of this regime, then, cannot be derived from its name, Marxist; or its heritage, the Comintern of the 1920s; or its occasional inspiration, Mao's third path. It must instead be understood in terms of an ideological unwillingness to acknowledge the rise of capitalism in the West Bengal countryside: more Chayanovian than Leninist; a tactical loathing for industrialization: more Gandhian than Marxist; and a deployment of formidable myths: more populist than parliamentary in its guise of democracy.

Urban Revivals

The Left's launching of a New Economic Policy in the early 1990s marks a break with the neopopulist imaginary. It envisions new alliances with urban capitalists and, at the fringes of Calcutta, an implicit endorsement of the transformations of agricultural land into urban use. And yet, as I have argued, a closer look at urban developmentalism reveals that it is continuous with the Left's old populisms. I interpret what is happening on the fringes of Calcutta as precisely another attempt to forge a "dialectical unity," to subvert the issue of class struggle. Here lies the significance of CPM leader Subhas Chakravorty's Smithian narrative of the "invisible hand" of real-estate promoters. Here also lies the impetus for the intricate footwork of land transactions that seeks simultaneously to smash and to resurrect loyal constituencies through complex cycles of evictions and resettlements.

If the *panchayats* are the key rural site where populist hegemonies are consolidated and contested on a daily basis, where is urban developmentalism negotiated? Chatterjee (1997, 171) argues that "the CPM has not been able to successfully open up a new institutional space for the daily transaction of public demands in urban areas." But my research shows that this is not the case, that in fact there are institutional sites where the regime is secured and concretized, and in ways that parallel rural control and discipline. I am referring not only to the neighborhood clubs that play such a crucial role in squatter settlements and party colonies but also to the entire gamut of patronage mechanisms that mediate access to resources in Calcutta.

Patronage politics is of course not new to Calcutta. Nor is it the exclusive realm of the Left Front. During the 1950s, for example, the ruling Congress party had built up a formidable machinery of clientelist politics. It is in this sense that Kothari (in Ghosh 1981, 30) called the Congress a "system" rather than a party. Chatterjee (1997, 183–84) traces the institutional roots of political mobilization even further back—to the revolutionary societies and clubs of the 1920s (see also Haithcox 1971, 25–27). At the present moment of regime politics, such institutional mechanisms have been perfected. Perhaps more than the clubs, it is the tactic of vesting that has structural congruence with the role of *panchayats*—the flexible merging of formal state action and informal party mobilization.

On the one hand, its ambiguities have allowed the regime tremendous flexibility in forging territorialized political alliances. On the other hand, the very idea of vesting maintains old class enemies, the myth of rampaging landlords, and thus distracts attention from the immediate inequalities of urban developmentalism. When squatters are evicted, as in the Mukundapur evictions, the blame comes to rest not on the shoulders of foreign investors or the CPM but rather on the nineteenth-century landlord and his mythical agent, Bihari Mondol, thereby legitimating the evictions. It is thus that urban developmentalism has been launched, not as a sharply felt break with existing political loyalties but rather as a new "dialectical unity" where antagonistic and warring interests are reconciled, albeit clumsily.

Such forms of dialectical unity at the point of the urban are not wholly new. They show up, for example, in the historicized planning techniques of the regime and indeed of the region. The dominant discourse of Calcutta plans has been of a core-periphery model, with a primate city sucking dry its hinterland. With the problem defined thus, the inevitable planning solution has come to be seen as the inversion of this hierarchy, through well-balanced countermagnets and growth centers (*Basic Development Plan* 1966–1986, 415). Here, the metropolis is most often presented through organic analogies whether it is in the complex multicellular structure envisioned by the Ford Foundation's Basic Development Plan or in the 1971 CMPO proposal for a multinucleated metropolis (Chatterji 1990, 147). Such spatial vocabularies have been appropriated by the Left Front to conveniently fit its neopopulist rhetoric (Government of West Bengal 1989, 11). In the Left's planning efforts, the problem has been further diagnosed as the hand of a central government that is "bourgeois-landlord-dominated, corrupt, traditionally stagnant" and "in collaboration with foreign monopoly capital" (Basu 1983, 19).

What is the city that is thus recuperated? It is, as de Certeau (1983, 94) would say, a universal and anonymous subject: the "city" as a proper name to which it becomes possible to attribute all the functions and predicates that were previously scattered and assigned to many different real subjects. If the agrarian myth allows the creation of a *Sonar Bangla,* then the rhetoric of a "dying city" makes possible the dream of an urban revival, a banner under which all can be united. The spatial imaginary of the regime is thus unshakably populist, advancing what Gore (1984, 226) would evaluate as an ecological fallacy: "An equation of individual interests with territorial interests under the assumption that developments which in an aggregate sense benefit a group of people will benefit each individual in the group equally."

A *Bhadralok* Party

I have been arguing that the populist logic and mechanisms of the Left Front cannot be interpreted as the failure of state capacity. Instead, they are

part of a successful regime strategy, where success generates its own contradictions such as the marginalization of the rural-urban poor and an impasse in urban development. Similarly, the urban materialization of the
regime—in patronage politics, informal vesting, territorial factionalism—
cannot be simply diagnosed as a failure of metropolitan planning institutions. It is clear that the administration of both the Calcutta municipality through the Calcutta Corporation and of the region through the CMDA
has been plagued by fragmentation, conflict, and even jurisdictional chaos
(Sivaramakrishnan and Green 1986, 149–50). However, it is also clear that
these institutions have been the arena of regime formation, and specifically
of the consolidation of the social basis of the regime: a Bengali *bhadralok*. If
the coupling of party and state has taken place in and through planning
institutions, then such a knotting of power has a distinctive sociocultural
idiom, one that has historical roots in the region. In taking a quick look at
this history, I am not making an argument about the historical continuity of
a social group and its timeless culture. Instead, my concern is with the historically perfected techniques of lived hegemony, with the regime as a social institution that, in Ferguson's words (1990, 12), is "always structured
but never determined."

In many ways, Calcutta was the original site of British colonialism,
bearing the dubious honor of being capital of British India for many years.
But like most colonial endeavors, the economic expansion of the city had
as much to do with indigenous elites as it did with colonialist forces (Hasan
1992, 75). While Bengali elites invested heavily in urban landholdings, including in the so-called White Town, pan-Indian business communities
like the Marwaris became key players in commerce and trade, usually in
comfortable partnerships with the British (Sinha 1990; Hasan 1992, 73).
By the late nineteenth century the Calcutta Municipal Corporation had
emerged as a key site of elite collaboration and conflict. The introduction
of representative rule in the corporation in 1875 opened the doors to indigenous participation (Ray 1979, 2). The Bengali elite, like the British,
sought to use the Corporation as a means of protecting their property interests (McGuire 1983). By 1899 the British were so concerned about their
share of municipal power that they passed the Calcutta Municipal Act in
order to ensure an effective representation to the European mercantile
community (Bhattacharya 1991, 11).

The waning of the economic strength of the Bengali elite is a well-
known story. The *zamindari* system, while granting unprecedented power
to agrarian landlords, was also wracked by an impoverishment of tenants
that hindered the extraction of revenue (Bagchi 1992). And in Calcutta the

British were successful in limiting indigenous ownership of industries and companies (McGuire 1983, 13). When World War I provided new economic opportunities for indigenous participation, Marwari elites, who had hitherto been key intermediaries in the "great bazaar of Calcutta" (Sinha 1990), became the region's industrialists (Goswami 1990, 89).

But, within the constraints of colonial rule, the Bengali elite remained in charge of the region's political institutions, specifically the Calcutta Corporation. There are a few important features of this history that shed useful light on the current regime. By the early twentieth century the region came to be characterized by a disjuncture between economic and political power. As the Marwaris gained ascendancy in the industrial and commercial sectors, so were they excluded from political deliberations. The Bengal National Chamber of Commerce and Industry (BNCCI), for example, catered mainly to the Bengali elite and formed close ties with the Bengal Provincial Congress Committee. In 1925 the Marwari elite formed a separate Indian Chamber of Commerce (ICC), looking to the central Congress leadership for support and patronage (Mukherjee 1987, 111–12). In other words, the separation of political and economic elitism also had a spatial basis in the emerging geography of the nation, with a Bengali political elite articulating a regional interest and Marwari entrepreneurs striking national affiliations.

Not surprisingly, in postcolonial India Marwari business houses established unchallenged dominance over West Bengal's urban and industrial economy, while Bengali political groups controlled the region's politico-administrative apparatus. In characterizing the region's present history as a "regime politics," I have implied that there are new alliances between the Bengali Left Front and Marwari investors, as in the Udayan housing development. But there is also a sense in which Calcutta defies the conventional notion of a regime as growth coalitions between political and economic elites. Even at the moment of liberalization, the historicized (and ethnicized) separation of these two structural elements remains obvious, with the Left continuing to pursue its populist mobilizations often to the detriment of its own development projects. If there is a developmental drive to the regime, then it is one that is perhaps more usefully situated in the state itself rather than in an economic elite. The striking aspect of New Communism is the transformation of the state into a site of market activity, into a real-estate developer. To the extent that this remains limited to the state, this is also a Bengali project.

I am making an argument, then, about the social basis of the regime as well as its cultural repertoire of techniques. In doing so, I am pinpointing the regime as the materialization not of a Bengali but of a *bhadralok* interest, that is, a particular cultural elite that emerges in the crucible of the nationalist struggle. I have earlier shown how this *bhadralok* identity is deeply masculinist, articulating regime and family through an ideal of domesticity. Here, I am concerned with two other aspects of such cultural elitism.

First, Bengali communism has always negotiated a space, at times clumsily, between revolutionary Leninism and bourgeois nationalism (Seth 1995). In the founding moments of the movement, a bitter debate had been waged between Lenin and M. N. Roy, one of the leaders of Bengali Marxism, at the 1920 Comintern Congress. Lenin had maintained that as the spearhead of a nationalist, anti-imperialist movement, Gandhi was a revolutionary; whereas Roy had insisted that "as a religious and cultural revivalist he was bound to be reactionary socially, however revolutionary he might appear politically" (Haithcox 1971, 33). Ironically, communism as it took hold in Bengal combined with the cultural and religious revivals of a nationalism seeking to establish a spiritually pure "motherland" free of the material corruptions of the West. Kohli's (1992, 375) comment about the CPM as "a Bengali party" has to be interpreted in light of such histories. This is a legacy of parochial nationalism that imparts a particular, and particularistic, accent to its cry of "Delhi *Chalo*" and its charges of urban bias. Neopopulisms are of course not unique to the Left Front. Banaji (1994) and Gupta (1998) note how agrarian populisms often seek to recover a rural "Bharat" in contrast to an urban-industrial "India." In the case of West Bengal, the specificity of this recovery rests in a cultural idiom, in the recuperation of a Bengali peasantry oppressed by the machinations of non-Bengali imperialists and monopoly capitalists. Of course, the view to Delhi obscures a close look closer to home.

Second, as key moments of the nationalist movement in Bengal, like *swadeshi*, were elitist movements, so is Bengali communism inherently *bhadralok*, deriving from the nationalist desires of an urban elite. Herein lies clues to the pastoral imaginary of the Left, lurking within which is possibly what Haithcox (1971, 252) identifies as M. N. Roy's Marxist disdain for the peasantry. In current iterations of the Left, such disdain has been transformed into the paternalism of populist mobilizations and democratic centralism.

Not surprisingly, urban developmentalism has been cast in the idiom of a *bhadralok* nostalgia for a lost city of charm and grace, most clearly evident in Operation Sunshine. Political columnist Barun Sengupta asked, Why did the Left Front put and keep these hawkers in place for thirty years, make fortunes off them, and then "kick them in their stomachs" (*Bartaman*, 7 December 1996)? But, given the material basis of the regime, this seeming anomaly is in fact predictable. The transition from the revolutionary zeal of the United Front to the circumscribed reformism of the Left Front is not solely a product of the need to adapt to the dictates of parliamentary democracy, as interpreted by a number of observers (Herring 1989; Kohli 1997). Instead, I am arguing that the creation of an agrarian myth and of an urban revival were moves foreshadowed in the sociocultural history of the regime.

Operation Sunshine thus reinscribed the urban poor as bourgeois shopkeepers, unworthy of *bhadralok* patronage. In a stylish volume put together in record time and made available during the twenty-year celebrations of the Left Front, Subhas Chakravorty (1997, 5–6) wrote:

> The word "hawking" does not exist in Bengali. It is an English word that refers to itinerant traders. We did not evict hawkers. We evicted illegal shopkeepers who had invaded public space.

Somen Mitra (1997, 11), then head of the opposition party, the Pradesh Congress, concurred: "I disagree with the government in the suddenness of the evictions. But I agree that it was absolutely necessary. These were no longer poor, needy traders. They had become commercialized—they were renting out space, they owned multiple stalls, and they had ties with large merchants."

Kanti Ganguly (1997, 212) entered a plea for the city's *sadharan manush,* the common public: "They have a right to these roads and pavements, you know. I once helped hawkers invade the sidewalks. I was wrong. They were helpless refugees then. Now, they do not need this kind of help. We must end the politics of patronage that has kept them here for so long."

As the poor were deemed corrupt, so were the new inheritors of the *bhadralok* city defined. The word *bhadralok* is appropriately polyvalent, signifying not only a cultural elite but also meaning "gentlemanly." In the Operation Sunshine publicity volume, the city's cultural elite lauded the CPM's political courage and hailed the return of the city of their childhood, polite and clean. If Calcutta had seen a proliferation of unruly *pablik* claims (Kaviraj 1997), then Operation Sunshine sought to recover a middle-class public, subject to civic control. After the hawker evictions in Shyambazar, a middle-class resident wrote in a Bengali daily:

> The stalls had mushroomed, crowded against each other. It was like hell, dirty, smelly, dark, and dingy. In the evenings, the smoke from the diesel generators would sting our eyes and suffocate our lungs. Suddenly, as if in a miracle, all of this is gone. I am enjoying my walk on these empty sidewalks so much that I feel as if I have

been suddenly transported to a foreign land, to the city of my
childhood (*Anandabazar Patrika*, 28 November 1996)

But the *bhadralok* city has also been constantly contested, not only
by the claims of the rural-urban poor but also through territorial factionalism. The history of the Calcutta Corporation during colonialism reveals
that it was an important instrument of patronage, prefiguring the regime
politics of the late twentieth century. And it was also wracked by competing
factions, known as *dals,* through which played out the ideological and material struggles of the nationalist movement (Mukherjee 1987, Ray 1979). As
I have already noted, in terms of indigenous representation, the Corporation
was exclusively Bengali, bypassing the economic interests of Marwari entrepreneurs. However, it is also important to note that by the 1930s the
Corporation came to be dominated by Bengali Hindus. Communal tensions
were so heightened that Muslim leaders formed a separate Muslim Chamber
of Commerce in 1932 (Ray 1979, 1209). By 1937 the breakaway faction had
managed to establish the Fazlul Haq ministry with British support. The
chance of a broad anti-British coalition in the municipal arena was thus
undermined (Ray 1979, 183). Also initiated was a bitter turf battle between
Corporation and state government, a struggle that would repeatedly play
out in the region, during the United Front years and more recently with the
Trinamul's victory in municipal elections.

I raise the history of communal factionalism because such issues have
become of pressing concern in contemporary India. If liberalization can be
thought of as a new regime of regulation, as markets that despite the
rhetoric of the invisible hand require a "visible fist" (Watts 1994, 375), then
the sociocultural basis of such hegemonies has to be uncovered. By pointing out how the unmapping of Calcutta makes possible various market
practices, some of which inhere in the apparatus of the state itself, I have argued that informality constitutes a crucially important mode of regulation
for the liberalizing regime. But there is also an emerging body of evidence
that suggests that the violent transformation of informal land and housing
markets is inextricably linked to communal violence, to the violence that is
the nation. Thus, Appadurai's (2000) work on the 1992–93 riots[19] shows how,
in Bombay, urban informality became the key site of religious and ethnic
warfare—from the demolitions of unauthorized residential dwellings in
Muslim areas by the Municipal Corporation to the overwhelming violence
against the Muslim poor. Urban space was thereby violently rewritten as
"sacred, national and Hindu" (Appadurai 2000, 647). Here, it is hard to separate out the rituals of communal hatred from the rituals of the market.

In the case of Calcutta, Das (2000) makes a somewhat different case about the 1992 communal riots. He provocatively argues that unlike past Calcutta riots,[20] and unlike the blatant fundamentalism of the 1992 explosions in other Indian cities, Calcutta witnessed "a land-grabbing riot under a communal garb" (301). Thus, he shows how in some areas the riots facilitated the eviction of Muslims from slums whose land values had dramatically increased (297). And in others, promoters benefited from the clearing of slums, though this time the perpetrators were homeless Bangladeshi Muslim day-laborers evicting Hindu bustee-dwellers (293).

Here, the much-lauded communal peace of the Left Front can be cynically interpreted as a willingness to allow all communal factions to violently carve out their own markets. Yet there is a difference between the foot soldiers of such movements and the sociocultural basis of the regime. As *Sonar Bangla* belongs to the *panchayats* rather than to the peasantry, so Calcutta belongs to the institutions of a culturally elitist regime rather than to the informal sector that is frequently mobilized in landgrabs. As Bengali nationalism, swathed in the saffron garbs of *swadeshi,* cast the nation in the image of a mother-goddess, so Bengali communism can only speak of social upliftment in the idiom of Sanskritization:

> Leftism in Bengal is parasitic upon a whole cultural heritage among the Bengali intelligentsia in which patriotism has been intimately tied with a distinctly religious (and needless to say, upper-caste Hindu) expression of the signs of power, in which the celebration of the power of the masses has been accompanied by an unquestioned assumption of the natural right of the intelligentsia to represent the whole people . . . (Chatterjee 1997, 4).

In the Calcutta of New Communism, it is the promise of a *bhadralok* city— unapologetically elitist, implicitly masculinist, and quietly Hinduist—that has inaugurated a hegemonic project of city-making.

Calcutta Requiem

I started this chapter with a dream of tombstones because this trope specifies the dynamics of hegemony. I have accordingly argued that the unmapping of Calcutta's fringes makes possible the territorialized flexibility of the regime, securing political acquiescence in and through tremendous volatility. This is not the spatiality of the oligarchic conspiracies that, inspired by *Chinatown,* I had set out to uncover. Rather, this is a more insidious hegemonic formation reminiscent of what Ferguson (1990, 19) identifies as an "anti-politics machine": "how the outcomes of planned social interventions can end up coming together into powerful constellations of control that were never intended and in some cases never even recognized, but are all the more effective for being subjectless." Shah's "dream of tombstones" is a counterhegemonic discourse precisely because it imagines a different spatiality, the subversive possibilities of drawing a map, of marking places, of speaking about space.

But this idea of citizenship is in and of itself a specific sociocultural construction, invoking an ordered and orderly *civitas*. It bears striking similarity to the liberatory trope of knowable land records and orderly land markets that is embodied in the World Bank's (1991) urban agenda for the 1990s. One of the examples ironically cited in the agenda is the Institute of Local Government and Urban Studies, which was founded in Calcutta in 1982 with support from the World Bank to train municipal employees in creating transparent land markets. Such transparency is much needed in Calcutta, but my research also shows the tremendous limits of such World Bank efforts. The "unmapping" of the city cannot be simply seen as a failure of "public accountability" (as do, for example, Chakravorty and Gupta 1996), a rationalist ideal gone awry. In a context where it is impossible to fix the rules and regulations of landownership and land use, the very idea of the "public" is subject to unlimited negotiability.

Indeed, in Calcutta, unmapping is the basis of persistent poverty, but it is also what affords the possibility of life and livelihood. Shah's dream would in fact spell the death of the rural-urban poor. It would enforce the land rights of a public citizenship without the *pablik* claims to shelter. My use of his motif possibly signals my own complicity—ethnographic and otherwise—in the *bhadralok* city, knowable through the regulatory fiction of a "dream of tombstones."[21] However, I hope that as I have upheld this ideal, so have I interrogated it. If I have evoked the possibility of transparent space, easily mapped and navigable at this moment of globalization, then my constant use of the term "liberalization" has been a counterpoint to this rhetoric, an indication of the frictions of space and power. An unmapped Calcutta is not about a deviant set of urban norms, and not even about localized norms redolent with the rich diversity of place. Rather it is about the territorialized processes through which power and powerlessness are normalized on an everyday basis.

In contrast to the "dream of tombstones," I would like to imagine unmapping as lived hegemony by drawing on a favorite allegory, one that I have often interpreted as indication of how the apparatus of modernist power is perfected through the techniques of tradition and myth.[22] My story comes from Gabriel García Márquez's novel *One Hundred Years of Solitude*.

Set in a phantasmic town called Macondo on the edge of a vast South American swamp, the novel details the events following the appearance of "Sir Francis Drake, the pirate."

At one point, the town comes to be inflicted with a plague that leads to the loss of memory. As the town slowly loses its collective memory, one of its leaders conceives of a formula: he writes down words on pieces of paper and attaches them to the respective objects. Soon all objects are thus labeled: table, chair, and so forth. But then he realizes that these labels make no sense if people forget the use of the objects. And so he is more explicit. He hangs a sign on the cow that says, "This is the cow. She must be milked every morning." And he creates two important signs—one that marks the town, "Macondo," and the other that says "God Exists."

After a while even these instructions are not enough to retain for the town the meaning of the written word. The residents then turn to the village fortune-teller. She had used her cards to tell the future. Now she has to use the cards to tell the past. The town, García Márquez writes, begins to live a past reconstructed as the uncertain alternatives of the fortune-teller's cards.

This, like an unmapped Calcutta, is a place where the future is made possible through the impossibility of remembering an authentic past, where living is made possible through the impossibility of labeling and naming.

Disruptions

A way out of the dualisms in which we have explained our bodies and our tools to ourselves. This is a dream not of a common language, but of a powerful infidel heteroglossia. . . . It means both building and destroying machines, identities, categories, relationships, spaces, stories. Although both are bound in the spiral dance, I would rather be a cyborg than a goddess.

Donna Haraway, "A Manifesto for Cyborgs"

Wipe your hand across your mouth, and laugh;
The worlds revolve like ancient women
Gathering fuel in vacant lots.

T. S. Eliot, "Preludes"

If ethnographies are spatialized interventions in fields of power, as depicted in my attempt to recover an unmapped Calcutta, then so are they negotiations, often clumsy, of space and place. I started my narrative of the city with a story about my encounter with a particular kind of public in a globalized Calcutta: the imaged public of the 1997 book fair, the remaking of the regime's sociocultural identity and material basis in the crucible of liberalization. I preface this closing chapter with one of my many negotiations of the *pablik*.

One fieldwork afternoon, underneath a blazing sun, I roamed the platforms of Dhakuria station in South Calcutta, searching for commuters. As the crowds swelled, I weaved my way carefully, taking on the performative identity that marked my ethnographies: deliberately shabby clothes, ragged slippers, sweaty hair pulled tightly back, a cloth bag, no note-taking, just genuine interest. I squatted on my haunches, avoiding the filthy platform, and started to talk to a commuter from a village deep in the southern reaches of the delta.

We were soon loudly interrupted by a middle-aged man, another commuter, but one whom I fixed in my mind as a middle-class clerk. I emphasize this "fixing" because it clearly shaped how I responded, with great hostility, to his presence. "Why are you asking the 'public' questions?" he shouted at me. The question was posed in Bengali, and he pronounced public as *pablik*. I retorted that it was none of his business: "What makes you the moral keeper of the public?" It had been a long day and I went on to tell him that if these women were lying dead on the platform, he would most likely simply step over them and continue with his journey. Why the sudden interest? Our shouting match turned into quite a public spectacle until my initial research subject intervened: *"Babu,"*[1] she said, turning to him, "why are you bothering yourself with women's issues? We are talking about women's topics. They will only embarrass you, and besides they are not really of any importance, are they?" Flustered, my middle-class clerk turned away, and the predominantly male crowd that had gathered around us lost interest as well.

And so I began to pose my litany of questions: about her village, about her work in Calcutta, about her family. To each she replied with a continuing narrative of widowhood. In fact, she elaborately detailed her husband's moment of death at the hands of a ferocious man-eating tiger that restlessly roamed the boundaries of their village. I had heard similar stories from other commuter women, and once again I was puzzled by this description of primeval forests and prowling tigers. I pondered the gravity of villages teeming with widows whose husbands had thus lost their lives: what a dangerous place the Sunderbans[2] must be!

But amidst the talk of death and dying I noticed that she wore all the traditional symbols of a married Hindu woman: the *sindur*, the bangles. Why did her narrative of Hindu widowhood not match up with her social emblems? She was, in Shah's imaginary, marked territory. As I turned to ask her this, her train rolled in. Through the push of the crowds, she shouted to me: "I have to get home and cook for my husband and children." "Oh, you remarried!" I proclaimed, relieved at the simple explanation. She laughed, and while boarding the train, said:

No *memsahib,*[3] I have to cook for my only husband, the one who gets eaten every day by a man-eating tiger while I wait at this station, parched and dusty, while I lose my breath on the trains, and walk through the muddy fields. He dies every day as I traverse this space. It is a terrible death for the tiger is always so hungry.

Since then, on hot afternoons in breathless South Calcutta stations, I often allow myself to mistake the frenzy of the local trains and the cacophony of its public for the roar of a majestic Bengal tiger—not one that is on display as the last stalwart of an endangered species in zoos around the world, but instead one that restlessly roams the imaginary of an unnamed woman.

Idioms of Critique

I tell the story of the man-eating tiger to show how words can undo. This is a narration of death, one that turns what seems to be a husband's willing unemployment into a gory death. This is also a narration of critique, one that recasts the questions of life and death in the most poignant of ways.

There are three reasons why I have been so drawn to this story, why I have chosen to present it as a moment of disruption. First, it is an instance of speaking. If other genres of speech, such as *adda*,[4] can be seen as important social practice, marking what Chakrabarty (1999, 144) designates as "homosocial space," the "phallic solitude" of a male bourgeoisie, then this particular narration is an interesting appropriation of the realm of speech. And it is a narration that overflows, that exceeds, demonstrating the inherently critical possibilities of a gendered subject: "a conception of the subject as multiple, rather than divided or unified, and as excessive or heteronomous vis-à-vis the state ideological apparati and the sociocultural technologies of gender" (de Lauretis 1987, x).

Second, the story of the man-eating tiger is distinctively spatialized. One way of thinking about this space is as a multiple and differentiated public, what Fraser (1990) terms "subaltern counterpublics." This, then, is a space of critique, engendered by the specific conditions of rural-urban commuting, a point I will return to later in this section. Yet another way of designating the spatiality of the narration is as the "between," the "spatiotemporal interval of *differance* essayed by Derrida," a "suspended moment" (Alarcón et al. 1999, 14). I borrow the terminology of being between because it provokes ideas about how identities are negotiated rather than determined, how they are deferred rather than guaranteed. And yet, in this case, the "between" is not simply metaphorical or imagined space: its material basis is the overflowing trains that move between city and countryside, a liminality that disrupts neat spatial categories and developmental teleologies. It exists in relation to, but beyond, the geography of urban populism. It exists in relation to, but beyond, the coherence of agrarian Bengal.

Third, the story is in fact a conversation. It is a story told by an unnamed commuter to a city girl in the peasant idiom of man-eating tigers.

Herein lies the spatial imaginary of ethnographic dialogues, one that defies interpretive closure. If postcolonial feminists have urged a speaking with the subaltern, rather than a listening to or speaking for (Spivak 1987), here is one such instance. But what is this "speaking with"? A tongue-in-cheek anecdote that makes fun of the city girl who readily imagines primeval forests and victimized peasants? A scathing critique of patriarchy told with great sophistication? It is the impossibility of separating out these various strands that complicates the ethnographic project. And it is thus that I have titled my Calcutta ethnography a requiem. The quintessential requiem is perhaps Mozart's—one that was left incomplete, possibly completed by an unknown hand, and whose ultimate authorship remains contested. So is it with my stories. It is in this spirit that I take a closer look at the idioms of critique that disrupt the hegemonic project of patronage and poverty that I have outlined.

Babuization

The domestication of Calcutta's rural-urban poor is not a seamless web of class and gender oppressions. In fact, the various dimensions of domestication point to the politics of poverty: how poverty is reproduced through the contingent and open-ended contestation of social identities. I have argued that squatter settlements are moments of persistent poverty, sites at which the logic of double gendering secures the domesticated consent of the poor. Yet this suturing of family and regime is not free from disruptions. Let me identify some key types of disruption.

One disruption, as epitomized by the man-eating tiger story, is the narration of illness and death as metaphorical representations of abandonment and polygamy. If unemployed men invoked the diseased and exhausted body as legitimation of their withdrawal from the labor force, then commuter women deployed the same theme. At times the explanation of illness or death would provide a socially honorable context for wage-earning work and rural-urban commuting. In the masculinist setting of a squatter settlement, the myth of natural tragedy allowed women to don the honorable guise of a poor widow.

But the trope of the incapacitated male body also often becomes a key element of gendered critique, particularly in the narrations of commuter women. In contrast to the mantle of widowhood, commuter women boisterously joked about the death of their husbands. Like the narrator of the man-eating tiger story, they were less concerned with the significations of widowhood and more interested in spinning an account of death, male death. When pressed on how and why they wore the symbols of marriage, they would rowdily state, "Well, our husbands are useless, so they might as well be dead." Such idioms of critique indicate a break with the gentle widowhood of squatter women and are worth a closer look.

In the squatter settlements, one word dominates: *bekar.* It is a word that means unemployed, possibly even useless. Through their participation in masculinist patronage, squatter men have recoded the word as signifying the rejection of menial labor and the adoption of meaningful work, worthy of heads of households. This hegemony of meaning persists unchallenged in the squatter settlements. However, on the commuter trains, poor working women advance a fundamentally different understanding of *bekar.* They use the term to explicitly or implicitly refer to sexual impotency, presenting male unemployment as an undermining of sexual capability and power.

A powerful symbol in such idioms of critique is the figure of the *babu,* the lazy, pleasure-loving, middle-class Bengali urbanite. Domestic servants refer to their employers as *babus,* but commuter women go a step further, reinscribing their husbands as *babus:* "We work all day long and they stay at home. They have become just like the *babus* we work for."

This process of signification is a crucial struggle over meanings. The concept of *babu,* a construct with deep roots in the cultural politics of the region, is double-loaded in its gendered meanings. On the one hand, it refers to the middle class as male, situating class oppressions within a larger structure of patriarchy and thereby merging hegemonic and marginalized masculinities. On the other hand, it constitutes elite and poor men as effeminate and weak, incapable of being manly, thereby unsettling both sets of masculinities.

In contrast, commuter women defined themselves as androgynous, simultaneously participating in male and female realms. At the end of an afternoon in Jadavpur station, twenty different commuter women said almost in unison: *"Amra purush ebong meye* [we are simultaneously men and women], earning for the household like a man and taking care of the house like a woman."

Calcutta's journalists describe the commuter women as barely human, the "automatic washing machines" of the city, strange fusions of woman and machine. I came to see them as Haraway's (1990) cyborgs, reassembled selves erected on the disassembly of socially constructed differences, a destabilization of the goddess myth. They weren't *grihalakshmis,* goddesses of the home, and they were proud of it.

But commuter women also have a sense that they are not automatic washing machines, of the tangible realities of their bodies. In fact, in their discourses they turn their tired body into a symbol of class and gender oppressions. In particular, they lash out at the time-body discipline of domestic work, likening it to factory work. They describe the delicate balance between commuting and taking care of the household as a double shift with enormous burdens and responsibilities. Citing the example of salaried work where *babus* are entitled to weekly holidays, commuter women emphasize that they need to take at least a day off each week: "If we don't get some rest, how will we continue to work? We must rest our bodies for this is what feeds us."

Such idioms of critique are especially important in the broader considerations of feminized work. There is now a massive body of research that demonstrates how the project of capitalism is also a body project, a gendered surveillance and control of the laboring body. How can such body projects be exceeded? As Harvey (1998, 404) asks, "If bodies are always made into docile bodies, or if we are all now cyborgs, then how can we measure anything outside of that deadly embrace of the machine as extension of our own body and body as extension of the machine?"

Feminist research indicates that body projects are also strategies of disruption. The very gendered and racialized logics that are used to produce domesticated bodies can also be used to challenge and subvert regimes of discipline (Hossfeld 1990) or at least to create a "different semiotics of production" (Rofel 1992). The issues raised by commuter women in their body discussions accordingly seek to transform the insidiously intimate structures of domestic work into a rationalized work setting with "objective" rules and norms. In doing so, they must be seen as not only working but also as "performing work" (McDowell and Court 1994). Such notions of performativity have dominated recent feminist debates and yet have also bypassed poor working women, as if poverty is a natural rather than naturalized state. As the commuters "*babu*ize" their husbands, as they claim rest for their aching limbs, they perform a gender and class identity, challenging its certainties and limits.

Men Not Allowed

What is striking about commuter women is not only their discursive critiques but also their daily engagement in political action. Every day thousands of poor women travel ticketless on the trains to and from Calcutta and are militant in their refusal to buy tickets. While male ticketless commuters are at times arrested by checkers, female commuters are aware that they can use gendered techniques to ward off harassment by male ticket checkers. They therefore crowd into the "Men Not Allowed" compartments of local trains. The railway administration has tried to deal with the problem by hiring female ticket checkers, but the women commuters have been extremely aggressive in their responses:

> Let them arrest us all. There isn't enough space in the hold for all of us.

> When she came to fine me I said, take off your coat and give it to me so that I'll have your job. Then only will I be able to afford the fine.

> You want to arrest me? First get my children from the village. We'll all stay in your jail and you can feed us.

Male commuters have a very different response to the issue of ticket checking. Not only were male commuters eager to maintain the impression of being law-abiding travelers but they also devised elaborate mechanisms to avoid checkers when they could not afford to buy tickets, such as traveling on late-night trains. As I have discussed earlier, there are significant occupational and wage differentials between male and female commuters,[5] such that the careful maintenance of masculinist pride in this case might have as much to do with class status as with gendered identity. Within the heterogeneity of Calcutta's rural-urban interface, among the multiple strands of commuting that link city and countryside, ticketless travel remains a distinctive practice of poor women.

Figure 5.1. "Men Not Allowed"—commuter women on the southbound journey, Baghajatin station.

Figure 5.2. Waiting for the train to arrive in the shade of Sandhyabazar, Jadavpur station.

I am convinced that the ability of commuter women to resist, critique, and challenge has to do with the experience of commuting, of being together with women who are strangers from strange villages but who are intimate in that the conditions of their lives are agonizingly similar. Commuter women form a collectivity in sites where they gather, such as waiting points on platforms and on the trains. This collective identity is extremely fluid, changing constantly as women come and go, but it nevertheless has a vibrant energy. It is thus that I would find it impossible to have a solitary conversation with a commuter woman. Invariably, others would join in, often rowdily, spinning a noisy dialogue. Or, when asked about their lives and work, commuter women would rarely respond about their individual experiences. Instead, they repeatedly attempted to create a grand narrative, weaving together the experiences of friends, acquaintances, and strangers, convinced that despite the obvious diversity, there was an overarching homology.

Commuting, then, creates a specific embodied subjectivity with its own set of discursive critiques and political practices. The experience can be understood in terms of Young's (1990) "politics of difference," an environment of physical inexhaustibility where difference, the presence of strangers, is unavoidable. The tangible experience of traveling on the overflowing trains has a distinct texture—a sense not only of one's own body but also of other bodies, jostling against one's own, usurping space. While such journeys create a sense of self as different from others, the boundaries of distinction are constantly violated and refashioned. It is in this dialectic of self and otherness that commuter women articulate a collective identity.

Does the daily crossing of borders create the possibility of a space of freedom for poor women? The rowdy discourses of commuter women, their unflinching challenge to state authority on the matter of ticketless travel, seem to point to a politics of resistance. Most striking is the ability of commuter women to articulate and press claims vis-à-vis the state, defining ticketless travel as an entitlement of citizenship. Their most common statement is this: "We vote and therefore why should we have to pay for what we cannot afford?" This politics of entitlement reverberates in domestic spheres through their severe critiques of male irresponsibility and occasionally allows them to imagine less oppressive conditions of work.

But more important, it points to an unanticipated "surplus," that which cannot be fully contained within the ideas and ideals of citizenship and community. What is interesting about their resistance on the trains is not just the articulation of a specific narrative of citizenship but the site at which this articulation occurs. It is a wholly new and contingent positionality, different from the household, workplace, and political community. In fact, it is impossible to speak of even a community/commonality on these restless trains. The disruptions that occur at this moment of surplus, in the "presence of strangers," point to the unanticipated ways in which citizens construct cities, and possibly new meanings of citizenship.

In this sense, the appropriation of "Men Not Allowed" spaces by commuter women points to the territorial negotiation of public/*pablik* realms. Their noisy chatter fills South Calcutta stations; in Jadavpur they take over the stalls of Sandhyabazar as they lie shuttered and vacant in the afternoon heat; and their rowdy presence on the trains creates deep discomfort for the "ladies" who were meant to occupy the genteel compartments of the local trains. In other words, the commuter women come to occupy the bourgeois spaces of the normalized public, and they do so with a sense of entitlement and belonging.

I write of this as unanticipated spatiality because it exists outside the geographies of domestic work and rural-urban households that I had first set out to map. Yet there are important resonances here with the socio-spatial practices of domestic workers in other settings. Constable (1997), for example, shows how Filipinas in Hong Kong remain strictly circumscribed within the domestic realm of servanthood but also inhabit a public, urban space every Sunday. As Filipinas congregate in Central District on their days off, they challenge the spatial boundaries of class, gender, and race. Despite "public" outrage, Constable writes, "they demand to be seen and they refuse to be moved." It is this that Yeoh and Huang (1998, 599), in the context of Singapore, designate as the "little tactics of habitat." They write not so much about resistance or negotiation as of the everyday "styles" that reconfigure space. And yet such "styles" are inextricably linked to the politics of citizenship. As members of a diaspora subject to intense state supervision, Filipina domestics in Singapore nevertheless manage to articulate a territorialized subject-position, one that unsettles the originary myth of one nation while staking a claim to an original other. As one Filipina, Lorna, put it:

> I do remember one time when we went shopping in Woodlands . . . I was trying to buy a towel and then this guy [the seller] instead of introducing what he was selling, he told me, "Why you Filipinos *ah*, you just come here to work you know, and you buy things cheap cheap" . . . I was really insulted but the first word that came from my mouth was, "You Singaporean, you think you are the biggest people in the world but you don't have your own land, you don't have your own house. Even though I am a maid, if I go back now [to the Philippines], I have a place to stay." (Yeoh and Huang 2000, 424, emphasis in original)

There are many levels at which Lorna's statement can be interpreted. The irony of a poor Filipina ridiculing the material basis of Singaporean nationhood, state-provided housing (Castells et al. 1990), is an interesting disruption of geopolitical hierarchies. Her proud assertion can also be read as a claim of citizenship, not unlike that of Ranjan and other Calcutta squatters. Lorna also evokes another provocative squatter figure, that of sixteen-year-old Nida, who is the youth leader in the Reclamation squatter settlement of Manila. Vividly portrayed in a 1991 documentary, *On Borrowed Land*,[6] Nida, in the face of evictions, declares in an unfaltering tone, "I refuse to be called a squatter. I am Filipina. One cannot be a squatter in one's own country."

What is to be made of this Third World claims-talk? If I see in the narrations of the commuter women a possibility of critique—of employer, husband, and state—I also see in it the recital of hegemonic consent. Indeed, it is precisely in the idiom of critique that one can locate the traces of domestication, the renewal of domesticity and *domus*, home and nation. As Lorna unravels the myth of Singapore, so she consolidates another myth: that of a Philippines where she—poor, working Filipina—has a right to space.

The Recital of Consent

In the case of commuter women, domestication comes in the form of domestic work, which continues to be a point of production with low wages, little job security, and no benefits. In Calcutta, domestic work as a segment of the informal labor market is becoming increasingly tight. As more and more poor women turn to the city for livelihood, the competition for jobs becomes ever more severe. Older commuters complain about the influx of young girls and women willing to accept lower and lower wages. New commuters detail the hardships of a job search, describing the stranglehold of well-established commuters on the labor market. In city neighborhoods there is a marking of territory, with each commuter staking claim to specific employer houses. Increasingly, these boundaries are transgressed by new commuters who are willing to work not only on a low-paid, part-time basis but also on a piece-rate basis, per bucket of clothes washed or room mopped. Such conditions mean that there is little possibility of a collective politics of organization and bargaining. Here, the persistence of poverty through the persistence of feminized livelihoods is amply evident.

In a regional context of severe unemployment, commuter women remain ghettoized in such feminized occupations, processes I have already detailed. Let me simply add that while I did not study domestic work as a point of production, it became apparent from the ethnographic record that commuter women failed to challenge either the relations of production or the relations in production that mark this arena of work. It was obvious that the only tactics they could deploy at the workplace were similar to what Hsiung (1996, 139) has called "wrangling": a verbal struggle aimed at resisting "undefined but potentially limitless claims on their labor."[7] Such tactics barely alter the overwhelming structural burdens of rural-urban commuting and the growing informalization of domestic work. Indeed, despite their self-inscription as androgynous, commuter women repeatedly described their wage-earning work as feminine: "*sansarer kaj* [household work]—we do not know how to do anything else; we simply take care of our households and other households."

How can such self-devaluations be reconciled with the rowdy claims that I earlier presented? Moreover, why are commuter women able to articulate idioms of critique within the liminal space of the trains, in the presence of strangers, but unable to concretize this critique in the intimate spaces of domestic work and domesticity? I will show later how such processes of domestication are most evident at the site of squatting, such that even the critiques advanced by commuter women are rarely voiced and heard in the hegemonic space of masculinist patronage and feminized livelihood. For the moment, however, I want to focus on how and why the very disruptions produced by commuter women reveal, and even reinforce, structures of hegemony.

In some ways, I am presenting the story of the man-eating tiger as a narration of modernity. I mean this in several different ways: that the narration is in and of itself an artifact, it is data (Ferguson 1999). It is indication that the modern is not simply a static object of narration; rather, modernity is always narrated, and thus always ambivalent and contested. And the story is a critical expression of the experience of modernity, articulated in a peasant idiom. In this sense, it resonates with other moments of resistance, for example Ong's (1987) detailing of how young women workers disrupted and even shut down production lines in Malaysia through incidents of spirit possession, thereby challenging industrial discipline and control through the moral symbols of peasant life.

Ong goes on to conclude that the tactic of spirit possessions did not contribute to a broader reworking of an inequitable social order. This is partly the argument that I have been making about the structural limits of domestic work. But I want to take this point further by arguing that the very idiom of critique reinforces paradigms of power. In doing so, I draw on a provocative example that comes from Mary Beth Mills's (1995) ethnography of an agrarian community in northeast Thailand. Mills shows how the experience of modernity is formulated and negotiated in "traditional" vocabularies. She describes a scene in the early 1990s where villages throughout the region came to be stricken by a mass hysteria around "widow ghosts"—sexually voracious spirits that were feared to be assaulting and killing men. To ward off the ghosts, villagers erected massive wooden penises outside their homes, and many of the men began to engage in cross-dressing. The hysteria, Mills argues, was related to the dramatic changes brought about by new forms of industrial work, migration, and consumerisms. The trope of widow ghosts was a critique of this rapid incorporation into late capitalism.[8]

Here, then, is an instance of the lively negotiations of meanings and practices that constitute the experience of modernity, modernity in Marshall Berman's sense of a "paradoxical unity." Here also is evident the performative aspects of gender (Butler 1990). But as Mills rightly notes, what is being critiqued is not so much capitalism as the perceived modernization-driven mutation of gender relations. The figure of the migrant woman is thus turned into that of the dangerous widow ghost who has the sexual power to undermine male vitality. Ong and Peletz (1995, 244–45) interpret Mills's findings in this way: "Because widow ghosts do not 'take issue' with capitalism and modernity and do in fact confine their 'critique' to the transformation of gender relations that is linked to capitalism, they simultaneously resist and bolster the very structures against which they are arrayed."

In this spirit, I see the story of the man-eating tiger, and indeed the larger genre of commuter critique, as marked by an idiom that reinforces two paradigms of power. The first element is the consolidation of a peasant myth, of a magical southern delta where the figure of the Royal Bengal tiger looms large. In some ways, this is a broader regional myth, and one with an interesting historical genealogy. Chakrabarty (1999, 122), for example, discusses how in the 1920s the symbolism of the Bengal tiger eating *sahibs* was prevalent in the nationalist *addas* of the Calcutta *bhadralok*. If the commuter critiques can be seen as a "social grammar,"[9] then perhaps this language is subject to multiple social uses and is clearly not "authentically" subaltern.[10] Such forms of inauthenticity do not undermine the import of the critique. But the idiom does naturalize the agrarian economy, displacing anxiety about poverty and landlessness into a narrative about inevitable and "natural" tragedy. As in Holmes's (1989) compelling account of peasant-workers in Friuili, the "enchantment" of the world serves to reveal the essence of sociocultural power. If Butler (1990, 140) has shown how gender is created through "stylized repetition of acts," in this case, agrarian hegemony is consolidated through the imitative and repetitive aspects of mythical narration.

The second idiomatic element that I am concerned with relates to the normalization of gender roles and relations. The story of the man-eating tiger is in many ways a legitimation of wage-earning work and the public presence of women through the moral legitimacy of widowhood. Indeed, in imagining their husbands as dead, commuter women reveal the intractability of their patriarchal households. While the "*babu*ization" of husbands reads as a provocative disruption of masculinist power, it also makes clear that commuter women can rarely stake claims against either employers or husbands. Through their own words, they reinscribe gender binaries as a class divide, difficult to bridge and perhaps impossible to challenge.

Let me reiterate that I am not making an argument about the inevitable disjuncture between speech and action, between the astounding critique on the station platform and the train ride to seemingly acquiescent domestic work. Rather, in keeping with a well-established framework of critical thought (Bourdieu 1991; Butler 1991), I am interpreting speech as material and symbolic practice, hence my concern about its content and form. To speak in ways that enchant the agrarian realm, to speak in ways that maintain marital status as the primary arbiter of rights and claims, is to produce hegemonic consent in the very act of critique.

In this sense, the idiom of citizenship seems to present a different genre of narration. Commuter women refuse to buy tickets because they are voting citizens; Ranjan asserts the right to shelter as a right of citizenship; and Lorna, Filipina domestic in Singapore, claims the home that she is entitled to in her homeland. Surely these are disruptions of the established order! To understand why the idiom of citizenship, like the narration of naturalized widowhood, recites consent, it is necessary to return once again to the volatile geography of New Communism.

The Socio-Spatial Order

I gingerly picked my way through the piles of rubble the bulldozers had left behind. It was 5 August 1997. And the squatter settlement of Patuli, in the southeastern fringes of Calcutta, was a wasteland (Figure 5.3). A day earlier the police had moved in, with "war-like urgency," and demolished all quarters and shanties occupied by squatters. For hours the police closed off roads to the settlement and, with the help of CPM leaders and cadres, systematically evicted the squatters. CMDA officers confirmed that 700 homes and almost 2,000 informal additions and shacks had been razed. The squatters had not provided any resistance (*Bartaman*, 5 August 1997). By the time I arrived at Patuli, many of the evictees had left. But there was still a steady exodus from the settlement—families, handcarts loaded with bundles of belongings, familiar faces. Allottee houses and units loomed incongruously amidst the smashed bricks of squatter units. An eerie silence had descended on the place, and the squatters whom I had come to know now just wanted to be left alone: "Please don't take any photographs of us in this condition. It is humiliating. Haven't we been humiliated enough?"

Only ten days before, in the same settlement, Ranjan had declared to me with great certainty, "If one is a citizen, one can't be homeless." Replayed in the heat and rubble of that August day it was less a statement vindicating the success of the informal sector and more an indication of the specific vulnerabilities of a regime of shelter. It was especially poignant because it was made at a moment of what had seemed to be great security—in a squatter settlement that had matured through the patronage of the Congress party and that was slated for the regularization of land titles. All through 1997 Patuli had seemed to contradict the familiar story of squatter evictions and resettlements.

Indeed, Patuli had presented the possibility that opposition parties like the Congress could disrupt the territorial power of the regime and even bring a measure of stability to the informal housing market. On the fringes, as the Left Front expanded its developmental alliances, so the Congress secured new electoral constituencies, mobilizing sharecroppers and squatters in the bid for land rights. It could be said that the hegemony of the

Figure 5.3. Evictions at Patuli settlement. The units that were spared were those already taken back by allottees.

regime had created inevitable contradictions that permitted it "to be criticized on its own terms" (Scott 1985, 317). The meteoric success of Mamata Banerjee, first as a Youth Congress leader, and more recently as founder of the Trinamul Congress party, rests to a large extent on the electoral support of squatters, evicted hawkers, and sharecroppers. In particular, it seemed that the current moment of India's coalition woes had created a need for election readiness on the ground and accordingly more negotiating room for the rural-urban poor.

How, then, do I tell the story of how and why once again what seemed disruptive turned out to be a consolidation of sociospatial order? How then do I tell of how and why once again what seemed fraught with ambivalence, what seemed volatile, was in fact chillingly static and quietly complicit?

Layers

I first stumbled across the Patuli settlement on a visit to an informal market established by the side of VIP Road on the southeastern fringes of the city. The market's untidy shacks were squeezed haphazardly in front of a walled housing complex of four-story walk-ups. The vendors at the market pointed me to the "quarters," which turned out to be a massive core housing project. It was a surreal landscape with rows of crumbling one-room core units, informal additions patched together with bamboo and tarpaulin, punctuated with a few formalized and obviously middle-class houses. I was to spend many months at Patuli, researching its various stakeholders: squatters, formal owners, party leaders, legislative representatives, and state officials. My account of Patuli is an interweaving of these narratives and their continuities and disjunctures.

If there is any consensus regarding Patuli, it is that it was built by the CMDA, with World Bank funding, in the late 1970s as a mixed-income housing project. The final allottees were selected through a lottery system, but most were unwilling to take possession because of the poor state of infrastructure in what was then a desolate part of the urban region. Watching the project lie vacant, the construction workers, many of them migrants from the villages of South 24-Parganas, began to take over as squatters. They chiefly occupied the core units that had been built for Economically Weaker Sections (EWS) and Low Income Groups (LIG). Over the years they were joined by friends and family, and by the mid-1980s their numbers had swelled to about a thousand families (*Asian Age,* 24 November 1996).

The squatters were at first CPM supporters, voting for the party in various elections. But starting in 1990, as the area began to develop, many of the original allottees began to express interest in taking possession of the occupied quarters and even formed a *Nagarik Samiti,* or citizen's committee, with the support of the CPM. Squatter leader Suren Banerjee provided detailed descriptions of the CPM's allegedly gruesome strategies of eviction:

> It was in 1991 that we decided we could not take it any more. CPM *goondas* [strongmen] had been beating us up, destroying our houses for a while by then. They would smash the cooking-pots of our women and terrorize us. We were used to it. Buddhadeb Bhattacharjee[11] had made us promises that we were going to be able to live here but nothing had happened. Then one day in December, one of our women was out collecting fuel wood. We can't afford to buy wood and so we must forage for it. She was pregnant. Some CPM men assaulted her, kicked her repeatedly in the stomach, and then left her just lying there half-dead.

"They came to me in 1991 and invited me to a town hall meeting, pleading with me for help," said Gobinda Naskar, Pradesh Congress leader, in one of my first interviews with him regarding the Patuli matter. He continued, "Given the possibility of evictions, I decided to file a High Court case on their behalf. They were homeless, they had been here since 1982, they deserved the right to these homes." Sachin Mukherjee, a former Naskar supporter who later switched to the Youth Congress faction, claimed credit: "In

1991 when the CPM was trying to evict the squatters and they came to Gobinda Naskar, I was given the responsibility for the High Court case. I was able to procure a stay order to stop any immediate evictions."

Such actions of the Congress won them a stable group of voters in Patuli. Suren Banerjee, squatter leader, admitted that the squatters were Left Front supporters in their villages: "For many years, we voted for the CPM, but now the Congress has helped us. They filed a High Court case on our behalf. They fought it all the way to the Supreme Court. The CPM councillors and leaders are all on the side of the allottees."

Not surprisingly, the High Court ruled against squatter claims to land. The Congress then embarked on a different tactic, convincing the Minister of Urban Affairs and the CMDA to consider selling some of the EWS and LIG units to squatters. Congress leaders like Gobinda Naskar promised to find easy installment loans from the State Bank of India for the squatters (*Asian Age*, 24 November 1996). "I will mortgage my own house to provide for them, my poor brothers and sisters," insisted Sachin Mukherjee. In one of his interviews with me, Pankaj Banerjee, Congress MLA, detailed the formation of a multiparty committee headed by the CMDA: "The committee is going to oversee the distribution of 900 core houses among the squatters. We are drawing up the lists. The government could not evict the squatters all of this time because of our opposition. And now, it is a rare case of the regularization of squatter claims to public land."

The CMDA saw it as an instance of exceptional generosity. S. K. Bhattacharya, Director of General Operations, emphasized: "The Minister is doing this with the sentiment that he would be helping the poor though these squatters had done little to deserve any sympathy. On the contrary, they have taken over the core houses through illegal occupation and even initiated legal action against us."

The newspapers passed the verdict: the state government had finally "bowed its head" to the illegal occupants (*Bartaman*, 17 February 1997; *Asian Age*, 8 April 1997).

Such forms of patronage politics have served the Congress well in the Calcutta metropolitan area. It is hard to isolate the precise role of constituencies of poor migrants and semiformal sharecroppers in the electoral calculus. However, what is clear is that during the last decade the Congress has increasingly presented a serious challenge to the Left Front in the Calcutta agglomeration. But lurking in the shadows of Congress dominance is an intricate and contending set of claims to land, and to the legacy of the Congress party itself. Patuli's history cannot be told except through the history of these claims.

Genesis Stories

"We built these quarters, you know," said Jinnah, an elderly man from the Basanti area of South 24-Parganas, as I sat talking to him and his wife in front of their two-room EWS quarter one lazy spring afternoon: "But after they were completed, they lay vacant for so long. *Goondas* were destroying what we had built. Thieves were stealing doors and windows. Some of us had no place to live. We were living in Park Circus, by the railway lines. And so we moved in. It was to the benefit of the *sarkar,* you see. The whole place would have been destroyed otherwise."

The genesis story that Jinnah had constructed was a common narrative in Patuli. Again and again, migrants detailed how they had worked on the construction of the project, how they had watched it being vandalized—from commuter trains back and forth to their villages, from other squatter settlements—and how they had moved in to save the project from the hands of miscreants. Such stories were a crucial element in how squatters claimed a stake to the quarters and were often echoed in newspaper accounts: "Many of the non-allottees were masons who had built the units . . . But, from 1989–90, when the allottees started taking possession, these people refused to evict the quarters. 'We came here to clean the jungles for you. How can you throw us out after 12 long years without any compensation?' they argued" (*Asian Age,* 24 November 1996).

This claim of having settled the land and protected the quarters is precisely what underpins the shift in terminology from "squatter" to "non-allottee," the shift in connotation from illegality to semilegality.

When the Patuli squatters filed cases with the High Court with the help of the Congress, they invoked a second claim to the quarters. They argued that the EWS and LIG units of the quarters had been built for low-income families. Indeed, the lottery had specified extremely low incomes as cutoff points for qualification. But, Sachin Mukherjee, Congress leader, emphasized, "Those who applied hid their incomes. They lied. And in any case, they never took possession. They stayed away because they did not like projects. There was no infrastructure, no services, and the middle classes did not like this."

Pankaj Banerjee, Congress MLA, confirmed: "After the squatters lost the High Court Case, I requested the Minister of Urban Affairs not to evict them because these were precisely the low-income groups the project was supposed to serve."

"The allottees who live here are not poor," alleged Suren Banerjee, squatter leader. "They have been selling property to developers and making a great deal of money, even though this is illegal. And why shouldn't they? They bought a unit for Rs 10,000 and now it is worth over Rs 100,000. Soon this area will be full of highrises. This is why they want to get rid of us, because of how valuable this land has become. The CPM is a part of this— their cadres are greedily buying up this land."

These three interconnected claims formed the core of squatter demands for regularization: that they built and protected the quarters, that they meet the original EWS and LIG eligibilities, and that the legal allottees are in effect *rentiers*, raking in large profits on the land.

The narratives of the squatters and the Congress sharply contrast with those of CPM cadres, leaders, and supporters. Amal Mazumdar, a mid-ranking CPM cadre, said, "The squatters are illegal occupants. They took over this land by force. But they are of course poor and ignorant people. They were instigated to do so by political clubs."

The allottees almost unanimously characterized the squatters as violent miscreants. Jharna, an allottee, talked to me while she supervised the finishing touches to the second floor of her new house: "I have given up hope with them. When we first moved here I first tried to start a women's group supported by the CPM. But they are uncivilized and uncouth. They don't deserve our attention. The men are always drunk. And there is so much violence. I was advised by the party not to expand my house until these people are kicked out."

The Urban Development Ministry, under fire for poor amenities in many of the suburban townships, placed the blame on the squatters. The Minister, Ashok Bhattacharya, argued that because of the squatters they had been unable to make any improvements (*Bartaman*, 18 March 1998).

The formation of the bipartisan committee seemed to produce something close to a consensus around one issue: that nine hundred squatter families were going to be given the opportunity to purchase their units from the CMDA. The local CPM councillor and head of the allottee Nagarik Committee, Ujjal Chatterjee, was the dissenting voice, emphasizing in his interviews with me in May that the committee had made no firm recommendations and had no obligations to regularize any of the squatters. But S. K. Bhattacharya, Director of General Operations, CMDA, who had been appointed head of the committee by the Urban Development Minister, confirmed that they were planning to regularize nine hundred families, emphasizing that this would be an opportunity to recover some costs.

Why 900? Bhattacharya shared the CMDA's records with me: 2,240 allotment letters had been originally issued in the early 1980s. Of these, 1,839 allottees had responded, leaving 401 unclaimed units. But many of these

1,839 allottees had not been able to take possession. One of the key working rules of the committee was that all allottees who were still interested in taking possession should be allowed to do so immediately. They thus determined that about 900 units could be made available for regularization of squatter claims. But by all estimates, in 1998 there were more than 2,000 squatter families in Patuli, occupying units as well as vacant plots. How, among these 2,000 families, were 900 lucky ones going to be chosen? Ujjal Chatterjee, the CPM councillor, said that the minister had suggested holding a lottery among the nonallottees, but most committee members chose instead to draw up lists. What were these lists and how were they devised?

The Politics of Lists

"We are creating a list of all families with their occupations, income, length of stay," explained Pankaj Banerjee, Congress MLA, during our first interview, "because we want to establish authentic claims. We will also use these lists to arrange easy installment loans for the beneficiaries." Amal Mazumdar, CPM leader, argued: "It is crucial to create a list. CMDA rules state that only those who do not own any property within a twenty-kilometer radius of the site can be eligible."

The ownership of property? Wasn't it self-evident that the squatters were poor and landless? How and why was this even an issue in regularization? But Suren Banerjee, squatter leader, confirmed that the list was being drawn up on the basis of who owned how much land in their native villages: "We keep track of everything . . . Who votes in which election for whom and where. Who owns how much land? There are 2,000 families but we will be able to easily eliminate 1,100 to come up with 900 genuine cases."

Suren Banerjee's words came as a huge surprise to me. My research indicated that less than 1 percent of the Patuli squatters owned any cultivable land at all in their villages. Many did not even own a homestead plot. High-ranking Congress leaders from Gobinda Naskar to Pankaj Banerjee confirmed my findings repeatedly, referring to the squatters as a "homeless" population.

As the events of the next few months unfolded, I began to realize that the list was a critical exclusionary tool, a way of exacting political allegiance and eliminating competitors. The process of "verification" soon turned into at best a set of negotiations and at worst an opportunity for strong-arm tactics. Each faction of the Congress generated its own list, as did the CPM. "It is a blatant misuse of the process," complained S. K. Bhattacharya: "How can we proceed if there are multiple 'genuine' lists? We have done our own survey also and there is only a 15 percent overlap between all of these lists and our survey. Each group is simply putting in the names of its own follow-ers. At the settlement, they are trying to evict other groups and bring in new people. It is a mess."

The contestations surrounding the Patuli list were a part of long-standing conflicts between two factions of the Congress party. When the squatters had first allied with the Congress, they had approached Gobinda Naskar, a mid-ranking leader in the Pradesh Congress Committee, a state-level Congress organization. Over the years a second faction emerged with-in the settlement, with allegiance to the Youth Congress. Sachin Mukherjee, the key grassroots link between the squatters and the Congress, as well as Suren Banerjee, the spokesperson for the squatters, both switched loyal-ties to the Youth Congress. They established ties with Pankaj Banerjee, a MLA with Youth Congress leanings, who in turn had firm connections with Mamata Banerjee. The settlement came to be divided into two clear fac-tions with separate hierarchies of party bosses.

For both factions the regularization list became a crucial tool in mo-bilizing and consolidating popular support. Youth Congress cadres alleged that Naskar's supporters were making false promises that all Pradesh Con-gress followers would be regularized. Ranjan, a Youth Congress supporter, said angrily, "When the waters were muddy, when we were struggling, Naskar would never show up. Now that the water is clear, he has shown up to enjoy his own reflection in the water. He has been taking photographs, creating his own identity cards, and telling people that these cards will get them units. Lies, all lies."

In contrast, Naskar blamed the Youth Congress for the High Court verdict: "We had a strong case, but they went and filed a second case for a smaller group of people, all full of false names. They raised all of this money but Sachin Mukherjee pocketed most of it. The second case jeopardized any chances of winning in court."

The factionalism at Patuli can only be understood in the context of regional and national struggles within the ailing Congress party. In West Bengal in the early 1980s, the Youth Congress, under the leadership of the popular Mamata Banerjee, established itself as a serious political player. Mamata was somewhat of a rebel within the Congress, accusing the Pradesh Congress, under Priya Ranjan Das Munshi, and later under Somen Mitra, of favoritism and authoritarianism in the selection of electoral candidates (Sengupta 1987; 1997). To this effect, she repeatedly lodged complaints with the All India National Congress. In 1997 the conflict between Mamata and Somen Mitra intensified, with Mamata declaring a boycott of Congress or-ganizational elections.

Mamata's obstinacy derived in considerable part from the growing possibility of a Left Front–Congress alliance at the national level to stave off the rise of the BJP and other fundamentalist parties. All through the summer of 1997 she staged massive rallies and lashed out at Somen Mitra and his followers. Political commentators observed that despite her unprecedented and unparalleled ability to draw crowds, national leadership continued to support Somen Mitra, recognizing him as the leader of the West Bengal Congress. Such alliances must in turn be understood within the context of national struggles for organizational leadership[12] (*Bartaman*, 28 July 1997).

These national and regional conflicts reverberated through Patuli, ineluctably linking the struggle for regularization with the battle for the soul of the Congress in West Bengal. As Mamata visited the settlement for the first time and urged her supporters to continue their mobilization work, the violent clashes between the Pradesh and Youth Congress factions began to intensify. The irreconcilable differences between the two factions provided the CPM with an opportunity they had not had for years: the chance for evictions.

In late July, when CMDA officers tried to execute a High Court order by taking possession of two quarters, a large group of rioting squatters, led by Congress leader Sachin Mukherjee, charged the officers and their police protectors, forcing them to retreat (*Bartaman*, 23 July 1997). Police officers claimed that they were attacked by a mob of almost a thousand, armed with daggers and revolvers (*Asian Age*, 23 July 1997; *Telegraph*, 23 July 1997). At a public meeting of the CPM South 24-Parganas District Committee, Subhas Chakravarty and Kanti Ganguly asked the squatters to leave peacefully, agreeing to help those who would leave voluntarily (*Ganashakti*, 26 July 1997). In fact, the proceedings of this meeting laid the groundwork for the evictions that were to follow in a few days. CPM leaders stressed that the Congress had been playing games with the squatters and that this was why evictions were inevitable. Echoing the statement he had made to me a few months earlier, Amal Mazumdar, Krishak Samiti leader, said, "If they had stayed loyal to us, we would have given them homes, services and security" (*Ganashakti*, 26 July 1997).

On 4 August 1997 the cadres of the CPM, the party of the poor, donned CMDA badges and zealously directed bulldozers to demolish squatter-occupied units (*Bartaman*, 4 August 1997). The bourgeoisification of Calcutta's margins was thus consolidated—by a *bhadralok* party, incidentally leftist, and keen to protect the gentlemanly interests of a new Bengali suburban middle-class.

Patuli reveals a series of fissures and cracks. For one thing, the politics of lists makes it amply clear that, in this case, squatter claims did not coalesce into an urban social movement. Rather, competing factions of squatters were tenuously incorporated into a fragmented project of populist mobilization. Neither the factionalism of the CPM nor the splitting in half of the Congress has boded well for the rural-urban poor. Indeed, Patuli squatters were imbricated in a political field that was almost indistinguishable from that of the colonies or other CPM-dominated settlements. While the squatters had some room to negotiate with different parties and factions, they were ultimately subject to the same logic of volatile populism articulated in the same oppressive mechanisms of masculinist patronage. It is thus that over and over again I wrote in my fieldnotes: "On the ground, I cannot tell one party apart from the other."

The irony of Patuli is that only a few days after the evictions, Mamata staged her most stunning rally yet, drawing a sea of Congress workers and supporters in sheer defiance of the AICC Plenary that was being held in Calcutta. At the rally she launched a separate organization, and a few months later she consolidated it as a new regional party called the Trinamul Congress. Declaring an outright war against the CPM, she pledged outside support to the BJP, going on to sweep Calcutta in the 1998 parliamentary elections (*Asian Age*, 25 February 1998; *Bartaman*, 26 February 1998), sorely weakening the Congress in West Bengal (*Bartaman*, 4 March 1998). The Trinamul managed to procure from the BJP a host of concessions, a "Bengal Package," drawn up by Mamata, that included her pet initiatives (*Asian Age*, 19 March 1998).

But the rise of the Trinamul, and Mamata's newfound channels of political access, proved inconsequential to the fate of settlements such as Patuli. The much-touted "Bengal Package" did not include a single mention of the regularization of squatter or peasant claims, the very basis of Mamata's popular mobilization in South Calcutta, her parliamentary district.

Ranjan had said:

If one is a citizen, one cannot be homeless.

In the wake of the Patuli evictions, I was struck by the disjuncture between this claim and the reality of his being rendered homeless. Perhaps, as Breman[13] recently suggested, there is another way of framing Ranjan's statement:

If one is homeless, one cannot be a citizen.

It is in this sense that Castells (1983, 212) writes about squatting as a "dependent city, a city without citizens." In a similar spirit, the rowdy assertion of the commuters can be rephrased as well:

> We vote, so why should we pay for what we need but cannot afford?
>
> *We cannot afford what we need, and thus we vote.*

Hegemony through Volatility

How and why do the rural-urban poor consent to the conditions of their oppression? How and why do they actively participate and constitute the project of hegemony and indeed the regime itself? The answers to such questions are already present in the chapters that I have presented, but let me take a moment here to gather up the pieces.

The rural-urban poor whom I have introduced through ethnographic evidence—distress migrants and commuters—are not only landless but also poor; not just poor, but also persistently poor. The shift in emphasis from landlessness to poverty signals a more complex ensemble of vulnerabilities, many of which the migrants and commuters themselves locate in urban struggles for livelihood and shelter. This is not to say that the issue of persistent poverty does not inevitably implicate the Left Front; it is instead to emphasize the difference between evaluating such things as land reforms and working through the social logic of the regime.

The persistence of poverty can be thought of as "a hegemonic formation," an ensemble of relatively stable social forms (Mouffe 1988, 90). I see this formation as articulating two key elements: the regime and the family. By the regime, I refer to the populisms of the Left Front—its specific political mobilizations as well as the mechanisms through which these alliances are secured. By the family, I mean the logic of double gendering, the coherence of the feminization of livelihood and the masculinization of politics. I use the word "family" rather than "household" because I wish to indicate the importance of the ideal of the family—historicocultural discourses of domesticity—as well as the material practices of negotiation within a diversity of household forms.

The feminization of livelihood is a key feature of persistent poverty because it manifests and maintains oppressive structures of employment as well as patriarchal elements of the regime. By emphasizing how the depoliticization of women's work occurs on a daily basis through the dynamics of masculinist patronage, my research shows that such domestications are negotiated through lived practices rather than imposed through the structure of reforms and agendas. The daily renewal of legitimacy happens on the one hand through the flexible deployment of spatialized patronage as in the colonies; and on the other hand through the suturing of family and regime. I use the term "suturing" to indicate a wound, a raw scar, that requires a process of what Williams (1977, 112) calls "lived hegemony."

How and why is masculinist patronage a lived hegemony? Because through it, to borrow Willis's (1977, 174) words, "structures become sources of meaning." We know from the substantial work on urban politics in the context of poverty that this daily renewal happens through populist mobilization—in squatter settlements, through the contingent granting of the claim to shelter and urban services. What I have been equally concerned with is the mutual constitution of regimes of the state and regimes of the family, with the making and remaking of subject-positions and position-takings.

> Far from patriarchy and its associated values being an unexplained
> relic of previous societies, it is one of the very pivots of capitalism
> in its complex, unintended preparation of labor power and repro-
> duction of the social order. It helps to provide the real human and
> cultural conditions which in their continuously deconstructed,
> reconstructed, fragile, uncertain, unintended and contradictory
> ways actually allow subordinate roles to be taken on "freely" within
> liberal democracy. (Willis 1977, 151)

Much has been written about how, in a West Bengal countryside marked by class inequalities, the Left has implemented a "dialectical peasant unity" through the everyday presence of local cadres (Rogaly 1998) and through the "management" of development (Webster 1992, 144). A similar form of "management" takes place in Calcutta through the urban network of neighborhood clubs and party offices. But such forms of discipline and control cannot be understood without taking account of its resonances in "private" sites of power, which is to say, in households. What is negotiated in the political community, in clubs, and party offices is electoral loyalty in the form of class and gender subject-positions. And what is negotiated within migrant households is gender relations, which act as the terms on which participation in the regime is possible. It is thus that masculinist patronage articulates regime and family, establishing continuities in hegemonic practices within and between households.

And it is thus that amidst the rowdy rebellions and active appropriations, hegemony is stealthily perpetuated. It is imperative to emphasize that this hegemonic formation, the suturing of regime and family, is not guaranteed. The mechanism of articulation—masculinist patronage—is itself what

Willis (1977, 174) would call a "necessary uncertainty." The idea of "lived hegemony" draws attention to processes of consolidation as well as to the possibilities of disruption. But as the stabilization of the hegemonic formation is never complete or conclusive, so the disruptions are never guaranteed. In the case of Calcutta's squatters, it is clear that the daily renewal of hegemony has taken on rather insidious forms and that the disruptions have been rather benign. I locate the persistence of poverty at precisely this intersection of stabilized oppressions and harmless rebellions.

The broader discussions of hegemony have implied that those marginalized from such structures of power might be able to resist hegemonic forms of meaning-making. In a spirit that resonates with feminist ideas of "speaking from the margins,"[14] Bourdieu (Bourdieu and Wacquant 1992, 173) interprets Virginia Woolf:

> . . . how, by ignoring the illusion that leads one to engage in the
> central games of society, women escape the *libido dominandi* that
> comes with this involvement, and are therefore socially inclined
> to gain a relatively lucid view of the male games in which they ordi-
> narily only participate by proxy.[15]

At first glance, the feisty critiques of Calcutta's commuter women strongly resemble such disruptions. Yet, as I have argued, the very form and tropes of disruption consolidate class and gender hegemony. If Carney and Watts (1990) are arguing that workers can manufacture "dissent," gendered dissent, then I am arguing that the very idiom of dissent can reproduce and recite consent.[16] This is perhaps most evident in the feminist debates on globalized work that interpret the negotiation of sexual and social freedoms by young women workers as both forms of resistance and as a consumerist desire that ensures self-discipline (Ong 1987). Some of the most compelling research shows how such desires are produced through the multinational factories that promote prescriptive models of femininity (Tiano and Ladino 1999) as well as by the state, as in the case of China's "democracy of consumption" (Zhang 2000). In these cases, what at first glance seems to be a lively challenge to the normative category of "working daughter" turns out to be a consolidation of another norm: that of the gendered consumer-worker interpellated in both the global assembly line and the global commodity chain.

Similar issues are at stake in the rich and sophisticated Latin American debates about the gendered dimensions of social reproduction. For example, in the context of Peru, Radcliffe (1993) shows how the state promoted a middle-class Hispanic model of femininity. In other words, different regimes of power were also regimes of gender. Her work provocatively demonstrates the ways in which squatter and peasant women deployed these models of gender in struggles against the state, thereby gaining access to land and services. In a similar vein, Hays-Mitchell (1995, 455) writes, "Poor urban women in Peru . . . generate their own 'counterhegemonic' identities by invoking the same identity that the state deploys of them as the epitome of national subjects—that is, as good mothers—in order to signal opposition and resistance to the state's inadequacies and/or excesses."

And yet the limits of such motherist politics are quite obvious, particularly in its reinforcement of the normative identity of motherhood. While this does not undermine the successes of such forms of mobilization, it does indicate the paradigm of power that remains intact. Thus, Abu-Lughod (1990, 315) suggests that various forms of resistance should be strategically read as revealing forms of power rather than as signs of human freedom.

Indeed, in an era of neoliberal restructuring, the state and parastatal apparatus of development have reappropriated such gendered models of political negotiation. If motherist politics can be read as counterhegemony, it is also now being put to instrumental use in the new consensus on enablement and self-help. These paradigms rehearse the form and rhetoric of urban social movements—grassroots mobilizations, women-oriented community development, self-management—and yet they are clearly products of a historical moment of late capitalism marked by the brutal retrenchment of social programs and services.

Cartographies of Hegemony

How and why do disruptions seal the deal? What is the specificity of squatting as a site of social reproduction that on the one hand leads to rowdy mobilizations but on the other hand produces hegemonic consent? In the case of Calcutta, I would argue that the answers to such questions rest in the spatiality of hegemony, in the volatile geography of urban populisms. This is also a "necessary uncertainty" of sorts, one where the uncertainty created through an unmapping of the city necessitates obedient participation in structures of patronage.

It is not surprising, then, that amidst the desperate spaces of a dying city I found hope in what at first seemed the most oppressive of sites—the claustrophobic, overflowing commuter trains. The ultimate embodiment of dehumanizing capitalism showed signs of life and living. In its unanticipated geography, this realm indicates, as Pile (1997, 2) notes, that "resistance might have its own distinct spatialities" that are not simply mirror images of geographies of domination.

But there are other spatialities that shape the territory of my research. The commuter trains are but one site in a larger articulation of rural and urban labor and housing markets. Thus, the very notion of a feminization of livelihood points to the social basis of informality as well as the territoriality of labor flows. In this case, domestic work is much more than a gendered point of production. Its very ingredients include the incorporation of landless peasant households into the urban informal sector, the material basis of social reproduction, and the metaphorical and political space of the nation-state.[17] It is in this sense that it becomes impossible to talk about the feminization of livelihood without a discussion of the masculinization of politics and of the latter without an analysis of the regional geography of the regime.

In other words, if I have argued that the commuter trains are a site of disruption, setting aside the issue of what those disruptions might mean, I am now arguing that squatter settlements embody a site of hegemonic formation. In doing so, I do not mean to imply an unqualified structural difference between commuters and migrants, between social reproduction in rural and urban locations. In light of the massive body of West Bengal research on the hegemonic role of *panchayats* and other institutions of populist mobilization, it is most likely possible to make an argument about how commuter women are implicated in rural institutions and structures that parallel those of squatter settlements. However, this space has remained beyond the boundaries of my research project. Despite my ethnographic involvement in certain commuter villages, the scope of my investigation did not include the "daily renewal of legitimacy" in the West Bengal countryside, mainly because this is an argument that has already been made with great force. Instead, I have sought to explain the quite fantastic territorialized flexibility of the regime in a liberalizing Calcutta, and its practices of hegemony.

I have hitherto told a story about the mutual constitution of region and regime, showing how the "present history" of the regime is manifested in an urban developmentalism, and how the key alliances and strategies of the regime have become territorialized with unprecedented intensity. In other words, this is a regime of accumulation such that its consolidations and contradictions are evident at the sociospatial level of the urban.[18] Another way of framing this would be to say that if regimes of accumulation are processes of regulation (Goodwin and Painter 1997), then such processes are inevitably spatial.

Jessop (1997, 72) argues that the regulationist approach to regimes requires a better understanding of "the ethico-political dimension to regulation." In emphasizing how regimes of accumulation are also regimes of the family, I have sought to elaborate this ethicopolitical content of hegemony. However, the case of Calcutta makes it clear that such regimes are also what Linda McDowell (1999) would call "regimes of place." Earlier I presented masculinist patronage as the Faustian bargain that lies at the heart of hegemonic formation; I am now invoking another meaning of the Faustian bargain: the "tragedy of development" (Berman 1982, 40). This is more than simply the bleeding of "human sacrifices" (64); rather, it is the "creative destruction" inherent in urban capitalism, the renewal of value through cycles of removal and resettlement. Indeed, Berman (72–75) argues that the Faustian bargain must be located not only in capitalism but equally in the utopian dreams of socialism—in the "immense construction site" that has become the "stage for world history in our time."[19]

Such is the territoriality of Calcutta's New Communism. It is in this "immense construction site" that the persistence of gendered poverty, the recital of hegemonic consent, must be located. In an unmapped space, in the "regime of place," the rigidities of class and gender hierarchies are produced through incredible flexibility. The "necessary uncertainty" of hegemony on the one hand makes possible the uncertain negotiation of claims to land and shelter, but on the other hand makes impossible the certain articulation of secure and regularized titles and rights. Thus the importance of the Patuli case, as an example of disruption and as an instance of hegemonic formation. It is this analytical pathway that makes evident how urban politics in a liberalizing Calcutta produces deep antagonisms, but not transformative struggles.

I have argued that the ethicopolitical content of this hegemony, the social logic of this regime, is simultaneously gendered and spatialized. By this I mean not so much the ways in which spaces, like the rural-urban interface, are gendered but rather that gender is itself constituted in and through space. The analytical shift from the social construction of space to the spatial construction of the social (Massey 1992, 70; see also Rose 1993) is an important one. It is a question that Sayer (1989, 257) raises of Willis's work, asking how place and region play a part in the consolidation and negotiation of hegemony so deftly portrayed by Willis, a point not directly addressed by the work itself. Is there something about this locality, "this place" at "this time," that shapes the logic, mechanisms, and possibilities of hegemonic articulation? In the case of an unmapped Calcutta, it is clear that there is a distinctive spatiality to a hegemony that is, as Jackson (1985, 828) would put it, "of the city" rather than simply "in the city."

There is also another aspect of such spatialities that is important—that

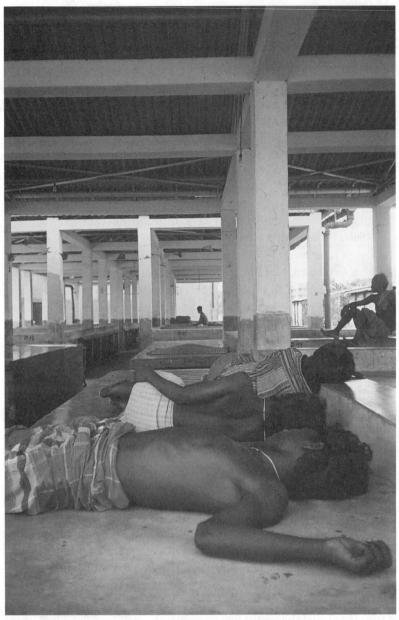

Figure 5.4. The freshly constructed CMDA market hall at the Patuli settlement, awaiting use by new middle-class residents.

space is neither a container nor an outcome of social processes.[20] As Massey (1995, 284) has argued in her extension of Mouffe's (1988 1995) ideas of hegemony, along with identity and power, spatiality is more usefully thought of as a "third interactive dimension." In the case of Calcutta's regime politics, the unmapping of the city can at one level be interpreted as an "institutional fix" that is also a "spatial fix" (Peck and Tickell 1994), the mode of regulation par excellence:

> We might say that the mode of regulation constitutes . . . the superficial "map" by which individual agents orient themselves so that the conditions necessary for balanced economic reproduction and accumulation are met in full. (Lipietz 1994, 339)

Quite provocatively, in Calcutta, unmapping becomes this map.

And yet this spatial fix does not do away with what Lipietz (339) identifies as the "radical uncertainty" that inheres in regimes of accumulation. As in the case of that key element of hegemonic formation, masculinist patronage, the spatial volatility of urban populism generates its own contradictions and uncertainties. If I have hitherto highlighted how these uncertainties guarantee the hegemonic consent of the poor, here I need to reiterate that the regime remains damned by its own historicized logic of territorialized flexibility. This is not simply another Faustian bargain, because here the "tragedy of development," of persistent poverty and unrelenting spatial evictions, is emptied of its developmental content. Here, then, is an idiom, a spatial vocabulary of hegemony, that contradicts and sabotages the content of regime projects. Analytically, I have not designated such instances as disruptions of hegemony because there is no ethicopolitical content to this sabotage other than that of hegemonic consolidation. At the margins of Calcutta, the core is always present. Perhaps a few lines from my field journal during the last week of fieldwork will indicate the spirit of this spatiality:

> I am of the city, of the uncanny urbanism that allows me to imagine only in the idiom of urban space. I have felt my soul stretched tight, fading behind city blocks. I have written in and of the grime of a thousand masquerades.[21]

> But here on the fringes, where I have spent much of my days during this past year, the city itself fades. It stutters to a halt amidst green fields. It is soothed by the deep shade that the trees cast. The city seeks to constitute itself in the piles of bricks awaiting use in the construction sites. But one rainstorm and the countryside creeps back in, through stealthy moss and stubborn blades of paddy.

We stop to buy a bunch of spinach and pumpkins from the peasant by the side of the highway. It's called the Bypass for it is meant to by-pass the city.

I am not of the city. Because the city does not exist at its core, not in the throngs of downtown, not in the gated residences of Alipore, not in the crumbling splendor of its colonial past, not in the dust and traffic of bulging thoroughfares. The city is here on the fringes. In the pasture.

It is terrifying in its presence for its presence leaves few traces. It is horrific in its brutality for it leaves no ruins amidst the pastoral beauty. This is not a history that I can tell on a grid, through street names and wards and mansions. Here, history overwhelms and de-fies, stretching to the horizon, dominant in its unmarked form. The city is the most ruthless at the moment of its greatest invisibility.

Postscript(s)

How is a city to be narrated? A city that at its surface is a multifarious collage, and, at closer look, ubiquitous in its depth?[1] What should be the culmination of such narrations?

In the multiple forms that this narrative has taken, I have struggled with the ways in which I have to end in writing what I dare not otherwise end—an intimate connection with the city of my birth, and the iconic city of "Third World" gloom.

In this postscript to a requiem I present the multiple endings that I have composed, each with a somewhat different mandate, each highlighting a different dimension of the project. Instead of sorting through the various conclusions, I present them all, showing how the first is ongoing, a master ending of sorts that incorporates all other endings; the second is one that expects a future; the third is one that I abandoned; and the last is the future that can never be written with finality.

I

If a requiem is as much an act of composition, evoking pleasure, as it is a performance of death, then my compositional strategies have emerged within a transnational cartography. My first ending, that which encompasses all others, makes explicit this location, for it is situated at the intersection of home and field, research and teaching, Calcutta and Berkeley. It is inspired by a pedagogic conversation with my students about the 1950 Kurosawa film *Rashomon*. The exchange took place in the context of a course I taught on gender and Asia, one that sought to provide not only the quite obvious gendered look at Asia but also a critical examination of the very trope of Asia itself. We examined the historicized diversity of development and urbanization that constitutes contemporary Asia, the diasporas that have dis-placed Asia, and the construction of Asia from themes of the "Oriental girl" to recent debates about the "Asian miracle." There are interesting resonances with my discussion of Calcutta, which has also involved analyzing both the historical specificity of sociospatial norms and the normalization of geopolitical power.

Rashomon is a site constituted through four conflicting narratives of a rape and murder. In the narrations—by a bandit who is the perpetrator, the woman, her husband who dies, and a woodcutter who observes the incident—the "truth" is constantly reinscribed. Rape becomes seduction, murder becomes honorable suicide, valiant men fighting an intricately choreographed duel become bumbling idiots, scrambling on the forest floor. In one, the woman is weak, at the mercy first of the bandit's desire and then her husband's contempt. In another, she is manipulative and cunning, moving from sobbing tears to deriding laughter in a heartbeat.

One of the pieces that my students read to frame the discussion of *Rashomon* was a scathing critique by Bordo (1990, 143) of postmodernism. Fearing the paralysis of a "gender-scepticism," Bordo rejects postmodernism's "dizzying accumulation of narratives." How, then, are we to deal with a text like *Rashomon*? With narratives that compete and collide such that acts of rape and murder become subject to relativist doubt? Does the truth rest in the voice of the Woman? In some scientific evidence that trumps the narratives? Kurosawa himself seems to privilege the account of the woodcutter, perhaps because he is the only observer who does not participate in the events, though even that is questioned. *Rashomon* ends on a humanist note, asserting the goodness of human nature through the motif of an abandoned baby who is adopted by the woodcutter. The woodcutter does the right thing[2]—and is therefore perhaps right.

As my students sorted through the *Rashomon* narratives, they searched for the similarities. There was one overwhelming commonality between the four, and this was the gendered idiom of narration. Interpreting *Rashomon* in light of Berger's (1972) analysis of "ways of seeing," they noted how the figure of the woman was constituted in the act of representation.[3] Even in the woman's own narrative, she presents herself as defined and shaped through the piercing and hateful gaze of a husband who no longer loves that which has been defiled through rape/seduction. Berger's work links up in important ways with longstanding feminist debates about representation and power, which indicate how women are the "grounds of debate" rather than the subjects or objects of debate (Mani 1990). In *Rashomon* the rape is incidental: what is debated is the woman's character and her role in initiating the chain of events that lead to her husband's death. In other words, she is rendered elusive and iconic, always re-presented, spoken for.

Can we say no more about *Rashomon*? Is there no alternative to clever postmodern strategies and humanistic naïvetés? I would like to suggest that another way of interpreting *Rashomon* is as the narration of power that arises from the disjunctures between the four narratives. If this is a "truth," then it has as much to do with *how* it said and by *whom* as it does with *what* is said. Put another way, these are narratives that can only be understood in light of the social hierarchies in which they are implicated and which they constitute through representation. The reinscription of rape as seduction by both bandit and husband can then be seen as a gendered truth, one that points to the impossibilities of meaningful sexual consent under conditions of dominance.[4] Or the contrast between the bandit's story of an honorable duel marked by a Samurai aesthetics of fighting and the husband's story of a honorable suicide serves to maintain an overarching idiom of masculinist honor.

I see this interpretation of disjunctures as the spirit, albeit unintentional, of this book. In my narration of gender and the city, both categories have revealed their inherent heteronomy. To use Scott's (1990) conceptualization of gender, these are categories that "overflow." I stress the intersection of gender and space because I have been concerned with a gendered subject that can only be recovered through its embodiments, in this case labor and housing. This is a subject that is not only the site of differences but is also constituted in and through different sites. The dramatic contradictions and slippages that have marked the territory of my Calcutta research make apparent such sociospatial multiplicities.

However, I do not see this as postmodern fragmentation or relativism. Rather, it indicates the space-geometries of hegemony, the traces of which inhere in the disjuncture between narratives. And so the discrepancies and silences of poverty measures tell us about the vulnerabilities of the rural-urban poor in West Bengal. Indeed, the invisibility of the rural landless in the official narrative, one that conflates cultivable agricultural land with homestead plots, confirms an agrarian structure dominated by the middle peasantry and a neopopulist party agenda seeking to perpetuate the myth of *Sonar Bangla*. Similarly, the invisibility of women workers at a moment of high female labor force participation shows how the economic landscape is constituted through the "feminization" of the informal sector. The striking disjuncture between how "mothers" are publicly mobilized and the "private" narratives of immoral and promiscuous working women reveals the patriarchy of the regime, how populist strategies consolidate rather than challenge gender hierarchies. The inscription of male unemployment by men as a type of work, as what allows them to participate in party politics, its reinscription by women as sexual impotence, and even as a gory death, points to a critique, but one that barely disrupts such gendered realities.

This, then, is the politics of poverty, one that requires moving beyond profiles of poverty to a critical epistemology of class and gender hierarchies. I have attempted to meet such mandates in my methodological framing of poverty. In the broadest sense this project deployed a Janus-faced fieldwork strategy. One face involved using methods like life histories to position subjects through their own voices. The reverse, pursued simultaneously, entailed resituating subjects in a historicized field of social and political contestations, which was, as Smith (1989, 170) would say, "open at the other end." Such "fields" are inherently spatialized and, indeed, the disjunctures made evident through the ethnographic method reveal the configurational dimension of space (Crang 1992, 532). One aspect of this geometry of power is the map of land rights. There are competing stories about land precisely when there are competing systems of land tenure and conflicting claims to land (Krueckeberg 1999). In the case of Calcutta, I have shown how such competing land narratives indicate a fluidity of land titles, an ambiguity that makes possible diverse land uses while limiting secure rights to territory. The movement back and forth between personal and social histories, from consensus to disjuncture, has been an attempt to hold ethnography and political economy in tension, one way of doing what Sayer (1989) rather cautiously calls a "critical" regional geography.

Perhaps such tensions are most evident in the dynamics of squatting. The life histories maintain the myth of household headship by mythicizing migration and squatting as territorial conquest. However, the stark disjuncture between these masculinist stories and the fragility of squatting indicates the consolidation of hegemony, that "moment of articulation." Ranjan's proud claim of citizenship, his critique of American democracy, must be thus interpreted—in light of the rhetorical devices of a leftist mobilization that deploys Western imperialism as a convenient foil for its regional chauvinism. Ranjan's inability or unwillingness to anticipate the brutal future reveals the ideology of housing, one that mystifies the spatial circuits of this commodity. There are historically perfected techniques at work here, which serve to domesticate the rural-urban poor at the very moment of mobilization. At the margins of a liberalizing Calcutta, it is the bourgeois city that is always waiting to be asserted. Ranjan's illusion is the faith that the city is constituted through his frontier story, unsullied by the spatial histories of hegemony.

This is a master ending. It is so because instead of seeking to neatly resolve all possible endings, it maintains as important and legitimate the different narratives of the city. In this spirit, I present three other conclusions, each linked to the other in a territory that is as much that of the geopolitics of research as it is of millennial Calcutta. The city lurks in and in between these postscripts.

II

I am a city planner. When I write about cities, I implicitly, even insidiously, introduce another project: that of social change and action. I do not do so to legitimate knowledge. Policy is not simply that which emerges as the inevitable conclusion to knowing, somehow making it all worthwhile. Rather, I do so because the narration of cities, mine, is marked by the distinctive anguish of the modern, the modern as an interventionist and transformative imagination. There are glimpses of this anguish all through this book, one that seeks to at once uphold and undermine "expectations of modernity,"[5] expectations that there will be progress, improvements, change. It is thus that I have grappled with the very apparatus of the modern, the *how* of cities, the *how* of knowledge, knowing that I have been imagining the resurrection of a city in the act of writing its requiem.

Let me then put on the table the ways in which each of the three thematic chapters of this book: on poverty, on gendered strategies of livelihood and shelter, and on the urban dimensions of liberalization, are undergirded by certain policy concerns. My discussion is deliberately brief, meant to signal and indicate, rather than detail.

In chapter 2 I argue that the politics of poverty is equally a politics of categories. Through an examination of competing discourses and measures of poverty, I have shown how knowledge is linked in complex ways to institutional action.[6] Indeed, the concern with "unmapping" informs much of my research. When I first started researching landlessness in West Bengal, I wrote in my field journal in great surprise:

> It is rather astonishing that despite a communist government with
> a political platform of agrarian reformism, and a formidable data-
> producing bureaucracy, West Bengal does not produce a single, re-
> liable indicator of rural landlessness.

I am no longer "astonished," for I have come to see the conflation of agricultural and homestead land as congruent with the Left's broader strategies of "dialectical peasant unity." If there are no class differences between agricultural laborers and middle peasants, if there is no need for the separate

unionization of agricultural laborers, then why should fine-grained definitions of landlessness matter? The regime's claim that there is no movement
of landless migrants into Calcutta, that all commuters come from landed
families—a claim repeated to me many times in party offices and in planning bureaucracies—rests precisely on flexible interpretations of the idea of
landlessness. These deficits in "public" information in fact mark a specific
institutional logic. They embody the very spirit of the regime.

> The management of names is one of the instruments of the man-
> agement of material scarcity, and the names of groups . . . record
> a particular state of struggles and negotiations over the official
> designations and material and symbolic advantages associated
> with them. (Bourdieu 1991, 240)

In this sense, my attempt to bring into view the rural landless and
women workers can be seen as a remanagement of names, what Sandercock
(1998) calls a "planning historiography" that draws attention to the erasures
and exclusions of the "official story." New subjects are thereby named and
engendered.

But in studying poverty I have also sought to provide what Holston
(1998, 55) calls an "ethnographic conception of the social." Here, the techniques of naming and mapping cannot suffice, for what is required is an
understanding of the very ways in which categories of knowledge are defined
and contested. This is a shift, as Fraser (1989) notes, from "needs" to "discourses about needs." There are two reasons why such an analytical move
is important for policy analysis and formulation. First, ethnographies bring
to light unanticipated processes and geographies. For example, Kandiyoti
(1999) shows how while surveys imply that researchers are already familiar
with the sociospatiality of poverty, ethnographic investigations can reveal
some of the most crucial aspects of deprivation and survival.

Second, the ethnographic attempt to confront the apparatus of planning, its very mechanisms of knowledge-gathering and policy-implemen-
tation, makes possible interventions in fields of power. If institutions are
the "rules of the game" (Van Arkadie 1989), then policy-making has to be as
concerned with how these rules are formulated and challenged as with the
outcomes of the game. Here, ethnographies become social interventions,
moving beyond what Harvey (1978, 231) calls "planning the ideology of
planning" to even possibly "planning the reconstruction of society."

In chapter 3 I take on the social basis of urban informality, emphasizing the gendered dimensions of housing and labor struggles. My intention
in doing so is partly to write against the paradigm of women-oriented com-

munity development, which has currently gained popularity. From a kinder and gentler World Bank to the shelter debates of Habitat II, there has been a new emphasis on enabling the poor. Enablement explicitly celebrates the efficiency and equity benefits of the informal sector (de Soto 1989; 2000) and implicitly locates the sources of such benefits in the practices of poor women. As Roberts (1994) notes, this utopian recovery of Third World urban communities coincides quite neatly with the austerity agenda of neoliberalism. Indeed, neoliberalism is engendered through the new trope of the Third World poor woman, this icon of unfatigued efficiency. To her can be safely assigned the world's problems, from managing the size of the population to the ecofeminist goal of saving the natural habitat.

In light of my Calcutta research, there are two aspects of the enablement paradigm that I find especially troubling. The first is the mystification of the brutal commodifications of the informal sector. While the ideology of self-help invokes the symbol of the entrepreneurial poor, as Breman (1996, 12) cautions, such trajectories of successful self-employment are rarely evident in informality. Thus, the growing heterogeneity, and even polarization, of Calcutta's informal sector is consistent with the broader geopolitical trends of late capitalism. Here, informal housing and labor markets are the domain of the poor, a symbol not of marginality but rather of constant marginalization. And entrepreneurship rests not in the desperate struggles of the rural-urban poor but rather in the regime as it remakes itself in the market image of liberalization. Under such conditions it is hard to imagine poverty as civil society, rich in its social networks. As Abu-Lughod (1998, 231) rightly warns, content should not be confused with form, for the civil society made evident in the informal sector is divisive and exclusionary.

Second, while I have emphasized the need to take account of the feminization of livelihood and poverty, I find the feminization of policy to be deeply problematic. As Jackson (1996) notes, at the moment of neoliberal restructuring, the burden of coping has shifted to the shoulders of the poor, and particularly poor women. Indeed, feminist scholars have long shown that collective consumption has involved a "triple shift" legitimated through the icon of the "new socialist woman" (Croll 1981; Molyneux 1985). In the current context of austerity policies, the dismantling of the welfare state has been made possible through the feminization of collective consumption (Castells 1989; Peck 2001). Thus, while enablement promotes the idiom of mothers leading and managing communities, the content of the programs implies a growing burden of community work for poor women. Not only does this model of community development reinforce the interlinked structures of state, family, and global capitalism but it also creates new forms of

exploitation that need careful analysis. A useful notion of feminized poverty, Jackson and Palmer-Jones (1999) argue, would not conflate two distinct
disadvantages, gender and poverty, and would instead show how poverty is
a gendered experience. The feminization of poverty policy, as embodied in
enablement, maintains as intact both gender and poverty.

In chapter 4 I present the volatile land transactions that are shaping
Calcutta's rural-urban interface. Implied in such a focus is the whole question of land reforms. Indeed, much of the policy debates in West Bengal
have been concerned with just such an issue. However, the discussion has
always been around agrarian reforms, and, as I have earlier discussed, with
little agreement on what counts as landownership. Through life histories, I
have shown how migrants and commuters define land as operational agricultural land, thereby contradicting Lieten's (1996a) claim that homestead
plots ward off deprivation. In doing so, they reinforce a body of research
that emphasizes the importance of cultivable land in generating vigorous
growth linkages (Harriss 1992a; Saith 1992; Ranis and Stewart 1993). But the
life histories also underscore the obvious limitations of redistribution in a
land-poor state. Instead, they provocatively point to the need to think about
the city as a site of land reforms—as not just a destination of migration but
instead as a complex process of settlement.

In posing the issue of urban land reforms, I am also returning to my
analytical emphasis on the apparatus of the regime, its regulatory ambiguities and the resultant vulnerability of the poor and the impasse in development. Thus, a call for the regularization of land titles or of housing reforms
has to be in tandem with a careful understanding of the regulatory context
within which such reforms will be implemented. In some ways, the emphasis on regulatory reforms echoes the sentiments of recent debates about
Third World housing. If in the 1970s squatting was viewed as an instance of
urban populism, then in the era of structural adjustment, informal settlements came to be seen as efficient and equitable forms of housing delivery
(Dowall 1991). In this latter scenario, governments were conceived of as
partners, regularizing titles to land and providing services (Baross 1990, 79).
This idea of the state as a neutral mediator in conflicts over land, housing,
and services is part of a growing concern with urban governance, with sector capacity and state capability (Pugh 1997, 1575). In the case of Calcutta,
this has been evident in the longstanding World Bank efforts to strengthen
institutions such as the CMDA (McCarney 1989; Harris 1989).

The emphasis on governance, on regulatory reforms, is useful because it brings the state back into view. This is an important counterpart to
civil society concepts that see the urban poor as managing their environ-

ments with a great deal of autonomy (as in Douglass 1998). But the case of Calcutta shows, in stark detail, that the state cannot be assumed to be a neutral mediator, that it is inevitably a site of bitter everyday and extraordinary contestations. A striking and recent example of this is the failure of the World Bank to discipline West Bengal's *panchayats* and its eventual withdrawal from the fishery projects of South 24-Parganas. Despite all its attempts, the Bank remained unable to short-circuit the entrenched systems of patronage, and at times blatant corruption, through which many *panchayats* operate.

In other words, as civil society cannot be romanticized as a reservoir of resistance, so the state cannot be idealized as the source of justice. In the governance framework, the state is essentially a "solved political problem" free of power and contestation (Bowles and Gintis 1993). This, then, is an incarnation of the neoliberal assumption of the exogeneity of political and social structures, a sense of virgin institutions, unmarked by struggles, passions, and intrigues. If urban land and housing reforms are to act as a serious antidote to poverty, such assumptions have to be abandoned and careful attention has to be paid to how states, like markets, are shot through with practices of power.

Once again, my research has raised two relevant issues. First, the reform of the regulatory context can be a crucial axis of policy change that makes possible a set of enforceable land rights. However, as I have noted, a "mapped" Calcutta might mean the end of negotiable land claims; in other words, the death of the rural-urban poor. The techniques of regulatory reform cannot be separated out from their equity content. For example, mechanisms of vesting allow the state expropriation of land but remain vague on how this land should be used by the state (Bhargava 1983, ix). Such mandates can be turned into requirements that take account of housing needs. Or the patriarchal basis of land redistribution can be altered such that land and housing titles and sharecropper deeds are not limited to male heads of households. Berry (1993) notes that in a context of unlimited negotiability, "security" depends on the "terms" on which men and women participate in such negotiations. Regulatory reforms can alter the terms of the regime, thereby providing a measure of security.

Second, as land and housing reforms must assume a state that itself requires reform, so they must assume a state that is itself the site of market activity. Indeed, the large body of research on urban informality, be it on populist mobilizations or on land tenure systems, points to the ways in which states are implicated in informal markets. Thus, informal housing cannot be seen simply as the realm of subsistence activities. Rather, from commercialized squatting to informal subdivisions, land and housing is produced and exchanged in dynamic markets, and in many cases the state itself acts as a developer (Soliman 1996). In the context of liberalization, it seems that regulatory ambiguities have intensified the market role of states, as in the case of Calcutta, and other rural-urban interfaces such as Mexico City (Jones and Ward 1998). The vulnerabilities inherent in such market activities, in the peculiar markets created through "unmapping" and "extralegal" regulation, shatter both the neopopulist utopia of informality as an embodiment of self-help and the neoliberal myth of informality as a free and efficient market form.

III

For a very long time, this manuscript ended with the story of the man-eating tiger. I had written in an inevitability that led to the inexorable disruption of hegemony, and that left the story uninterpreted and unexplained. In my closing words, I left the commuter woman suspended between city and countryside, her words undoing the very categories through which I had established my account of poverty.

But this was an iconization that spoke less to the "field" of Calcutta and more to the location of my writing at "home" in Berkeley. Such is the geopolitics of this project, the "real economies of representation" (Barnett 1997, 151), and perhaps this was appropriate. However, in writing her in as a mythical figure able to make myths, I had managed to mystify my nostalgia, the nostalgia of a *memsahib* who saw in the peasant woman a lyrical and pure rebellion.

From my institutional location in Berkeley, I came to see her as inhabiting a liminal space, a space of freedom. Trains and buses themselves came to take on such meanings: they became, in Gordimer's (1979) prescient words about apartheid South Africa, places marked by inherent contradictions that inevitably threw up resolutions, unanticipated resolutions. I saw such disruptions particularly in gendered spaces, in Dill's (1988) account of the camaraderie that developed among African American domestics of the early twentieth century as they rode the bus to work; in the Saharan trains that have emerged as sites of trade bulging with women traders and their wares (*New York Times*, 16 April 2001).

In the transnational space of feminist research, I saw the commuter woman as the authentic subaltern from whom I could extract testimony.[7] I wrote the ending as an instance of what Spivak (1987) calls "speaking with," rather than "listening to" or "speaking for," the subaltern. But lurking in the shadows was a feminist desire to represent the unnamed commuter as representative, "speaking as." The politics of poverty is such that this "speaking as" can only be understood within the political economy of academic production, in that circulation of "other" as commodity. In the listening, I had chosen to bypass the ambivalences that marked the critiques of the commuter, insisting on seeing her as "intending subject" and not as "figured body." I am drawing here on Spivak's interpretation of Mahasweta Devi's stunning short story, "Douloti, the Bountiful." Spivak (1990a, 126) designates the subaltern, Douloti, as "the site of a real aporia." I had originally seen my unnamed commuter woman as resolutely undoing difference through *differance*—a slip-sliding of meaning that could undermine categories of power. But perhaps, like Douloti, she was an aporia.

Aporia as doubt, that which plagues all epistemologies and thus never completely known to me.[8] Aporia as *a-poros* or pathway, a conduit, a pathway of trampling feet on the teeming trains, down muddy village paths and the burning asphalt of city streets. Aporia as the affectation of being at a loss for what to say, an affectation that maintains the regimes of family, state, and place. My ending presented this affectation as valorized speech (Barnett 1997) and naturalized the site of aporia "through the practices of locale and location" (Probyn 1990). Spivak designates Douloti as "aporia" because at the moment of tormented dying she yearns to return "home," to the very home that had sealed her fate. In the story of the man-eating tiger there is a similar nostalgia,[9] but it is one that is as much mine as that of the commuter woman. In writing a requiem for the city, perhaps I too had sought to recover a pristine home, the *desh*—both countryside and country—much mythologized by squatters and commuters, and institutionalized in the leftist imaginary.

And so, as the second ending was written for permanence, so were these lines on a momentary whim. These are the footnotes to that abandoned ending, Berkeley footnotes to a Calcutta story.

Home/land

You are no longer mine:
The stories that I tell
Are of your poor
The silences I forever keep
Are of your women
The gestures I imitate
Are of your dissidents.
But you,
You are no longer mine.

I am held prisoner by your figures
The bent coolie
The harried clerk
Framed in the white-heat
Blanched of desire.
I search for you in every face I meet
Elsewhere
Making do
With second-hand urbanity
Reclaiming from temperate rain
Tropical passions
Distilling from ghettoes
The pain of your slums.
What respite do I seek in you
When you are no longer mine?

IV

There are futures anticipated in my narration of the city, one of which I have not dared to fully write:

In the winter of 2000–2001 I made my most recent trip to the fringes of the city. Yes, the city was here. *Bhadralok* Calcutta, fit for a communism for the new millennium.

Patuli had been transformed into a landscape of suburban homes,

with finality. Quite a few of the colonies had disappeared without a trace. The land was like a tabula rasa, erased clean but ready for development. Across the street from where Mukundapur once stood, the highrises of Udayan stockily spanned the horizon, littering the highway and green meadows with concrete, brick, dust, and the tired sun-burnt bodies of hundreds of workers.

A few months later, in the state assembly elections of May 2001, Jyoti Basu's handpicked successor, Buddhadeb Bhattacharjee, would reclaim the fringes, shattering Congress's strongholds and capitalizing on the rhetoric of liberalization. Kanti Ganguly would win a seat not far from Noyon's village. His ministerial jurisdiction would be defined as the southern delta, concretizing the rural-urban interface that I had grappled with for so long.

Is this an ending, a final mapping of an unmapped city, where the informal city is succeeded by a formalized landscape of townships named in a leftist vocabulary, built and lived with capitalist fervor?

But, north of the bustle of Udayan, out of sight, I know that there are old plots of land, fenced in, quietly farmed by sharecroppers. The signs promising new projects are by now rusted and bent, a fitting tombstone for this hostage territory.

In the eerie calm of a noonday suburb, the regime and its contenders continue to morph and fracture, jostle and fragment. As Patuli is stamped "allotted," and thus legitimate, as the informal subdivisions lay out their plot lines in the wake of the last paddy crop, so waiting in the wings is another Ranjan seeking to claim his shelter, and perhaps even CMDA bulldozers awaiting orders for a new round of evictions.

If this is an ending, like my narrative of the city, it can only be one of multiple and irreconcilable iterations.

Methodological Appendix: Research Strategies and Data Sources

Locating the Urban Poor

As detailed in chapter 2, the research project started out with a focus on distress migration. In order to locate such households in Calcutta, three methods were used:

1. Analysis of secondary data, specifically urban surveys of pavement-dwellers, squatters, slum-dwellers, and informal sector workers conducted by the Calcutta Metropolitan Development Authority (CMDA) as well as by independent researchers and NGOs (Banerjee 1985; Shaw 1985, 1988; Jagannathan and Halder 1988–89; Unnayan 1983, 1996; Roy et al. 1992; Chakrabarti and Halder 1992; Sen 1992; Ghosh 1992; Dasgupta 1992).
2. Interviews with the authors of some of these studies and heads of relevant government agencies (listed below).
3. Independent scouting trips that lasted a month to follow up on locations indicated by such surveys, particularly the Unnayan studies of squatter settlements. On such trips, I kept simple tallies for each settlement using the following matrix.

Name	Male/ Female	Source of Migration	Year of Migration	Housing Status	Employment

The scouting trips yielded two conclusions that were important stepping-stones for the next phases of the project. First, it became clear that regularized slums had residents who were well-established migrants, many of whom had migrated to the city thirty to thirty-five years ago. There was also a great deal of employment and income diversity in these settlements. Such patterns were borne out by the urban surveys. Accordingly, I excluded slums as well as settlements of Bangladeshi refugees from the study.

Second, in the case of squatting it was almost impossible to find any of the settlements identified in the surveys. They had for the most part been demolished or relocated. Accordingly, I devised a strategy for looking for new squatter settlements by identifying vacant pieces of urban land. Much of this involved locating and investigating land bordering drainage canals, highways, and railway lines—common topographical and infrastructural elements associated with squatting in Calcutta. Again, at each settlement, I tallied preliminary information to get a sense of migration histories, employment patterns, and squatting rights. Given the scale of this project, I limited my search to the wards of South Calcutta and the southeastern fringes of the Calcutta agglomeration.

In total, I collected preliminary information in twelve squatter settlements, finally choosing three as sites of research. All twelve squatter settlements were composed primarily (98 percent) of recent migrants from South 24-Parganas district. The three settlements were chosen on the basis of their diverse locations and squatting histories. In all three cases, I was keen to ensure that I would have independent access to the settlement, unmediated by political parties, NGOs, or community organizations.

List of Interviews on Spatial Locations of the Urban Poor in Calcutta

1. Animesh Halder, Head of Planning, Calcutta Metropolitan Development Authority, multiple interviews
2. Koely Roy, Unnayan, multiple interviews
3. Ashim Das, Unnayan, multiple interviews
4. Arun Deb, Unnayan
5. Nirmala Banerjee, Professor, Centre for Social Science Studies, multiple interviews
6. Dipak Rudra, Food Commissioner, Government of West Bengal
7. Nandita Chatterjee, Executive Officer, Calcutta Metropolitan Development Authority, multiple interviews

Squatter Settlements

The three squatter settlements that I selected were the following:

1. *Jadavpur*: a settlement of seventy households lining the railway tracks at a South Calcutta station. An informal market of
fifty stalls also bordered the settlement. The settlement has
been in existence for more than thirty years but has witnessed

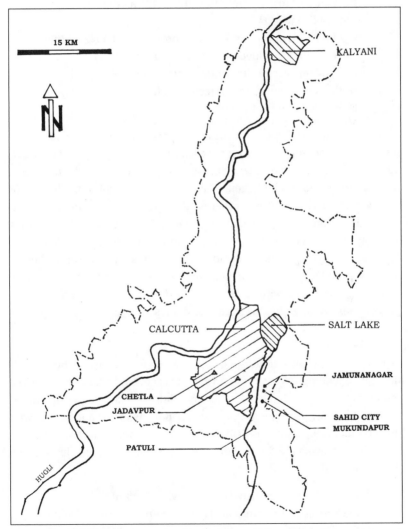

Figure A.1. Map of the Calcutta Metropolitan District, showing fieldwork sites
(squatter settlements and resettlement colonies).

cycles of evictions. Most of the current households migrated to Calcutta during the last twenty-five years.

2. *Chetla*: a settlement of about 800 households along the putrid canals of the Port Trust in residential South Calcutta. Much of the settlement dates to the early 1980s, although there are sections that are older. Most of the families that live here migrated to Calcutta about ten to fifteen years ago and relocated from other squatter sites to the settlement during the last five to ten years.

3. *Patuli*: a CMDA sites and services project that had been built on the southern fringes of the city in the late 1970s and had been taken over by about 2,000 squatter households. The settlement of squatters started soon after the project was completed and continued all through the 1980s.

As explained in chapter 2, the Jadavpur settlement also led me to numerous resettlement colonies on the eastern fringes of Calcutta. I conducted research in three: Jamunanagar, Sahid City, and Mukundapur (Figure A.1). All three colonies had been established by the CPM in the late 1970s and over time had been used as sites for the periodic resettlement of squatters. In 1997 Jamunanagar had approximately 1,000 households, including 160 households that had been relocated from the Jadavpur settlement to Jamunanagar in the late 1980s. Sahid City was smaller, with about 400 households. Mukundapur had approximately 600 squatter households. Resettlement plot sizes varied between 1 and 2.5 *kathas*, with residents paying corporation taxes but not having formal land titles.

Research Strategy

I spent a total of eleven months moving back and forth between the four settlements, spending at least one day a week in each. I did not live in any of the settlements but spent ten to twelve hours a day in them. I was accompanied most of the time by a research assistant, Rita Bose, who was not familiar with the settlements but had done field research on informal sector workers.

The following are the research strategies that I deployed in all of the four settlements.

1. Preliminary tallies, listed in the previous section, with as many residents as possible. I followed up by close-ended interviews where I would fill out a questionnaire (included at the end of this section) either during or after the interview. As discussed in previous chapters, this structured method,

while useful in providing a general sense of the settlement, was extremely limited in revealing the dynamics of poverty. Thus, the bulk of research in the settlements was composed of open-ended qualitative methods.

2. Open-ended interviews and life histories with eighty-seven households. In the case of each household, interviews with all adult members were conducted, and conducted separately. Often children, particularly working children, were also interviewed.

3. Ethnographies with twenty-five households, of which twenty were in the squatter settlements and five in Jamunanagar. These are households that I got to know well over the eleven months, where I met with members many times in various contexts and where I also had an ethnographic presence in family life.

4. Interviews with squatter leaders in each settlement.

5. For the last four months of the project, I expanded my research to cover the party and state apparatus. This included interviews with the party cadres, political representatives, and state bureaucrats involved with each settlement. In cases like Patuli, where the fate of the settlement was changing rapidly from day to day, multiple interviews were conducted with each informant at different points in time. In seeking to develop an ethnographic conception of the regime, I also maintained an ethnographic presence in clubs and party offices and alongside party cadres and politicians as they engaged in community organizing.

List of Interviews for Patuli Settlement

(does not include squatter leaders, allottees, and all interviewees who declined to have their names formally included in this list)

1. Jhini Sinha, *Asian Age* reporter, who first broke the story of possible formalization, multiple interviews
2. Pankaj Banerjee, Youth Congress leader and MLA, multiple interviews
3. Gobinda Naskar, Pradesh Congress leader
4. Ujjal Chatterjee, CPM leader and local Councillor
5. Sachin Mukherjee, Youth Congress leader, multiple interviews
6. Nandita Chatterjee, Executive Officer, Calcutta Metropolitan Development Authority, multiple interviews

7. Kanti Ganguly, CPM leader and Calcutta's Mayor in Council (Conservancy)
8. S. K. Bhattacharya, Director of General Operations, Calcutta Metropolitan Development Authority, multiple interviews
9. Former head of the CPM women's committee for the settlement; the committee was disbanded after a few months

List of Interviews for Jadavpur Settlement

1. Sumitra Dasgupta, CPM party officer, Falguni club
2. Amal Mazumdar, CPM party officer, East Jadavpur Local Committee

List of Interviews for Jamunanagar Settlement

(requests for anonymity have been honored)

1. Amal Mazumdar, CPM party officer, East Jadavpur Local Committee
2. Kanti Ganguly, CPM leader and Calcutta's Mayor in Council (Conservancy)
3. Chief Officer, Land Acquisition Cell, Calcutta Metropolitan Development Authority, multiple interviews
4. Land Records Officer, Land Acquisition Office, Government of West Bengal
5. CPM party cadres, Falguni club

List of Interviews for Chetla Settlement

(requests for anonymity have been honored)

1. CPM party cadres, Chelta party office
2. Aides to Ruby Datta, Congress leader and local Councillor
3. Port Trust Authority officials

Urban Land Development

The resettlement colonies drew my attention to the specific patterns of urban transformation occurring on Calcutta's southeastern fringes. In order to track and analyze these processes, I engaged in the following research strategies.

1. Search for land records and maps. As described in chapter 4, all through the research project I maintained a search for land records and official maps. This involved multiple meetings with officials at the Calcutta Metropolitan Development Authority, the Geographical Survey of India, the National

Atlas Services, the Land Records and Acquisition Cell of the
Government of West Bengal, and various real-estate developers. The most important interviews are listed below, taking into account requests for anonymity.

2. Analysis of all land-related incidents pertaining to the southeastern fringes in five important dailies over a period of two
years: *Anandabazar Patrika, Bartaman, Ganashakti, Tele-*
graph, Asian Age. Three of these are Bengali dailies, and two
are English. *Ganashakti* is the official paper of the Left Front.

3. Ethnographic presence in party offices of the CPM and
Congress parties, in land records offices of the CMDA and
Government of West Bengal, and in the offices of three real-
estate developers. This was not a daily presence but rather
a series of regular visits over the course of four months.

4. Tracking election results for the Calcutta metropolitan region
for the last five years.

List of Interviews on Urban Development of the Southeastern Fringes

(requests for anonymity have been honored)

1. Nandita Chatterjee, Executive Director, Calcutta Metropolitan Development Authority, multiple interviews
2. S. K. Bhattacharya, Director of General Operations, Calcutta
Metropolitan Development Authority, multiple interviews
3. Chief Officer, Land Acquisition Cell, Calcutta Metropolitan
Development Authority, multiple interviews
4. Liaison Officer, Calcutta Metropolitan Development
Authority
5. Land Records Officer, Land Acquisition Office, Government
of West Bengal
6. Officer in Charge of Vesting: Land Acquisition Office,
Government of West Bengal
7. Kanti Ganguly, CPM leader and Calcutta's Mayor in Council
(Conservancy)
8. Amal Mazumdar, CPM party officer, East Jadavpur Local
Committee
9. Pankaj Banerjee, Youth Congress Leader and MLA, multiple
interviews
10. Three different real-estate developers who own large pieces
of land in the southeastern fringes, multiple interviews

Commuters

At the urging of my squatter informants, I began to research commuting as a second manifestation of the rural-urban interface. There are many strands of commuting that link Calcutta to the surrounding countryside. I focused on one band within this sociospatial heterogeneity: the commuting of landless men and women from South 24-Parganas into five South Calcutta railway stations: Jadavpur, Dhakuria, Baghajatin, Garia, and Kalighat. Given the breathless pace of commuting and the fleeting presence of many of the commuters at the station, I had to rework some of my research strategies.

1. Open-ended interviews and life histories with seventy-two commuter households. However, unlike squatters, where I had access to different members of each household, in the case of commuters, this was often impossible. To remedy this situation, I chose a base village in South 24-Parganas, Bayarsin. Of the seventy-two households, twenty-two were from Bayarsin. By conducting fieldwork in the village, I was able to interview all members of these households.

2. Ethnographies of seven households. Six of these were from the twenty-two Bayarsin households. The seventh was a household where both husband and wife commuted and I had the opportunity to meet with them many times in Garia station.

3. Ethnographic presence at the commuter stations, especially during afternoon commute hours.

4. Interviews with railway administrators of the southern lines.

Bayarsin

Bayarsin is a village of 1,000 households in Taldi *Gram Panchayat* of the Canning block of South 24-Parganas. About 85 percent of Bayarsin's predominantly landless 1,000 households depend on commuting to Calcutta as a significant source of livelihood. I was referred to Bayarsin by officials at the Narendrapur Ramakrishna Mission, a religious organization that had been put in charge of a proposed World Bank fishery project in Taldi. I spent a month studying some of Bayarsin's commuting households through the following strategies.

1. Open-ended interviews with twenty-two households. Interviews were conducted with all members of each household.

2. Random sampling of households to obtain data on employment and commuting patterns.

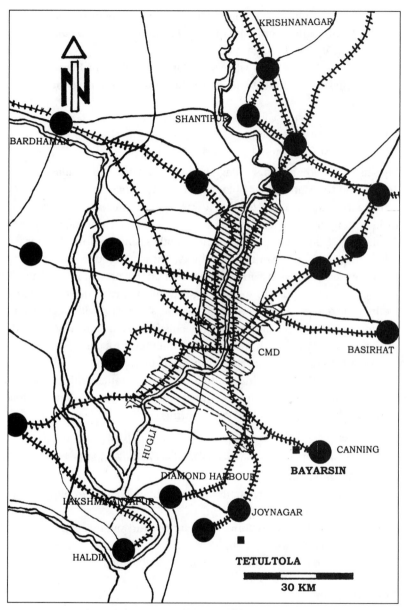

Figure A.2. Schematic map of Calcutta's important rural-urban commuting routes, indicating fieldwork villages.

3. Ethnographies of six households over a course of three weeks.
4. Multiple interviews with the *panchayat* head and two *panchayat* officials.
5. Multiple interviews with Narendrapur Ramakrishna Mission officials about the World Bank fishery project proposed for Taldi.
6. Analysis of Census data for the village.

Working Daughters

My search for a commuter village had first taken me to a village called Tetultola in the Mathurapur I block of South 24-Parganas (Figure A.2). On arriving in Tetultola, I realized that it was too far from any railway stations to allow daily commuting. But I soon discovered that a growing number of Tetultola's 135 households, most of them landless and destitute, had forged other urban linkages: working daughters. These are young girls, ranging from ages seven to twenty-one, who are sent off to work as full-time maids in Calcutta, rarely returning to the village during their years of wage-earning work. While the category of "working daughters" overlaps with migrant and commuter households, these girls form a distinct group. I have not included them in the data that I have presented, but they are a part of the general arguments that I make about the feminization of livelihood.

I spent only a week in Tetultola but kept in touch with two of the working daughters in Calcutta over the course of six months. In Tetultola my research strategies involved the following:

1. Ethnographic presence in one working-daughter household.
2. Open-ended interviews with members of four working-daughter households.
3. Random sampling of households to obtain data on employment patterns.
4. Interviews with the former *panchayat* head and two *panchayat* officials.
5. Analysis of census data.

Poverty Data

In investigating the various indicators that are used to measure and represent poverty in West Bengal, I drew upon the following data sources:

1. Census data on demographic change, occupational structure, and migration. The Calcutta office of the Census Bureau provided me with village-level data.

2. National Sample Survey data on employment, poverty, and landholdings, often published in *Sarvekshana*.
3. State-level Agricultural Census data on landholding and other rural indicators.
4. State-level statistics produced by the Government of West Bengal's Statistical Bureau, published annually in *Economic Review*, and occasionally summarized in the form of statistical abstracts.

Preliminary Questionnaire for Squatter Settlements

Name of Settlement _____

Location _____

Date of Interview _____

I. Identifiers

1. Name: _____
2. Address: _____
3. Sex:_____ Approx. age: _____
4. Marital status: _____ No. of HH members: _____
Notes: _____

II. Migration History

1. Originating Village:_____
2. Occupation:_____
3. Property Ownership: _____
4. Date of leaving village of self and HH: _____
5. Reason for leaving village:_____
6. Route to Calcutta:_____
7. Contacts for move: _____
8. Access to settlement, timing: _____
Notes: _____

III. Rural Ties

1. Connections with village
    a) Spatially stretched HH?_____
    b) Property ownership: _____

c) Remittances: _____

d) Visits: _____

Notes: _____

IV. Work and Income

1. Nature of paid work of self: _____

2. Nature of paid work of HH members: _____

3. Contacts and access to work: _____

4. Location of work: _____

5. Earnings of self and HH members: _____

6. Expenditures of self and HH members: _____

7. Savings, investments, debts: _____

8. Nature of unpaid work of self and HH members: _____

Notes: _____

V. Housing Conditions

1. Nature of shelter and amenities: _____

2. Process of settlement: _____

3. Tenure: _____

4. Upgrading: _____

5. Access to infrastructure: _____

Notes: _____

VI. Political Identity

1. Voting? Location? Mobilizing agents: _____

2. Contact with political parties (urban & rural): _____

3. Contact with government agencies: _____

4. Contact with NGOs: _____

5. Community involvement: _____

Notes: _____

Notes

1. Opening Moves

1. For a lively discussion of Kahn's building and how it has come to "represent" contemporary Bangladesh, see Vale (1992).

2. For a full discussion of this point, see Roy (2001b).

3. The Left Front, comprising various communist and socialist parties, is the ruling coalition in West Bengal. The lead party is the CPI(M)—the Communist Party of India (Marxist).

4. I owe this point to Nezar AlSayyad.

5. I am grateful to Derek Gregory for urging me to take a close look at *The Rumour of Calcutta*.

6. During the timespan of this research project, Buddhadeb Bhattacharjee was Minister of Information and Culture and Home (Police) Minister in the West Bengal government. He was later appointed Deputy Chief Minister and, in 2000, took over when Jyoti Basu, the Front's long-time leader, retired. In the State Assembly elections of 2001, he won the Jadavpur seat, sweeping the southeastern wards and fringes of the city.

7. The phrase comes from Chatterjee (1997).

8. The lines are from T. S. Eliot's (1917) poem "Preludes."

9. The term *babu* came into use during the colonial period to refer to a leisure-loving, urban, Bengali middle class. Later in the book I will discuss various appropriations of the term.

10. The social practice of informal conversations, seen as an important aspect of the region's public life. For more see Chakrabarty (1999).

11. All through this book I draw upon Spivak's (1987) idea of the "subaltern" as that which cannot be represented. Instead of seeking to find an "authentic" subaltern voice, I am concerned with the mechanics of voice and representation that are thereby put on the table (for more, see Kaplan and Grewal 1999).

12. A comment notoriously attributed to Rajiv Gandhi.

13. See for example Dasgupta's (1990) discussion of Samar Sen's poetry or of Sunil Gangopadhyay's imagery of a city with many paramours and ready consent in her loins.

14. For more on the "narration of the nation" see Bhabha (1990).

15. Dissenters wrote protest pieces in leading Calcutta newspapers, many of them critiquing the neglect of Hélène Cixous, who had accompanied Derrida on this visit. See, for example, Bagchi (1997).

16. The phrase is Jessop's (1994, 264).

17. Growth rates were particularly spectacular for foodgrains, 6.5 percent for the 1981–82 to 1991–92 period, compared with a national rate of 2.7 percent (Saha and Swaminathan 1994, A2). The source and nature of the growth remains subject to controversy (see Rogaly et al. 1995) with the Left Front attributing success to its agrarian reforms (*Economic Review* 1996–97).

18. Most of the West Bengal village-level studies are premised on the assumption that poverty is a spatially bounded process, that the rural poor negotiate survival within village boundaries. When this assumption is relaxed, as in Rogaly (1994), quite predictably it becomes clear that the rural landless engage in diverse forms of migration. The urban surveys hint at the rise of a new type of distress migration, involving the urban settlement of poor rural households. Such patterns are strikingly different from the interstate circular migration that has long characterized the region (de Haan 1994), as well as from the settlement of Bengali middle peasants in Calcutta slums (Shaw 1988; Chakrabarti and Halder 1990). Also significant is that the urban surveys indicate women as primary household earners (Roy et al. 1992), a pattern in sharp contrast to the low rates of female labor-force participation that characterize West Bengal (Banerjee 1985; Standing 1991).

19. For the transition debates, see Dobb (1963), Hilton (1976), and Brenner (1985). I do not mean to suggest that my research speaks to the fundamental disagreements that mark this body of work. Instead, I think that the spirit of these debates contains some important insights for the case of West Bengal.

20. The terminology is from Castells (1977).

21. More recently, bolstered by the East Asian experience, the idea of sectoral linkages between agriculture and industry has taken the shape of a development ideology, what Hart (1993) labels the "new agrarian optimism."

22. Of course, the Latin American research does not constitute a singular theoretical body. For example, de Soto's work has a strong neoliberal thrust (see Bromley 1990), while Castells, Perlman, Collier, and Eckstein are neo-Marxist in their analyses.

23. In chapters 3 and 4 I explain how and why I see important continuities between the Left Front and the "Bengali modern" that Chakrabarty (1994) uncovers in his analysis of colonialism and nationalism.

24. Jones and Ward (1998) make a similar point in their study of *ejido* reforms in Mexico City, a case that has striking resonances with Calcutta.

25. My work is in keeping with the feminist research on late capitalism: be it how economic globalization is being constituted through the feminization of work (Elson 1991; Standing 1999; Radcliffe 1999; Beneria et al. 2000), or how neoliberal restructuring is deepening the patriarchy of liberal democracies (Naples 1997; Fraser and Gordon 1998; Pateman 1998).

26. For a critique, see Mohanty (1988).

27. For a critique, see Jackson (1996).

28. For a repudiation of the "universal subject of Marxism," see Mouffe (1995).

29. For more on community as the basis rather than background of politics, see Hirschmann and di Stefano (1996, 9) and Phelan (1996).

30. For a critique of the "container" conception of space, see Gore (1984).

31. For a notion of home that interrogates the relation between identity and community, see Martin and Mohanty (1986).

32. For a discussion of deterritorialization, see Kaplan (1987) and Wolff (1995).

33. Kaplan's (1994, 139) reminder that "a politics of location" is useful as a way of deconstructing "the hegemonic use of the term gender" rather than as "reflection of authentic, primordial identities" is an important cautionary note.

34. For more on this see Bondi (1990), Crang (1992), and Duncan and Sharp (1993).

35. The critiques by Deutsche (1991) and Massey (1991) make this point.

2. The Politics of Poverty

1. The Calcutta Metropolitan District, at last count, comprised 2 municipal corporations, Calcutta and Howrah, as well as 37 municipalities and 165 nonmunicipal areas. The CMDA is the main authority charged with its supervision.

2. *Ganashakti,* the Left Front's newspaper, was a primary publication outlet.

3. Harriss (1993), for example, emphasizes that the production increases are linked to private investments in groundwater irrigation and have no apparent connection with agrarian reforms.

4. See also Mann and Dickinson (1980) and de Janvry (1981).

5. See also Marshall (1987).

6. Amis (1995, 147), for example, suggests the use of labor market as starting points in the study of urban poverty.

7. Kanti Ganguly, veteran CPM leader, and who at that time was Mayor-in-Council (Conservancy) of Calcutta. The *babu* is commonly used to refer to persons of the middle class.

8. For a discussion of *abhab* in the Bangladeshi context, see Kabeer (1994, 139).

9. Not surprisingly, when applied to my research populations, each poverty line yielded a different estimate of poverty among distress migrants and commuters, though on the whole these populations were overwhelmingly poor.

10. His conclusion is borne out by the village-level studies; see also Kohli (1997, 338).

11. One *bigha* is equivalent to one-third of an acre.

12. Pepsi—slang word for any kind of generic soft drink.

13. *Desher maya—desh* as country/countryside; *maya* as seduction/unexplained love.

14. Champahati: a village closer to Calcutta. There is an emerging trend among commuters of moving to villages closer to Calcutta.

15. Dhapa: an area on the eastern fringes of Calcutta.

16. Narendrapur: a rural town close to Calcutta.

17. Harriss (1993), for example, differentiates between those scornful of reformism (Mallick) and those willing to accept its limits (Lieten, Kohli).

18. Berry (1989, 1993) shows how social networks require considerable "investments" and might not therefore be as efficient and equitable as they have been made out to be.

19. Kabeer (1994) makes a similar argument about intrahousehold food entitlements.

20. *Da* as in elder brother, a mark of respect, shown toward all older persons, including employees.

3. Domestications

1. *Sardars*: construction foremen who both hire and manage day laborers.

2. As I have explained earlier, the term *babu* came into use during the colonial period to refer to a leisure-loving, urban middle class. But the term is also in common usage among the rural-urban poor to refer to middle-class households, such as the ones that employ domestic servants. In chapter 5 I will discuss the significance of Kanchan's attempt to label her husband a *babu*.

3. Mouffe uses this phrase in her various discussions of hegemony. See, for example, Mouffe (1988).

4. In her study of petty trading in Calcutta, Dasgupta shows that the most successful petty traders are those "tied" to agents and middlemen, usually of the same ethnic community, through credit or product advances. Self-employed "free" traders, on the other hand, are the poorest, usually consisting of women and Bengalis. Dasgupta (1992, 254) argues that Bengali traders, the late entrants into these occupations, were unable to establish such patron-client ties, thus losing out to other migrant groups.

5. The phrase is from Hochschild (1989).

6. But see also Chang and Groves (2000) for how some Filipinas resisted this "saintly" behavior.

7. Given the rather detailed documentation of *panchayat* politics, including the exclusion of the rural landless from this arena, I did not investigate the political activities of commuter men in any detail. Commuter women were unanimous in their rejection of village politics—that the *panchayats* are highly exclusionary and that they simply did not have the time to cultivate such favors. Thus, by masculinized politics I am referring primarily to the ways in which migrant men directly, and migrant women indirectly, negotiate access to squatter settlements.

8. Ray (1999, 10) defines this hegemonic political field as characterized by a "homogeneous political culture" and a "concentration of power."

9. Gobinda Naskar: an important leader of the Pradesh Congress faction of the Congress party.

10. For more on masculinities, see Chapman and Rutherford (1988), Hearn and Morgan (1990), and Jackson (1999).

11. Radcliffe brilliantly shows how peasant and squatter women deployed such hegemonic femininities back against the state. See also Hays-Mitchell (1995).

12. Craske argues that unlike state-sponsored mobilization, independent squatter organizations can challenge gender roles. But a closer look at her findings reveals the control of the Catholic Church over these organizations.

13. Stacey (1988) and Patai (1991) argue the impossibility of research that lives up to the standards of feminist ethics.

4. Dreaming of Tombstones

1. *Sindur*: the red powder used by married Hindu women on their forehead and in the parting of their hair to indicate their married status.

2. A pseudonym.

3. *Dada*: neighborhood boss, usually with political backing. *Dadagiri*: violent strategies used by *dadas* to maintain power.

4. *Dada*: in this use the term means elder brother, indicating respect.

5. *Benami*: literally meaning "false name." In West Bengal the term has come to be irrevocably tied to land reforms and the attempt on the part of landowners to conceal ownership by listing land in the name of fictitious relatives.

6. A special thanks to Oren Yiftachel for urging me to take a closer look at the debates in geography about regimes and modes of regulation.

7. A *katha* is approximately 720 square feet.

8. The Calcutta municipality operates through a mayor-in-council system, a hierarchy of elected and appointed positions, where elected ward councillors choose a municipal cabinet.

9. Suman: West Bengal's premier contemporary folk singer.

10. One *bigha* is equivalent to one-third of an acre and comprises twenty *kathas*.

11. The Urban Land Ceiling Act was recently repealed. The repercussions thereof are still not known.

12. Bagchi (1987, 599) writes, "If the basic data was not available, one wonders how could the transport planning group obtain land use and economic data which the other groups did not use or were not aware of?"

13. Among other things, Dembowski shows how the master plan for the CMD area is still not charted even though the CMDA was statutorily established twenty-seven years ago to do so; how the outline development plans required by the West Bengal Town and Country Planning Act of 1979 have never been formulated; how Geographical Survey of India maps of the area were unavailable throughout the 1990s; and how the various maps used in High Court and Supreme Court decisions are of varying and inadequate scale and tucked away in unpublished court files.

14. In the 2001 State Assembly elections, Kanti Ganguly did indeed win the seat from Mathurapur and was appointed a Minister of State with the portfolio of Sunderbans development, the South 24-Parganas region that I have demarcated as a crucial part of Calcutta's rural-urban interface.

15. The Congress party in West Bengal is divided between a Youth Congress and a Pradesh Congress. In August 1997 a large proportion of Youth Congress supporters and leaders, under the leadership of Mamata Banerjee, broke away from the Congress, forming a regional party called Trinamul Congress, which pledged outside support to the BJP coalition in power at the national level.

16. As I mentioned earlier, in 2000, Buddhadeb Bhattacharjee finally succeeded Jyoti Basu.

17. Delhi *Chalo*: "Let's move on Delhi," wage a struggle against the central government.

18. For an important critique of Lipton's theory of urban bias, see Byres (1979).

19. The communal riots that followed in the wake of the demolition of the mosque at Ayodhya.

20. His points of comparison are the riots of 1918, of 1926, and of 1946–47.

21. See Chakrabarty's (1991) critique of such ideals and complicities. I see Shah's dream of tombstones to be quite indicative of his particular social location

(class, ethnicity, and gender), and my use of the trope to be equally revealing of mine (possibly, class and profession).

22. For more on this argument, see Roy (2001b).

5. Disruptions

In the epigraph for chapter 1 I quote from T. S. Eliot's "Preludes" to evoke the "notion" of *bhadralok* Calcutta as "some infinitely gentle, infinitely suffering thing." These are the lines that dramatically follow, suggesting the cruelty of the city.

1. Her use of the term *babu* refers to his particular class status.

2. The Sunderbans is the southern delta of the Hooghly, famed for its mangrove swamps and as home of the endangered Bengal tiger.

3. As I discuss in chapter 3, the term *memsahib* means a foreign woman, but it is also one often used by domestic servants to refer to their female employers.

4. The social practice of informal conversation that is seen as a distinctive feature of the region's public life.

5. As I detailed in chapter 2, I studied only one band of rural-urban commuting: that of poor peasants from South 24-Parganas district. There is a great deal of middle-class commuting that connects Calcutta to surrounding districts, none of which I have taken on in this study.

6. *On Borrowed Land* (1991) was written and directed by Matthew Westfall as a master's thesis at the University of Southern California.

7. For similar strategies in the context of domestic service in the United States, see Dill 1988.

8. What is intriguing about the story is that, as Mills notes, the icon of the widow ghost derives not from some deep reservoir of peasant culture; rather it is a figure from a popular Thai soap opera, from a hypermodern circulation of images through media circuits.

9. I borrow this term from Holmes (1989, 46).

10. Ong and Peletz (1995, 244), in their introduction to Mills's essay, argue that the attack of the widow ghosts is a ritual dramatization of subalterns' fears. But Mills's work shows how this vocabulary is appropriated rather than "authentic." I cannot trace the roots of the man-eating tiger myth, and indeed I am not interested in proving its authenticity. But I do want to stress that the imaginary of the Sunderbans as primeval forest extends across classes and genders.

11. Once again, Buddhadeb makes an appearance, prefiguring his later electoral successes in the southeastern fringes and political power as leader of the regime.

12. For example, Kesri was seeking to secure his election to the chairmanship of the AICC and felt that Somen Mitra's faction was a sure hedge against his rivals, Sharad Pawar and Rajesh Pilot.

13. Jan Breman suggested this in his role as discussant at a symposium titled "Urban Informality in an Era of Liberalization" held at UC Berkeley in January 2001.

14. The phrase is of course that of bell hooks (1984).

15. Bourdieu is discussing Woolf's 1927 novel, *To the Lighthouse*. Similarly, Hart (1993), in her study of production politics in the Muda region of Malaysia, argues that peasant women, excluded from male structures of patronage, articulated critiques of the "master narrative." Or Carney and Watts (1990) show how in the wake of the implementation of an irrigation project in the Gambia, Mandinka women lost entitle-

ments to land and thus engaged in contentious negotiations of work relations and the conjugal contract.

16. Carney and Watts are writing in relation to Burawoy's (1979) famous treatise on "manufacturing consent."

17. The feminist research on domestic work is also concerned with how this point of production is tied up with the reproduction of the nation. See, for example, Radcliffe (1990), Constable (1997), and Yeoh and Huang (2000).

18. For more on issues of scale and space in regulation theory, see Lauria (1997, 6).

19. Berman, in keeping with his thesis of the "modernism of underdevelopment," goes on to make an argument about how, in developing countries, this has been a "pseudo-Faustian bargain" in that it did not work (1982, 76). As I have argued elsewhere (Roy 2001b), this is a deeply problematic interpretation of development and modernity, mystifying the "working" of capitalism in the West and reducing the complexity of modernization and modernism in the East to simplistic notions of mimicry and perversity.

20. Gregson et al. (1997, 196) call for the interrogation of conventional notions of space and place, for example, by moving from thinking about space and place as a preexisting location in which performances take place to how performances themselves constitute spaces and places. For a discussion of how feminist geography enlivens ideas of space and place, see Roy (2001a).

21. The phrases are imperfect derivations from T. S. Eliot's "Preludes" (1917).

Postscript(s)

1. This is a reference to my invocation of de Certeau (1984) in chapter 4.

2. A provocative comparison can be made here with Spike Lee's 1989 film *Do the Right Thing*, where the "right thing" itself is subject to a double consciousness, an ethical duality (see, for example, McKelly 1998).

3. Berger (1972, 47) famously states: "Men act, and women appear. Men look at women. Women watch themselves being looked at."

4. For an excellent discussion of such issues in the context of American slavery, see Hartman (1999).

5. This is the title of Ferguson's (1999) wonderful book.

6. For more on the knowledge-action link, see the work of Innes (1990).

7. Kaplan and Grewal (1999, 355–56) provide a useful critique of this "desire" for authentic testimony.

8. See Derrida (1993) for a discussion of aporia as spatiotemporal indeterminacy, and for the connections with *différance*.

9. Such nostalgias have been present in quite a few life histories. See, for example, Kartik's discussion of *desher maya* in chapter 2 or Mala's craving for her village in chapter 3.

Bibliography

Abu-Lughod, J. 1998. "Civil/Uncivil Society: Confusing Form with Content." In M. Douglass and J. Friedmann, eds., *Cities for Citizens*. New York: John Wiley and Sons.

Abu-Lughod, L. 1990. "The Romance of Resistance: Tracing Transformations of Power through Bedouin Women." In P. Sanday and R. Goodenough, eds., *Beyond the Second Sex: New Directions in the Anthropology of Gender*. Philadelphia: University of Pennsylvania Press.

Acharya, P. 1994. "Elusive New Horizons: Panchayats in West Bengal." *Economic and Political Weekly*, 29 January, 231–34.

Agarwal, B. 1990. "Social Security and the Family: Coping with Seasonality and Calamity in Rural India." *Journal of Peasant Studies* 17, no. 3: 341–412.

———. 1995. *Gender, Environment, and Poverty Interlinks in Rural India: Regional Variations and Temporal Shifts, 1971–1991*. Geneva: United Nations Research Institute for Social Development.

———. 1998. "Disinherited Peasants, Disadvantaged Workers: A Gender Perspective on Land and Livelihood." *Economic and Political Weekly* 33, no. 13: A2–A14.

Alarcón, N., et. al. 1999. "Introduction: Between Woman and Nation." In C. Kaplan et al., eds. *Between Woman and Nation: Nationalisms, Transnational Feminisms, and the State*. Durham: Duke University Press.

AlSayyad, N. 1993. "Squatting and Culture: A Comparative Analysis of Informal Developments in Latin America and the Middle East." *Habitat International* 17, no. 1: 33–44.

Amin, A. 1994. "Post-Fordism: Models, Fantasies, and Phantoms of Transition." In A. Amin, ed., *Post-Fordism: A Reader*. Cambridge: Blackwell.

Amis, P. 1984. "Squatters or Tenants? The Commercialization of Unauthorized Housing in Nairobi." *World Development* 12, no. 1: 87–96.

———. 1995. "Making Sense of Urban Poverty." *Environment and Urbanization* 7, no. 1: 145–57.

Anderson, P. *Lineages of the Absolutist State*. Verso: London.

Angel, S., et al. 1987. *The Land and Housing Markets of Bangkok*. PADCO.

Appadurai, A. 1984. "How Moral Is South Asia's Economy? A Review Article." *Journal of Asian Studies* 43, no. 3: 481–97.

———. 1989. "Small-Scale Techniques and Large-Scale Objectives." In P. Bardhan, ed., *Conversations between Economists and Anthropologists: Methodological Issues in Measuring Economic Change in Rural India.* Delhi: Oxford University Press.

———. 1996. *Modernity at Large: Cultural Dimensions of Globalization.* Minneapolis: University of Minnesota Press.

———. 2000. "Spectral Housing and Urban Cleansing: Notes on Millennial Mumbai." *Public Culture* 12, no. 3: 627–51.

Bagchi, A. 1987. "Planning for Metropolitan Development: Calcutta's Basic Development Plan, 1966–86—A Post-Mortem." *Economic and Political Weekly* 22, no. 14: 597–601.

Bagchi, Amiya. 1992. "A Comparative Perspective on Colonialism and Modes of Exploitation." In J. Breman and S. Mundle, eds., *Rural Transformation in Asia.* New York: Oxford University Press.

Bagchi, J. 1990. "Representing Nationalism: Ideology of Motherhood in Colonial Bengal." *Economic and Political Weekly* 25, no. 42–44: WS65–WS71.

———. 1997. "Unfairly Written Out of the Fair." *Telegraph,* 12 February, Fifth Column.

Bakan, D., and A. B. Stasiulis. 1997. "Negotiating Citizenship: The Case of Foreign Domestic Workers in Canada." *Feminist Review* 57: 112–39.

Banaji, J. 1994. "The Farmers' Movements: A Critique of Conservative Rural Coalitions." *Journal of Peasant Studies* 21, nos. 3–4: 229–45.

Bandyopadhyay, D. 1997. "Not a Gramscian Pantomime." *Economic and Political Weekly* 32, no. 12: 581–84.

Bandyopadhyaya, N. 1985. *Evaluation of Land Reform Measures in West Bengal: A Report.* Calcutta: Centre for Studies in Social Sciences.

Banerjee, D. 1996. "Industrialization Programme in West Bengal: Policy and the Problems—Some Lessons from Newly Industrializing Countries in Asia." In A. Raychadhuri and D. Sarkar, eds., *Economy of West Bengal: Problems and Prospects.* Calcutta: Allied Publishers.

Banerjee, D., and A. Ghosh. 1988. "Indian Planning and Regional Disparity in Growth." In A. Bagchi, ed., *Economy, Society, and Polity.* Delhi: Oxford University Press.

Banerjee, N. 1985. *Women Workers in the Unorganized Sector: The Calcutta Experience.* Hyderabad: Sangam Books.

———. 1989. "Trends in Women's Employment, 1971–1981." *Economic and Political Weekly* 24, no. 17: WS10–WS22.

Banerjee, S. 1990. "Marginalization of Women's Popular Culture in Nineteenth-Century Bengal." In K. Sangari and S. Vaid, eds., *Recasting Women: Essays in Indian Colonial History.* New Brunswick: Rutgers University Press.

———. 1997. *Jyoti Basu: The Authorized Biography.* New Delhi: Viking Press.

Bardhan, K. 1993. "Women and Rural Poverty: Some Asian Cases." In M.G. Quibria, ed., *Rural Poverty in Asia: Priority Issues and Policy Options.* New York: Oxford University Press.

Bardhan, P. 1983. *The Political Economy of Development in India.* Oxford: Basil Blackwell.

———. 1989a. "Poverty and Employment Characteristics of Urban Households in

West Bengal: An Analysis of the Results of the National Sample Survey, 1977–78." In G. Rodgers, ed., *Urban Poverty and the Labor Market: Access to Jobs and Income in Asian and Latin American Cities.* Geneva: ILO.

———, ed. 1989b. *Conversations between Economists and Anthropologists: Methodological Issues in Measuring Economic Change in Rural India.* New York: Oxford University Press.

Barnes, T. J., and M. R. Curry. 1992. "Postmodernism in Economic Geography: Metaphor and the Construction of Alterity." *Environment and Planning D: Society and Space* 10: 57–68.

Barnett, C. 1997. "Sing Along with the Common People: Politics, Postcolonialism, and Other Figures." *Environment and Planning D: Society and Space* 15: 137–54.

Baross, P. 1990. "Sequencing Land Development: The Price Implications of Legal and Illegal Settlement Growth." In P. Baross and J. Linden, eds., *The Transformation of Land Supply Systems in Third World Countries.* London: Avebury.

Basu, A. 1992. *Two Faces of Protest: Contrasting Modes of Women's Activism in India.* Berkeley: University of California Press.

Basu, J. 1983. Foreword. In *Significant Six Years of the Left Front Government of West Bengal.* Calcutta: CPI(M) State Committee.

———. 1997. *With the People: A Political Memoir.* Calcutta: UBS Publishers.

Basu, S. 1982. *Politics of Violence: A Case Study of West Bengal.* Calcutta: Minerva.

Baudelaire, C. 1869. *Paris Spleen.* Trans. Louise Varese. New York: New Directions.

Beck, T. 1994. "Common Property Resource Access by Poor and Class Conflict in West Bengal." *Economic and Political Weekly* 29, no. 4: 187–97.

Beneria, L., et al. 2000. "Globalization and Gender." *Feminist Economics* 6, no. 3: vii–xvii.

Benhabib, S. 1995. "Feminism and Postmodernism." In S. Benhabib et al., *Feminist Contentions: A Philosophical Exchange.* New York: Routledge.

Benton, L. 1989. "Homework and Industrial Development: Gender Roles and Restructuring in the Spanish Shoe Industry." *World Development* 17, no. 2: 255–66.

Berger, J. 1972. *Ways of Seeing.* London: Penguin Books.

Berman, M. 1982. *All That Is Solid Melts into Air: The Experience of Modernity.* New York: Penguin Books.

Bernstein, H. 1988. "Capitalism and Petty-Bourgeois Production: Class Relations and Divisions of Labor." *Journal of Peasant Studies* 15, no. 2: 258–71.

Berry, S. 1989. "Social Institutions and Access to Resources." *Africa* 59, no. 1: 41–55.

———. 1993. *No Condition Is Permanent: The Social Dynamics of Agrarian Change in Sub-Saharan Africa.* Madison: University of Wisconsin Press.

Bertaux-Wiame, I. 1981. "The Life History Approach to the Study of Internal Migration." In D. Bertaux, ed., *Biography and Society: The Life History Approach in the Social Sciences.* Sage Studies in International Sociology 23.

Bhabha, H. 1990. *Nation and Narration.* London: Routledge.

Bhalla, A., and F. Lapeyre. 1997. "Social Exclusion: Towards an Analytical and Operational Framework." *Development and Change* 28: 413–33.

Bhargava, G. 1983. *Socio-Economic and Legal Implications of the Urban Land (Ceiling and Regulation) Act, 1976.* New Delhi: Abhinav.

Bhattacharjee, B. 1991. Foreword. In B. Dasgupta et al., eds., *Calcutta's Urban Future: Agonies from the Past and Prospects for the Future.* Calcutta: Government of West Bengal.

Bhattacharya, D. 1993. *Agrarian Reforms and the Politics of the Left in West Bengal.* Ph.D. dissertation, University of Cambridge.

———. 1995. "Manufacturing Consent: CPM's Politics of Rural Reforms." In *Agricultural Growth and Agrarian Structure,* Report on the 1995 Workshop. Calcutta: Center for Social Science Studies.

Bhattacharya, M. 1991. "Municipal Calcutta: An Evolutionary Perspective." In B. Dasgupta et al., eds., *Calcutta's Urban Future: Agonies from the Past and Prospects for the Future.* Calcutta: Government of West Bengal.

Bhattacharya, N., and M. Chattopadhyay. 1989. "Time Trends in the Level of Living in Rural India: A Critical Study of the Evidence from Large-Scale Surveys." In P. Bardhan, ed., *Conversations between Economists and Anthropologists: Methodological Issues in Measuring Economic Change in Rural India.* Delhi: Oxford University Press.

Bhaumik, S. K. 1993. *Tenancy Relations and Agrarian Development: A Study of West Bengal.* New Delhi: Sage Publications.

Bondi, L. 1990. "Feminism, Postmodernism, and Geography: Space for Women." *Antipode* 22: 156–67.

Bordo, S. 1990. "Feminism, Postmodernism, and Gender-Scepticism." In L. Nicholson, ed., *Feminism/ Postmodernism.* New York: Routledge.

Bose, A. 1994. "Trends and Implications of Urbanization in India during the Twentieth Century." In A. Dutt et al., eds., *The Asian City: Processes of Development, Characteristics, and Planning.* Boston: Kluwer Academic Publishers.

Bose, P. K. 1995. "Sons of the Nation: Child Rearing in the New Family." In P. Chatterjee, ed., *Texts of Power: Emerging Disciplines in Colonial Bengal.* Minneapolis: University of Minnesota Press.

Bourdieu, P. 1977. *Outline of a Theory of Practice.* Cambridge: Cambridge University Press.

———. 1987. *Homo Academicus.* Stanford: Stanford University Press.

———. 1991. *Language and Symbolic Power,* ed. J. Thompson. Cambridge: Polity.

Bourdieu, P., and L. Wacquant. 1992. *An Invitation to Reflexive Sociology.* Chicago: University of Chicago Press.

Bowles, S., and H. Gintis. 1993. "The Revenge of Homo Economicus: Contested Exchange and the Revival of Political Economy." *Journal of Economic Perspectives* 7, no. 1: 83–102.

Boyce, J. 1987. *Agrarian Impasse in Bengal: Institutional Constraints to Technological Change.* Oxford: Oxford University Press.

Brass, T. 1997. "The Agrarian Myth, the 'New' Populism, and the New Right." *Economic and Political Weekly* 32, no. 4: PE27–PE42.

Breman, J. 1985. *Of Peasants, Migrants, and Paupers: Rural Labor Circulation and Capitalist Production in Western India.* Delhi: Oxford University Press.

———. 1989. "Extension of Scale in Fieldwork: From Village to Region in Southern Gujarat." In P. Bardhan, ed., *Conversations between Economists and Anthropologists: Methodological Issues in Measuring Economic Change in Rural India.* Delhi: Oxford University Press.

———. 1990. *Labor Migration and Rural Transformation in Colonial Asia.* Amsterdam: Free University Press.

———. 1996. *Footloose Labor: Working in India's Informal Economy.* New York: Cambridge University Press.

Brenner, R. 1985. "Agrarian Class Structure and Economic Development in Pre-Industrial Europe." In T. H. Aston and C. H. E. Philpin, eds., *The Brenner Debate: Agrarian Class Structure and Economic Development in Pre-Industrial Europe.* New York: Cambridge University Press.

Bromley, R. 1990. "A New Path to Development—The Significance and Impact of Hernando De Soto's Ideas on Underdevelopment, Production, and Reproduction." *Economic Geography* 66, no. 4: 328–48.

Burawoy, M. 1979. *Manufacturing Consent: Changes in the Labor Process under Monopoly Capitalism.* Chicago: University of Chicago Press.

———. 1985. *The Politics of Production.* London: Verso.

Burawoy, M., et al. 1991. *Ethnography Unbound: Power and Resistance in the Modern Metropolis.* Berkeley: University of California Press.

Butler, J. 1990. *Gender Trouble.* London: Routledge.

———. 1991. *Excitable Speech: A Politics of the Performative.* London: Routledge.

———. 1992. "Contingent Foundations: Feminism and the Question of Postmodernism." In J. Butler and J. Scott, eds., *Feminists Theorize the Political.* New York: Routledge.

Butler, J., and J. Scott, eds., 1992. *Feminists Theorize the Political.* New York: Routledge.

Byres, T. J. 1979. "Of Neo-Populist Pipe-Dreams: Daedalus in the Third World and the Myth of Urban Bias." *Journal of Peasant Studies* 6, no. 2: 210–37.

———. 1992. "The Agrarian Question and Differing Forms of Capitalist Agrarian Transition: An Essay with Reference to Asia." In J. Breman and S. Mundle, eds., *Rural Transformation in Asia.* New York: Oxford University Press.

Calcutta Metropolitan Planning Organization. 1966. *Basic Development Plan for the Calcutta Metropolitan District, 1966–1986.* Calcutta: CMPO.

Calvino, I. 1972. *Invisible Cities.* New York: Harcourt Brace Jovanovich.

Carney, J., and M. Watts. 1990. "Manufacturing Dissent: Work, Gender, and the Politics of Meaning in a Peasant Society." *Africa* 60, no. 2: 207–41.

Castells, M. 1977. *The Urban Question.* London: Edwin Arnold.

———. 1983. *The City and the Grassroots.* Berkeley: University of California Press.

———. 1985. *From "The Urban Question" to "The City and the Grassroots."* Working Paper 47, Urban and Regional Studies, University of Sussex.

———. 1989. *The Informational City.* Cambridge: Basil Blackwell.

Castells, M., et. al. 1990. *The Shek Kip Mei Syndrome: Economic Development and Public Housing in Hong Kong and Singapore.* London: Pion.

Chakrabarti, A., and A. Halder. 1990. *Slum Dwellers of Calcutta: Socio-Economic Profile, 1989–90.* Calcutta: CMDA.

Chakrabarty, D. 1984. "Trade Unions in a Hierarchical Culture: The Jute Workers of Calcutta, 1920–50." In R. Guha, ed., *Subaltern Studies VII: Writings on South Asian History and Society.* Delhi: Oxford University Press.

———. 1991. "Open Space/ Public Place: Garbage, Modernity, and India." *South Asia* 16, no. 1: 15–31.

———. 1994. "The Difference-Deferral of a Colonial Modernity: Public Debates on Domesticity in British Bengal." In D. Arnold and D. Hardiman, eds., *Subaltern Studies VIII.* Delhi: Oxford University Press.

———. 1999. "*Adda,* Calcutta: Dwelling in Modernity." *Public Culture* 11, no. 1: 109–45.

Chakraborty, S. 1991. "Extended Metropolitan Areas: A Key to Understanding Urban Processes in India." In N. Ginsburg et al., eds., *The Extended Metropolis: Settlement Transition in Asia.* Honolulu: Hawaii.

Chakravorty, S. 1997. "Operation Sunshine." In S. Lahiri, ed., *Operation Sunshine.* Calcutta: Bishwakosh Parishad.

Chakravorty, S., and G. Gupta. 1996. "Let a Hundred Projects Bloom: Structural Reform and Urban Development in Calcutta." *Third World Planning Review* 18, no. 4: 415–31.

Chambers, R. 1992. "Poverty in India: Concepts, Research, and Reality." In B. Harriss et al., eds., *Poverty in India: Research and Policy.* Delhi: Oxford University Press.

———. 1995. "Poverty and Livelihoods: Whose Reality Counts?" *Environment and Urbanization* 7, no. 1: 173–204.

Chandrasekhar, C. P. 1993. "Agrarian Change and Occupational Diversification: Non-Agricultural Employment and Rural Development in West Bengal." *Journal of Peasant Studies* 20, no. 2: 205–70.

Chang, G. 1994. "Undocumented Latinas: The New 'Employable' Mothers." In E. Nakano Glenn et al., eds., *Mothering: Ideology, Experience, and Agency.* New York: Routledge.

Chang, K., and J. M. Groves. 2000. "Neither 'Saints' nor 'Prostitutes': Sexual Discourse in the Filipina Domestic Worker Community in Hong Kong." *Women's Studies International Forum* 23, no. 1: 73–87.

Chapman, R., and J. Rutherford. 1988. *Male Order: Unwrapping Masculinity.* London: Lawrence and Wishart.

Chatterjee, M. 1990. "Town Planning in Calcutta." In S. Chaudhuri, ed., *Calcutta: The Living City.* Calcutta: Oxford University Press.

Chatterjee, P. 1990a. "The Nationalist Resolution of the Women's Question." In K. Sangari and S. Vaid, eds., *Recasting Women: Essays in Indian Colonial History.* New Brunswick: Rutgers University Press.

———. 1990b. "The Political Culture of Calcutta." In S. Chaudhuri, ed., *Calcutta: The Living City.* Calcutta: Oxford University Press.

———. 1992. "A Religion of Urban Domesticity: Sri Ramakrishna and the Calcutta Middle Class." In P. Chatterjee and G. Pandey, eds., *Subaltern Studies VII.* Delhi: Oxford University Press.

———. 1993. *Nationalist Thought and the Colonial World: A Derivative Discourse.* Minneapolis: University of Minnesota Press.

———. 1997. *The Present History of West Bengal.* Delhi: Oxford University Press.

Chatterji, M. 1991. "Settlement Pattern in the Calcutta Metropolitan Region: A Futuristic Vision." In B. Dasgupta et al., eds., *Calcutta's Urban Future: Agonies from the Past, Prospects for the Future.* Calcutta: Government of West Bengal.

Chayanov, A.V. 1966. *The Theory of the Peasant Economy.* Homewood: Richard D. Irwin.

Collier, D. 1976. *Squatters and Oligarchs: Authoritarian Rule and Policy Change in Peru.* Baltimore: Johns Hopkins University Press.

Connell, R. W. 1995. *Masculinities.* Berkeley: University of California Press.

Constable, N. 1997. *Maid to Order in Hong Kong: Stories of Filipina Workers*. Ithaca: Cornell University Press.

Cooper, F. 1983. "Urban Space, Industrial Time, and Wage Labor in Africa." In F. Cooper, ed., *The Struggle for the City: Migrant Labor, Capital, and the State in Urban Africa*. Beverly Hills: Sage.

Crang, P. 1992. "The Politics of Polyphony: Reconfigurations in Geographical Authority." *Environment and Planning D: Society and Space* 10: 527–49.

Craske, N. 1993. "Women's Political Participation in *Colonias Populares* in Guadalajara, Mexico." In S. Radcliffe and S. Westwood, eds., *Viva: Women and Popular Protest in Latin America*. New York: Routledge.

Croll, E. 1981. "Women in Rural Production and Reproduction in the Soviet Union, Cuba, and Tanzania." *Signs* 7, no. 2: 375–99.

Das, S. 2000. "The 1992 Calcutta Riot in Historical Continuum: A Relapse into Communal Fury?" *Modern Asian Studies* 34, no. 2: 281–306.

Dasgupta, B. 1984. "Agricultural Labor under Colonial, Semi-Capitalist, and Capitalist Conditions: A Case Study of West Bengal." *Economic and Political Weekly* 19, no. 30, A129–A148.

———. 1987. "Urbanisation and Rural Change in West Bengal." *Economic and Political Weekly* 22, no. 7, 276–87.

———. 1995. "Institutional Reforms and Poverty Alleviation in West Bengal." *Economic and Political Weekly* 30, no. 41, 2691–702.

Dasgupta, K. 1995. "A City Away from Home: The Mapping of Calcutta." In P. Chatterjee, ed., *Texts of Power: Emerging Disciplines in Colonial Bengal*. Minneapolis: University of Minnesota Press.

Dasgupta, N. 1992. *Petty Trading in the Third World: The Case of Calcutta*. Brookfield, Vt.: Avebury.

Dasgupta, S. R. 1990. "Calcutta in Twentieth-Century Literature." In S. Chaudhuri, ed., *Calcutta: The Living City*. Calcutta: Oxford University Press.

De Certeau, M. 1984. *The Practice of Everyday Life*. Berkeley: University of California Press.

De Haan, A. 1994. *Unsettled Settlers: Migrant Workers and Industrial Capitalism in Calcutta*. Hilversum: Verloren.

De Janvry, A. 1981. *The Agrarian Question and Reformism in Latin America*. Baltimore: Johns Hopkins University Press.

De Lauretis, T. 1987. *Technologies of Gender: Essays on Theory, Film, and Fiction*. Bloomington: Indiana University Press.

De Soto, H. 1989. *The Other Path*. New York: Harper and Row.

———. 2000. *The Mystery of Capital: Why Capitalism Triumphs in the West and Fails Everywhere Else*. New York: Basic Books.

Deere, C. 1990. *Household and Class Relations: Peasants and Landlords in Northern Peru*. Berkeley: University of California Press.

Dembowski, H. 1999. "Courts, Civil Society, and Public Sphere: Environmental Litigation in Calcutta." *Economic and Political Weekly* 34, no. 1–2: 49–56.

Derrida, J. 1993. *Aporias*. Trans. T. Dutoit. Stanford: Stanford University Press.

Deutsche, R. 1991. "Boys Town." *Environment and Planning D: Society and Space* 9: 5–30.

Dill, B.T. 1988. "Making Your Job Good Yourself: Domestic Service and the Construction of Personal Dignity." In A. Bookman and S. Morgen, eds., *Women and the Politics of Empowerment*. Philadelphia: Temple University Press.

Dirlik, A. 1997. "Critical Reflections on 'Chinese Capitalism' as Paradigm." *Identities* 3, no. 3: 303–30.

Dobb, M. 1963. *Studies in the Development of Capitalism*. New York: International Publishers.

Douglass, M. 1998. "World City Formation of the Asia Pacific Rim: Poverty, 'Everyday' Forms of Civil Society, and Environmental Management." In M. Douglass and J. Friedmann, eds., *Cities for Citizens*. New York: John Wiley and Sons.

Douglass, M., and J. Friedmann, eds. 1998. *Cities for Citizens*. New York: John Wiley and Sons.

Dowall, D. 1991. "Comparing Karachi's Informal and Formal Housing Delivery Systems." *Cities* 8, no. 3: 217–27.

Dreze, J. 1990. "Poverty in India and the IRDP Delusion." *Economic and Political Weekly* 25, no. 39, A95–A104.

Duncan, N., and J. P. Sharp. 1993. "Confronting Representations." *Environment and Planning D: Society and Space* 11: 473–86.

Echeverri-Gent, J. 1992. "Public Participation and Poverty Alleviation: The Experience of Reform Communists in India's West Bengal." *World Development* 20, no. 10: 1401–22.

Eckstein, S. 1977. *The Poverty of Revolution: The State and the Urban Poor in Mexico*. Princeton: Princeton University Press.

Ehrenreich, B. 1984. "Life without Father: Reconsidering Socialist-Feminist Theory." *Socialist Review* 73: 48–57.

Ehrenreich, B., and F. Piven. 1984. "The Feminization of Poverty." *Dissent* 31, no. 2: 162–70.

Elson, D. 1991. *Male Bias in the Development Process*. New York: St. Martin's Press.

EPW Research Foundation. 1993. "Poverty Levels in India: Norms, Estimates, and Trends." *Economic and Political Weekly* 28, no. 34: 1748–67.

Erlich, A. 1967. *The Soviet Industrialization Debate, 1924–1928*. Cambridge: Harvard University Press.

Escobar, A. 1992. *Encountering Development: The Making and Unmaking of the Third World*. Princeton: Princeton University Press.

Ferguson, J. 1990. *The Anti-Politics Machine: "Development," Depoliticization, and Bureaucratic Power in Lesotho*. New York: Cambridge University Press.

———. 1999. *Expectations of Modernity: Myths and Meanings of Urban Life in the Zambian Copperbelt*. Berkeley: University of California Press.

Fernandes, L. 1997. *Producing Workers: The Politics of Gender, Class, and Culture in the Calcutta Jute Mills*. Philadelphia: University of Pennsylvania Press.

Fernandez-Kelly, M. P., and A. Garcia. 1989. "Informalization at the Core: Hispanic Women, Homework, and the Advanced Capitalist State." In A. Portes et al., eds., *The Informal Economy: Studies in Advanced and Less Developed Countries*. Baltimore: Johns Hopkins University Press.

Fortmann, L. 1995. "Talking Claims: Discursive Strategies in Contesting Property." *World Development* 23, no. 6: 1053–63.

Frank, A. G. 1979. *Dependent Accumulation and Underdevelopment*. New York: Monthly Review Press.

Fraser, N. 1989. *Unruly Practices: Power, Discourse, and Gender in Contemporary Social Theory.* Minneapolis: University of Minnesota Press.

————. 1990. "Rethinking the Public Sphere: A Contribution to the Critique of Actually Existing Democracy." *Social Text* 25/26: 56–80.

Fraser, N., and L. Gordon. 1994. "A Genealogy of 'Dependency': Tracing a Keyword of the U.S. Welfare State." *Signs* 19, no. 2: 309–36.

Fraser, N., and L. Nicholson. 1990. "Social Criticism without Philosophy: An Encounter between Feminism and Postmodernism." In L. Nicholson, ed., *Feminism/ Postmodernism.* New York: Routledge.

Friedmann, H. 1978. "Simple Commodity Production and Wage Labor in the American Plains." *Journal of Peasant Studies* 6, no. 1: 71–100.

Furedy, C. 1987. "From Waste Land to Waste-Not Land." In P. Sinha, ed., *The Urban Experience: Calcutta.* Calcutta: Riddhi.

Gaiha, R. 1992. "Estimates of Rural Poverty in India: An Assessment." In B. Harriss et al., eds., *Poverty in India: Research and Policy.* Delhi: Oxford University Press.

Ganguly, K. 1997. "Sunshine-er Pore Abong Age (Before and After Sunshine)." In S. Lahiri, ed., *Operation Sunshine.* Calcutta: Bishwakosh Parishad.

García Márquez, G. 1970. *One Hundred Years of Solitude.* Trans. Gregory Rabassa. 1998 edition. New York: Perennial Classics.

Ghosh, A. 1981. *Peaceful Transition to Power: A Study of Marxist Political Strategies in West Bengal, 1967–77.* Calcutta: Firma KLM.

Ghosh, S. 1992. *Thika Tenancy in Bustees of Calcutta: A Study.* Discussion Paper 6, Department of Economics, Calcutta University.

Ghosh, S. K. 1991. "Calcutta's Urban Growth and Built Form." In B. Dasgupta et al., eds., *Calcutta's Urban Future: Agonies from the Past, Prospects for the Future.* Calcutta: Government of West Bengal.

Gilbert, A., and P. Ward. 1985. *Housing, the State, and the Poor.* Cambridge: Cambridge University Press.

Goodman, D., and M. Redclift. 1981. *From Peasant to Proletarian: Capitalist Development and Agrarian Transitions.* Oxford: Basil Blackwell.

Goodwin, M., and J. Painter. 1997. "Concrete Research, Urban Regimes, and Regulation Theory." In M. Lauria, ed., *Reconstructing Urban Regime Theory: Regulating Urban Politics in a Global Economy.* Thousand Oaks, Calif.: Sage Publications.

Gordimer, N. 1979. *Burger's Daughter.* New York: Viking.

Gore, C. 1984. *Regions in Question: Space, Development Theory, and Regional Policy.* New York: Metheun.

Goswami, O. 1990. "Calcutta's Economy 1918–1970: The Fall from Grace." In S. Chaudhuri, ed., *Calcutta: The Living City.* Calcutta: Oxford University Press.

Government of West Bengal. 1989. *A Review of the Industrial Scene in West Bengal.* Calcutta: Commerce and Industries Department.

————. 1995. *Statistical Abstract: West Bengal, 1994–95.* Calcutta: Bureau of Applied Economics and Statistics.

————. 1997. *Economic Review, 1996–97.* Calcutta: Government of West Bengal Press.

Gramsci, A. 1971. *Selections from the Prison Notebooks.* Trans. and ed. Q. Hoare and G. N. Smith. New York: International Publishers.

Greenough, P. 1982. *Prosperity and Misery in Modern Bengal: The Famine of 1943–44.* New York: Oxford University Press.

Gregson, N., et al. 1997. "Conclusions." In Woman and Geography Study Group, ed., *Feminist Geographies: Explorations in Diversity and Difference.* Harlow: Longman.

Grewal, I. 1996. *Home and Harem: Nation, Gender, Empire, and the Cultures of Travel.* Durham: Duke University Press.

Guha, R. 1992. "Discipline and Mobilize." In P. Chatterjee and G. Pandey, eds., *Subaltern Studies VII: Writings on South Asian History and Society.* Delhi: Oxford University Press.

Guhan, S., and B. Harriss. 1992. Introduction. In B. Harriss et al., eds., *Poverty in India: Research and Policy.* Delhi: Oxford University Press.

Gupta, A. 1998. *Postcolonial Developments: Agriculture in the Making of a Modern India.* Durham: Duke University Press.

Haithcox, J. 1971. *Communism and Nationalism in India: M. N. Roy and Comintern Policy, 1920–1939.* Princeton: Princeton University Press.

Hall, S. 1988. "The Toad in the Garden: Thatcherism among the Theorists." In C. Nelson and L. Grossberg, eds., *Marxism and the Interpretation of Culture.* Chicago: University of Illinois Press.

———. 1991. "Old and New Identities, Old and New Ethnicities." In A. King, ed., *Culture, Globalization, and the World-System.* Binghamton: State University of New York.

Haraway, D. 1990. "A Manifesto for Cyborgs." In L. Nicholson, ed., *Feminism/ Postmodernism.* New York: Routledge.

Harris, N. 1989. "A Comment on 'The World Bank Support for Institutional and Policy Reform in the Metropolitan Areas: The Case of Calcutta.'" *Habitat International* 13, no. 3: 19–22.

Harrison, M. 1977. "Resource Allocation and Agrarian Class Formation: The Problem of Social Mobility among Russian Peasant Households, 1880–1930." *Journal of Peasant Studies* 4, no. 2: 127–61.

Harriss, J. 1989a. "Knowing about Rural Economic Change: Problems Arising from a Comparison of the Results of Macro and Micro Research in Tamil Nadu." In P. Bardhan, ed., *Conversations between Economists and Anthropologists: Methodological Issues in Measuring Economic Change in Rural India.* Delhi: Oxford University Press.

———. 1989b. "Vulnerable Workers in the Indian Urban Labor Market." In G. Rodgers, ed., *Urban Poverty and the Labor Market: Access to Jobs and Income in Asian and Latin American Cities.* Geneva: ILO.

———. 1992a. "Agriculture/ Non-Agriculture Linkages and the Diversification of Rural Economic Activity: A South Indian Case Study." In J. Breman and S. Mundle, eds., *Rural Transformation in Asia.* New York: Oxford University Press.

———. 1992b. "Does the 'Depressor' Still Work? Agrarian Structure and Development in India: A Review of Evidence and Argument." *Journal of Peasant Studies* 19, no. 2: 189–228.

———. 1993. "What Is Happening in Rural West Bengal? Agrarian Reform, Growth, and Distribution." *Economic and Political Weekly* 28, no. 24: 1237–47.

Harriss-White, B. 1990. "The Intrafamily Distribution on Hunger in South Asia." In J. Dreze and A. Sen, eds., *The Political Economy of Hunger.* Oxford: Clarendon Press.

———. 1993. *Markets, Society, and the State: Problems of Marketing under Conditions of Small-Holder Agriculture in West Bengal.* Working Paper 28, Development Policy and Practice Research Group, Open University.

Hart, G. 1991. "Engendering Everyday Resistance: Gender, Patronage, and Production Politics in Rural Malaysia." *Journal of Peasant Studies* 19, no. 1: 93–121.

———. 1993. *Regional Growth Linkages in the Era of Liberalization: A Critique of the New Agrarian Optimism.* Working Paper 37. Geneva: ILO.

Hartman, S. 1999. "Seduction and the Ruses of Power." In C. Kaplan et al., eds., *Between Woman and Nation: Nationalisms, Transnational Feminisms, and the State.* Durham: Duke University Press.

Harvey, D. 1978. "On Planning the Ideology of Planning." In R. Burchell and G. Sternlieb, eds., *Planning Theory in the 1980s.* New Brunswick: Center for Urban Policy Research, Rutgers University.

———. 1989. *The Condition of Postmodernity: An Enquiry into the Origins of Cultural Change.* Cambridge: Blackwell.

———. 1994. "Flexible Accumulation through Urbanization: Reflections on 'Post-Modernism' in the American City." In A. Amin, ed., *Post-Fordism: A Reader.* Cambridge: Basil Blackwell.

———. 1998. "The Body as an Accumulation Strategy." *Environment and Planning D: Society and Space* 16: 401–21.

Hasan, F. 1992. "Indigenous Cooperation and the Birth of a Colonial City: Calcutta, c. 1698–1750." *Modern Asian Studies* 26, no. 1: 65–82.

Hays-Mitchell, M. 1995. "Voices and Visions from the Streets: Gender Interests and Political Participation among Women Informal Traders in Latin America." *Environment and Planning D: Society and Space* 13: 445–69.

Hearn, J., and D. Morgan. 1990. *Men, Masculinities, and Social Theory.* Boston: Unwin Hyman.

Herring, R. 1989. "The Dilemmas of Agrarian Communism." *Third World Quarterly* 11, no. 1: 89–115.

Hilton, R. 1976. *The Transition from Feudalism to Capitalism.* London: New Left Books.

Hirschmann, N., and C. Di Stefano. 1996. "Revision, Reconstruction, and the Challenge of the New." In N. Hirschmann and C. Di Stefano, eds., *Revisioning the Political: Feminist Reconstructions of Traditional Concepts in Western Political Theory.* Boulder: Westview Press.

Hochschild, A. 1989. *The Second Shift.* New York: Viking.

Holmes, D. R. 1989. *Cultural Disenchantments: Worker Peasantries in Northeast Italy.* Princeton: Princeton University Press.

Holston, J. 1998. "Spaces of Insurgent Citizenship." In L. Sandercock, ed., *Making the Invisible Visible: A Multicultural Planning History.* Berkeley: University of California Press.

hooks, b. 1984. *Feminist Theory: From Margin to Center.* Boston: South End Press.

Hossfeld, K. 1990. "Their Logic against Them: Contradictions in Sex, Race, and Class in Silicon Valley." In K. Ward, ed., *Women Workers and Global Restructuring.* Ithaca: Cornell University Press.

Hsiung, P. C. 1996. *Living Rooms as Factories: Class, Gender, and the Satellite Factory System in Taiwan.* Philadelphia: Temple University Press.

Hutnyk, J. 1996. *The Rumour of Calcutta: Tourism, Charity, and the Poverty of Representation.* New Jersey: Zed Books.

Indra, D., and Buchignani, N. 1997. "Rural Landlessness, Extended Entitlements, and Inter-Household Relations in South Asia: A Bangladesh Case." *Journal of Peasant Studies* 24, no. 3: 25–64.

Innes, J. 1990. *Knowledge and Public Policy: The Search for Meaningful Indicators.* New Brunswick, N.J.: Transaction Publishers.

Jackson, C. 1999. "Men's Work, Masculinities, and Gender Divisions of Labor." *Journal of Development Studies* 36, no. 1: 89–108.

———. 1996. "Rescuing Gender from the Poverty Trap." *World Development* 24, no. 3: 489–504.

Jackson, C., and R. Palmer-Jones. 1999. "Rethinking Gendered Poverty and Work." *Development and Change* 30, no. 3: 557–83.

Jackson, P. 1985. "Urban Ethnography." *Progress in Human Geography* 10: 157–76.

Jagannathan, V., and A. Halder. 1988. "Income-Housing Linkages: A Case Study of Pavement Dwellers in Calcutta." *Economic and Political Weekly* 23, no. 23: 1175–78.

———. 1988. "A Case Study of Pavement Dwellers in Calcutta: Occupation, Mobility, and Rural-Urban Linkages." *Economic and Political Weekly* 23, no. 49: 2602–5.

———. 1989. "A Case Study of Pavement Dwellers in Calcutta: Family Characteristics of the Urban Poor." *Economic and Political Weekly* 24, no. 6: 315–18.

Jessop, B. 1994. "Post-Fordism and the State." In A. Amin, ed., *Post-Fordism: A Reader.* Cambridge: Blackwell.

———. 1997. "A Neo-Gramscian Approach to the Regulation of Urban Regimes: Accumulation Strategies, Hegemonic Projects, and Governance." In M. Lauria, ed., *Reconstructing Urban Regime Theory: Regulating Urban Politics in a Global Economy.* Thousand Oaks, Calif.: Sage Publications.

Johnston, B. F., and P. Kilby. 1982. "Unimodal and Bimodal Strategies of Agrarian Change." In J. Harriss, ed., *Rural Development: Theories of Peasant Economy and Agrarian Change.* London: Hutchinson University Library.

Jones, G., and P. Ward. 1998. "Privatizing the Commons: Reforming the Ejido and Urban Development in Mexico." *International Journal of Urban and Regional Research* 22, no. 1: 76–93.

Jones III, J. P., et al. 1997. Introduction. In J. P. Jones III et al., eds., *Thresholds in Feminist Geography: Difference, Methodology, Representation.* Lanham, Md.: Rowman and Littlefield.

Joyce, J. 1916. *A Portrait of the Artist as a Young Man.* London: Egoist.

Judd, D., and P. Kantor, eds. 1992. *Enduring Tensions in Urban Politics.* New York: Macmillan.

Kabeer, N. 1994. *Reversed Realities.* Verso: London.

———. 1999. "Resources, Agency, Achievements: Reflections on the Measurement of Women's Empowerment." *Development and Change* 39: 435–64.

Kandiyoti, D. 1999. "Poverty in Transition: An Ethnographic Critique of Household Surveys in Post-Soviet Central Asia." *Development and Change* 30: 499–524.

Kaplan, C. 1987. "Deterritorializations: The Rewriting of Home and Exile in Western Feminist Discourse." *Cultural Critique* 6: 187–98.

———. 1994. "The Politics of Location as Transnational Feminist Critical Practice." In I. Grewal and C. Kaplan, eds., *Scattered Hegemonies: Postmodernity and Transnational Feminist Practices.* Minneapolis: University of Minnesota Press.

Kaplan, C., and I. Grewal. 1999. "Transnational Feminist Cultural Studies: Beyond the Marxism/Poststructuralism/Feminism Divides." In C. Kaplan et al., eds.,

Between Woman and Nation: Nationalisms, Transnational Feminisms, and the State. Durham: Duke University Press.

Kautsky, K. 1899. *The Agrarian Question.* Paris: Maspero.

Kaviraj, S. 1997. "Filth and the Public Sphere: Concepts and Practices about Space in Calcutta." *Public Culture* 10, no. 1: 83–113.

Khanna, S. 1989. "Long-Term Problems Remain." *Economic and Political Weekly* 24, no. 18: 958–60.

Kipling, R. 1920. "The City of Dreadful Night." In *From Sea to Sea: Letters of Travel.* New York: Doubleday, Page.

Kitching, G. 1982. *Development and Underdevelopment in Historical Perspective: Populism, Nationalism, and Industrialization.* New York: Metheun.

Kohli, A. 1987. *The State and Poverty in India: The Politics of Reform.* Cambridge: Cambridge University Press.

———. 1992. *Democracy and Discontent: India's Growing Crisis of Governability.* Cambridge: Cambridge University Press.

———. 1997. "From Breakdown to Order: West Bengal." In P. Chatterjee, ed., *State and Politics in India.* Delhi: Oxford University Press.

Koppel, B. 1991. "The Rural-Urban Dichotomy Reexamined: Beyond the Ersatz Debate?" In N. Ginsburg et al., eds., *The Extended Metropolis: Settlement Transition in Asia.* Honolulu: University of Hawaii Press.

Kostof, S. 1992. *The City Assembled: The Elements of Urban Form through History.* London: Thames and Hudson.

Krueckeberg, D. 1999. "Private Property in Africa: Creation Stories of Economy, State, and Culture." *Journal of Planning, Education, and Research* 19: 176–82.

Laclau, E., and C. Mouffe. 1987. *Hegemony and Socialist Strategy: Towards a Radical Democratic Politics.* London: Verso.

Lal, S. 1997. "Radical Soap Opera." *Telegraph,* 13 March.

Laslett, B., and J. Brenner. 1989. "Gender and Social Reproduction: Historical Perspectives." *Annual Review of Sociology* 15: 381–404.

Lauria, M. 1997. "Reconstructing Urban Regime Theory." In M. Lauria, ed., *Reconstructing Urban Regime Theory: Regulating Urban Politics in a Global Economy.* Thousand Oaks, Calif.: Sage Publications.

Leaf, M. 1993. "Land Rights for Residential Development in Jakarta, Indonesia: The Colonial Roots of Contemporary Urban Dualism." *International Journal of Urban and Regional Research* 17, no. 4: 477–91.

Lehmann, D. 1986. "Two Paths of Agrarian Capitalism, Or a Critique of Chayanovian Marxism." *Comparative Studies of Society and History* 28, no. 4: 601–27.

Lenin, V. I. 1899. *The Development of Capitalism in Russia.* Moscow: Progress Publishers (1967).

Lewis, W. A. 1954. "Economic Development with Unlimited Supplies of Labor." In A. Agarwala and S. Singh, eds., *The Economics of Underdevelopment.* Oxford: Oxford University Press.

Lieten, G. K. 1996a. "Land Reforms at Centre Stage: The Evidence on West Bengal." *Development and Change* 27: 111–30.

———. 1996b. *Development, Devolution, and Democracy: Village Discourse in West Bengal.* New Delhi: Sage.

Lipietz, A. 1994. "Post-Fordism and Democracy." In A. Amin, ed., *Post-Fordism: A Reader.* Cambridge: Blackwell.

Lipton, M. 1977. *Why Poor People Stay Poor.* Cambridge: Cambridge University Press.

———. 1988. *The Poor and the Poorest: Some Interim Findings.* Washington, D.C.: World Bank Discussion Papers.

Logan, J., and H. Molotoch. 1987. *Urban Fortunes: The Political Economy of Place.* Berkeley: University of California Press.

MacLeod, G., and M. Goodwin. 1999. "Space, Scale, and State Strategy: Rethinking Urban and Regional Governance." *Progress in Human Geography* 23, no. 4: 503–27.

Mallick, R. 1990. "Limits to Radical Intervention: Agricultural Taxation in West Bengal." *Development and Change* 21: 147–64.

———. 1993. *Development Policy of a Communist Government: West Bengal Since 1977.* New Delhi: Cambridge University Press.

Mani, L. 1989. "Contentious Traditions: The Debate on Sati in Colonial India." In K. Sangari and S. Vaid, eds., *Recasting Women.* New Brunswick: Rutgers University Press.

Mann, S. A., and J. M. Dickinson. 1980. "State and Agriculture in Two Eras of American Capitalism." In F. Buttel and H. Newby, eds., *The Rural Sociology of the Advanced Societies.* Montclair, N.J.: Allanheld, Osmun.

Marshall, P. J. 1987. "The Company and the Coolies: Labor in Early Calcutta." In P. Sinha, ed., *The Urban Experience: Calcutta.* Calcutta: Riddhi.

Martin, B., and C. T. Mohanty. 1986. "Feminist Politics: What's Home Got to Do with It?" In T. de Lauretis, ed., *Feminist Studies/Critical Studies.* Bloomington: Indiana University Press.

Massey, D. 1991. "Flexible Sexism." *Environment and Planning D: Society and Space* 9: 31–57.

———. 1992. "Politics and Space/Time." *New Left Review* 196: 65–84.

———. 1993. "Questions of Locality." *Geography* 78, no. 2: 142–49.

———. 1994. *Space, Place, and Gender.* Minneapolis: University of Minnesota Press.

———. 1995. "Thinking Radical Democracy Spatially." *Environment and Planning D: Society and Space* 13, no. 3: 283–88.

McCarney, P. 1989. "Building New Institutions for Metropolitan Planning." *Habitat International* 13, no. 3: 15–18.

McDowell, L. 1991. "Life without Father and Ford: The New Gender Order of Post-Fordism." *Transactions of the Institute of British Geographers* 16: 400–419.

———. 1992. "Speaking from Inside and Outside the Project." *Antipode* 24, no. 1: 56–72.

———. 1999. *Gender, Identity, and Place: Understanding Feminist Geographies.* Minneapolis: University of Minnesota Press.

McDowell, L., and G. Court. 1994. "Performing Work: Bodily Representations in Merchant Banks." *Environment and Planning D: Society and Space* 12: 727–50.

McGee, T. G. 1991. "The Emergence of Desakota Regions in Asia: Expanding a Hypothesis." In N. Ginsburg et al., eds., *The Extended Metropolis: Settlement Transition in Asia.* Honolulu: Hawaii.

———. 1995. "Eurocentrism and Geography: Reflections on Asian Urbanization." In J. Crush, ed., *Power of Development.* New York: Routledge.

McGuire, J. 1983. *The Making of a Colonial Mind: A Quantitative Study of the Bhadralok in Calcutta, 1857–1885.* Canberra: Australia National University Press.

McKelly, J. 1998. "The Double Truth, Ruth: 'Do the Right Thing' and the Culture of Ambiguity." *African American Review* 32, no. 2: 215–28.

Mellor, J. 1976. *The New Economics of Growth: A Strategy for India and the Developing World.* Ithaca: Cornell University Press.

Merrington, J. 1976. "Town and Country in the Transition to Capitalism." In R. Hilton, ed., *The Transition from Feudalism to Capitalism.* London: New Left Books.

Mills, M. B. 1995. "Attack of the Widow Ghosts: Gender, Death, and Modernity in Northeast Thailand." In A. Ong and M. Peletz, eds., *Bewitching Women, Pious Men: Gender and Body Politics in Southeast Asia.* Berkeley: University of California Press.

Mingione, E. 1994. "Life Strategies and Social Economies in the Postfordist Age." *International Journal of Urban and Regional Research* 18, no. 1: 24–45.

Minhas, B. S., et al. 1991. "Declining Incidence of Poverty in the 1980s: Evidence versus Artefacts." *Economic and Political Weekly,* 6–13 July, 1673–82.

Mitchell, T. 1988. *Colonising Egypt.* Cambridge: Cambridge University Press.

Mitra, A. 1963. *Calcutta: India's City.* Calcutta: New Age Publications.

———. 1977. *Terms of Trade and Class Relations: An Essay in Political Economy.* London: Frank Cass.

Mitra, S. 1997. "Footpath-Rasta Parishkar Kore Darkar Chilo (It Was Necessary to Clean Up the Sidewalks and Roads)." In S. Lahiri, ed., *Operation Sunshine.* Calcutta: Bishwakosh Parishad.

Mohan, R., and P. Thottan. 1992. "The Regional Spread of Urbanization, Industrialization, and Urban Poverty." In B. Harriss et al., eds., *Poverty in India: Research and Policy.* Delhi: Oxford University Press.

Mohanty, C. 1988. "Under Western Eyes: Feminist Scholarship and Colonial Discourses." *Feminist Review* 30: 61–88.

Molyneux, M. 1985. "Family Reform in Socialist States: The Hidden Agenda." *Feminist Review* 21: 47–64.

Moore, H. 1994. *A Passion for Difference.* Minneapolis: University of Minnesota Press.

Moore, M. 1984. "Political Economy and the Rural-Urban Divide, 1767–1981." In J. Harriss and M. Moore, eds., *Development and the Rural-Urban Divide.* London: Frank Cass.

Mouffe, C. 1988. "Hegemony and New Political Subjects: Toward a New Concept of Democracy." In C. Nelson and L. Grossberg, eds., *Marxism and the Interpretation of Culture.* Chicago: University of Illinois Press.

———. 1992. "Feminism, Citizenship, and Radical Democratic Politics." In J. Butler and J. Scott, eds., *Feminists Theorize the Political.* New York: Routledge.

———. 1995. "Post-Marxism: Democracy and Identity." *Environment and Planning D: Society and Space* 13: 259–65.

Mukarji, N., and D. Bandyopadhyay. 1993. *New Horizons for West Bengal's Panchayats.* Calcutta: Government of West Bengal.

Mukherjee, S. 1985. "The Bourgeoisie and Politics in West Bengal." In R. Chatterji, ed., *Politics in West Bengal: Institutions, Processes, and Problems.* Calcutta: World Press.

Mukherjee, S. N. 1987. "Bhadralok and Their Dals: Policies of Social Factions in Calcutta, 1820–56." In P. Sinha, ed., *The Urban Experience: Calcutta.* Calcutta: Riddhi.

Mukhopadhyay, S., and C. P. Lim. 1985. "Rural Non-Farm Activities in the Asian Region: An Overview." In S. Mukhopadhyay and C. P. Lim, eds., *Development and Diversification of Rural Industries in Asia.* Kuala Lumpur: Asian and Pacific Development Center.

Murdock, G. 1997. "Thin Descriptions: Questions of Method in Cultural Analysis." In J. McGuigan, ed., *Cultural Methodologies.* London: Sage Publications.

Nagar, R. 1997. "Exploring Methodological Borderlands through Oral Narratives." In J. P. Jones III et al., eds., *Thresholds in Feminist Geography: Difference, Methodology, Representation.* Lanham, Md.: Rowman and Littlefield.

Nakano Glenn, E. 1992. "From Servitude to Service Work: Historical Continuities in the Racial Division of Paid Reproductive Labor." *Signs* 18, no. 1: 1–43.

Naples, N. 1997. "The New Consensus on the Gendered Social Contract: The 1987–1988 U.S. Congressional Hearings on Welfare Reform." *Signs* 22, no. 4: 907–45.

Narayan, U., and M. L. Shanley. 1997. "Contentious Concepts." In M. L. Shanley and U. Narayan, eds., *Reconstructing Political Theory: Feminist Perspectives.* University Park: Pennsylvania State University Press.

Nath, V. 1994. "Poverty in the Metropolitan Cities of India." In A. Dutt et al., eds., *The Asian City: Processes of Development, Characteristics, and Planning.* Boston: Kluwer Academic Publishers.

Nossiter, T. J. 1988. *Marxist State Governments in India: Politics, Economics, and Society.* New York: Pinter Publishers.

Oi, J. 1986. "Communism and Clientelism: Rural Politics in China." *World Politics* 37, no. 2: 238–66.

Ong, A. 1987. *Spirits of Resistance and Capitalist Discipline: Factory Women in Malaysia.* Albany: State University of New York Press.

———. 1990. "State versus Islam: Malay Families, Women's Bodies, and the Body Politic in Malaysia." *American Ethnologist* 17, no. 2: 258–76.

———. 1991. "The Gender and Labor Politics of Postmodernity." *Annual Review of Anthropology* 20: 279–309.

———. 1999. *Flexible Citizenship: The Cultural Logics of Transnationality.* Durham: Duke University Press.

Patai, D. 1991. "U.S. Academics and Third World Women: Is Ethical Research Possible?" In S. B. Gluck and D. Patai, eds., *Women's Words: The Feminist Practice of Oral History.* New York: Routledge.

Pateman, C. 1998. "The Patriarchal Welfare State." In J. Landes, ed., *Feminism, the Public and the Private.* New York: Oxford University Press.

Payne, G. 1989. *Informal Housing and Land Subdivisions in Third World Cities: A Review of the Literature.* Oxford: CENDEP/ ODA.

Paz, O. 1991. *Configurations.* New York: New Direction Books.

Peck, J. 2001. *Workfare States.* New York: Guilford Press.

Peck, J., and A. Tickell. 1994. "Searching for a New Institutional Fix: The After-Fordist Crisis and the Global-Local Disorder." In A. Amin, ed., *Post-Fordism: A Reader.* Cambridge: Blackwell.

Perlman, J. 1976. *The Myth of Marginality: Urban Poverty and Politics in Rio de Janeiro.* Berkeley: University of California Press.

Phelan, S. 1996. "All the Comforts of Home: The Genealogy of Community." In N. Hirschmann and C. Di Stefano, eds., *Revisioning the Political: Feminist*

Reconstructions of Traditional Concepts in Western Political Theory. Boulder: Westview Press.

Pile, S. 1997. "Opposition, Political Identities, and Spaces of Resistance." In S. Pile and M. Keith, eds., *Geographies of Resistance.* New York: Routledge.

Pirenne, H. 1925. *Medieval Cities: Their Origins and the Revival of Trade.* Princeton: Princeton University Press (1952 edition).

Portes, A., et al., eds. 1989. *The Informal Economy: Studies in Advanced and Less Developed Countries.* Baltimore: Johns Hopkins University Press.

Pratt, G. 1997. "Stereotypes and Ambivalences: The Construction of Domestic Workers in Vancouver, British Columbia." *Gender, Place, and Culture* 4: 159–77.

Probyn, E. 1990. "Travels in the Postmodern: Making Sense of the Local." In L. Nicholson, ed., *Feminism/Postmodernism.* New York: Routledge.

Pugh, C. 1997. "Poverty and Progress? Reflections on Housing and Urban Policies in Developing Countries, 1976–1996." *Urban Studies* 34, no. 10: 1547–95.

Radcliffe, S. A. 1990. "Ethnicity, Patriarchy, and Incorporation into the Nation: Female Migrants as Domestic Servants in Peru." *Environment and Planning D: Society and Space* 8: 379–93.

———. 1993. "People Have to Rise Up—Like the Great Women Fighters. The State and Peasant Women in Peru." In S. A. Radcliffe and S. Westwood, eds., *Viva: Women and Popular Protest in Latin America.* New York: Routledge.

———. 1999. "Latina Labour: Restructuring of Work and Renegotiation of Gender Relations in Contemporary Latin America." *Environment and Planning A* 31: 196–208.

Ranis, G., and F. Stewart. 1993. "Rural Non-Agricultural Activities in Development: Theory and Application." *Journal of Development Studies* 40: 75–101.

Ranis, G., et al. 2000. "Economic Growth and Human Development." *World Development* 28, no. 2: 197–219.

Ray, A. 1996. "A Statistical Profile of Industrial Development in West Bengal." In A. Raychaudhuri and D. Sarkar, eds., *Economy of West Bengal: Problems and Prospects.* Calcutta: Allied Publishers.

Ray, R. 1999. *Fields of Protest: Women's Movements in India.* Minneapolis: University of Minnesota Press.

Ray, R. K. 1979. *Urban Roots of Indian Nationalism: Pressure Groups and Conflict of Interests in Calcutta City Politics, 1875–1939.* New Delhi: Vikas Publishing House.

Rich, A. 1984. "North American Time." In *The Fact of a Doorframe.* New York: Norton.

———. 1986. *Blood, Bread, and Poetry: Selected Prose 1979–1985.* New York: Norton.

———. 1991. "Here Is a Map of Our Country." In *An Atlas of the Difficult World.* New York: Norton.

Roberts, B. 1989. "Urbanization, Migration, and Development." *Sociological Forum* 4, no. 4: 665–91.

———. 1994. "Informal Economy and Family Strategies." *International Journal of Urban and Regional Research* 18, no. 1: 6–23.

———. 1995. *The Making of Citizens: Cities of Peasants Revisited.* New York: Arnold.

Rofel, L. 1992. "Rethinking Modernity: Space and Factory Discipline in China." *Cultural Anthropology* 7, no. 1: 93–114.

Rogaly, B. 1994. "Rural Labor Arrangements in West Bengal, India." Ph.D. dissertation, St. Antony's College, Oxford University.

———. 1997. "Linking Home and Market: Towards a Gendered Analysis of Changing Labour Relations in Rural West Bengal." *IDS Bulletin* 28, no. 3: 63–72.

Rogaly, B., et al. 1995. "*Sonar Bangla*? Agricultural Growth and Agrarian Change in West Bengal and Bangladesh." *Economic and Political Weekly* 30, no. 29: 1862–68.

———. 1998. "Containing Conflict and Reaping Votes: Management of Rural Labor Relations in West Bengal." *Economic and Political Weekly* 33, no. 42–43: 2729–39.

Romero, M. 1992. *Maid in the USA.* New York: Routledge.

Rose, G. 1993. *Feminism and Geography.* Minneapolis: University of Minnesota Press.

Roy, A. 2001a. "The Reverse Side of the World: Identity, Space, and Power." In N. AlSayyad, ed., *Hybrid Urbanism: On Identity in the Built Environment.* Westport: Greenwood/Praeger.

———. 2001b. "Traditions of the Modern: A Corrupt View." *Traditional Dwellings and Settlements Review* 12, no. 2: 7–19.

Roy, A. K. 1976. *Communism in Asia: A Study in Strategy and Tactics.* Calcutta: Progressive Publishers.

Roy, K., et al. 1992. "Rural-Urban Migration and Poverty in South Asia." *Journal of Contemporary Asia* 22, no. 1: 57–71.

Ruud, A. 1994. "Land and Power: The Marxist Conquest of Rural Bengal." *Modern Asian Studies* 28, no. 2: 357–80.

———. 1995. "Wealth, Power, and Status among CPM-Supporter Groups in Rural West Bengal." In *Agricultural Growth and Agrarian Structure, Report on the 1995 Workshop.* Calcutta: Center for Social Science Studies.

Saha, A., and M. Swaminathan. 1994. "Agricultural Growth in West Bengal in the 1980s." *Economic and Political Weekly* 29, no. 13: A2–A11.

Saith, A. 1992. "Asian Rural Industrialization: Context, Features, Strategies." In J. Breman and S. Mundle, eds., *Rural Transformation in Asia.* New York: Oxford University Press.

Salzinger, L. 1997. "From High Heels to Swathed Bodies: Gendered Meanings under Production in Mexico's Export-Processing Industry." *Feminist Studies* 23, no. 3: 549–74.

Sandercock, L. 1998. "Framing Insurgent Historiographies for Planning." In L. Sandercock, ed., *Making the Invisible Visible: A Multicultural Planning History.* Berkeley: University of California Press.

Sarkar, T. 1987. "Nationalist Iconography: Image of Women in Nineteenth-Century Bengali Literature." *Economic and Political Weekly* 22, no. 47: 2011–15.

Sayer, A. 1989. "The New Regional Geography and Problems of Narrative." *Environment and Planning D: Society and Space* 7: 253–76.

———. 1991. Behind the Locality Debate: Deconstructing Geography's Dualisms. *Environment and Planning A* 23: 283–308.

Scott, James. 1985. *Weapons of the Weak: Everyday Forms of Peasant Resistance.* New Haven: Yale University Press.

Scott, Joan. 1988. *Gender and the Politics of History.* New York: Columbia University Press.

Sen, A. 1981. "Ingredients of Famine Analysis: Availability and Entitlements." *Quarterly Journal of Economics* (August): 433–64.

———. 1988. "Family and Food: Sex Bias in Poverty." In T. N. Srinivasan and P. Bardhan, *Rural Poverty in South Asia.* New York: Columbia University Press.

———. 1990. "Gender and Cooperative Conflicts." In I. Tinker, ed., *Persistent Inequalities: Women and World Development.* New York: Oxford University Press.

———. 1992. *Inequality Reexamined.* New York: Russell Sage.

Sen, Asok. 1992. *Life and Labor in a Squatter Colony.* Calcutta: Centre for Social Science Studies.

Sengupta, P. 1989. "Politics in West Bengal: The Left Front versus the Congress (I)." *Asian Survey* 29, no. 9: 883–97.

———. 1997. "The 1995 Municipal Election in West Bengal: The Left Front Is Down." *Asian Survey* 37, no. 10: 905–17.

Seth, S. 1995. *Marxist Theory and Nationalist Politics: The Case of Colonial India.* New Delhi: Sage.

Shaw, A. 1988. "The Income Security Function of the Rural Sector: The Case of Calcutta." *Economic Development and Cultural Change* 36, no. 2: 303–14.

———. 1997. "Heart of the City." *Telegraph,* 24 June.

Sinha, P. 1990. "Calcutta and the Currents of History, 1690–1912." In S. Chaudhuri, ed., *Calcutta: The Living City.* Calcutta: Oxford University Press.

Sivaramakrishnan, K. C., and L. Green. 1986. *Metropolitan Management: The Asian Experience.* New York: Oxford University Press.

Smart, A. 1986. "Invisible Real Estate: Investigations into the Squatter Property Market." *International Journal of Urban and Regional Research* 10, no. 1: 29–45.

Smith, D. 1989. *The Everyday World as Problematic: A Feminist Sociology.* Boston: Northeastern University Press.

Smith, G. 1990. "Negotiating Neighbors: Livelihood and Domestic Politics in Central Peru and the Pais Valenciano." In J. Collins and M. Gimenez, eds., *Work without Wages: Domestic Labor and Self-Employment within Capitalism.* Binghamton: State University of New York Press.

———. 1994. "Towards an Ethnography of Idiosyncratic Forms of Livelihood." *International Journal of Urban and Regional Research* 18, no. 1: 71–87.

Smith, N. 1992. "New City, New Frontier: The Lower East Side as Wild, Wild West." In M. Sorkin, ed., *Variations on a Theme Park.* New York: Noonday Press.

Soliman, A. 1996. "Legitimizing Informal Housing: Accommodating Low-Income Groups in Alexandria, Egypt." *Environment and Urbanization* 8, no. 1: 183–94.

Spivak, G. C. 1987. "Can the Subaltern Speak?" In C. Nelson and L. Grossberg, eds., *Marxism and the Interpretation of Culture.* Urbana: University of Illinois Press.

———. 1988. *In Other Worlds.* New York: Routledge.

———. 1990a. "Woman in Difference: Mahasweta Devi's 'Douloti the Bountiful.'" *Cultural Critique* (Winter): 105–28.

———. 1990b. *The Post-Colonial Critic.* New York: Routledge.

———. 1993. *Outside in the Teaching Machine.* London: Routledge.

Stacey, J. 1988. "Can There Be a Feminist Ethnography?" *Women's Studies International Forum* 11: 21–27.

Stack, C. 1974. *All Our Kin: Strategies of Survival in a Black Community.* New York: Harper and Row.

Standing, G. 1999. "Global Feminization through Flexible Labor: A Theme Revisited." *World Development* 27, no. 3: 583–602.

Standing, H. 1991. *Dependence and Autonomy: Women's Employment and the Family in Calcutta.* New York: Routledge.

Stone, C. 1989. *Regime Politics: Governing Atlanta, 1946–1988.* Lawrence: University of Kansas Press.

Swyngedouw, E. 1997. "Neither Global nor Local: 'Glocalization' and the Politics of Scale." In K. Cox, ed., *Spaces of Globalization: Reasserting the Power of the Local.* New York: Guilford.

Thomas, F. C. 1997. *Calcutta Poor: Elegies on a City above Pretense.* Armonk, N.Y.: M. E. Sharpe.

Tiano, S., and C. Ladino. 1999. "Dating, Mating, and Motherhood: Identity Construction among Mexican Maquila Workers." *Environment and Planning A* 31: 305–25.

Tsing, A. 1997. "Transitions as Translations." In J. Scott et al., eds., *Transitions, Environments, Translations: Feminisms in International Perspective.* New York: Routledge.

United Nations. 1996. *Habitat Agenda and Istanbul Declaration: Second United Nations Conference on Human Settlement.* New York.

Unnayan. 1983. *Living on the Margins: A Preliminary Report on Marginal Land Dwellers in Calcutta.* Calcutta: Unnayan.

———. 1996. *Mapping the Urban Poor: Unrecognized Settlements in Selected Municipalities of Calcutta Urban Area.* Calcutta: Unnayan.

Vale, L. 1992. "Designing National Identity." In N. AlSayyad, ed., *Forms of Dominance.* Ashgate: Avebury.

Van Arkadie, B. 1989. "The Role of Institutions in Development." *Proceedings of the World Bank Annual Conference on Development Economics.* Washington, D.C.: World Bank.

Van Schendel, W., and A. H. Faraizi. 1984. *Rural Laborers in Bengal, 1880–1980.* Rotterdam: Erasmus University Press.

Vasudevan, H. 1997. "The Sources of Soviet Scepticism." *Asian Age,* 17 February.

Viswesaran, K. 1994. *Fictions of Feminist Ethnography.* Minneapolis: University of Minnesota Press.

Wacquant, L. 1997. "Three Pernicious Premises in the Study of the American Ghetto." *International Journal of Urban and Regional Research* 21, no. 2: 341–53.

Warde, A. 1988. "Industrial Restructuring, Local Politics, and the Reproduction of Labor Power: Some Theoretical Considerations." *Environment and Planning D: Society and Space* 6: 75–95.

Watts, M. 1994. "Development II: The Privatization of Everything." *Progress in Human Geography* 18, no. 3: 371–84.

———. 1996. "Development III: The Global Agrofood System and Late Twentieth-Century Development (or Kautsky Redux)." *Progress in Human Geography* 20, no. 2: 230–45.

Webster, N. 1990. "Agrarian Relations in Burdwan District, West Bengal: From the Economics of Green Revolution to the Politics of Panchayati Raj." *Journal of Contemporary Asia* 20, no. 2: 177–211.

———. 1992. "Panchayati Raj in West Bengal: Popular Participation for the People or the Party?" *Development and Change* 23, no. 4: 129–63.

Weiner, M. 1978. *Sons of the Soil: Migration and Ethnic Conflict in India.* Princeton: Princeton University Press.

Westergaard, K. 1986. *People's Participation, Local Government, and Rural Development: The Case of West Bengal.* Copenhagen: Center for Development Research.

Williams, R. 1973. *The Country and the City.* New York: Oxford University Press.

———. 1977. *Marxism and Literature.* New York: Oxford University Press.

Willis, P. 1977. *Learning to Labor: How Working-Class Kids Get Working-Class Jobs.* New York: Columbia University Press.

Wilson, E. 1991. *The Sphinx in the City: Urban Life, the Control of Disorder, and Women.* Berkeley: University of California Press.

Wilson, F. 1993. "Workshops as Domestic Domains: Reflections on Small-Scale Industry in Mexico." *World Development* 21, no. 1: 67–80.

Wolf, D. 1992a. *Factory Daughters: Gender, Household Dynamics, and Rural Industrialization in Java.* Berkeley: University of California Press.

———. 1992b. "Feminist Dilemmas in Fieldwork." *Frontiers* 13, no. 3: 1–8.

Wolff, J. 1995. *Resident Alien: Feminist Cultural Criticism.* New Haven: Yale University Press.

World Bank. 1991. *Urban Policy and Economic Development: An Agenda for the 1990s.* Washington, D.C.: World Bank.

Wright, M. W. 1999. "The Dialectics of Still Life: Murder, Women, and Maquiladoras." *Public Culture* 11, no. 3: 453–74.

Yeoh, B., and S. Huang. 1998. "Negotiating Public Space: Strategies and Styles of Migrant Female Domestic Workers." *Urban Studies* 35: 583–602.

———. 1999. "Spaces at the Margins: Migrant Domestic Workers and the Development of Civil Society in Singapore." *Environment and Planning A* 31: 1149–67.

———. 2000. "Home and Away: Foreign Domestic Workers and Negotiations of Diasporic Identity in Singapore." *Women's Studies International Forum* 23, no. 4: 413–29.

Young, I. 1990. The Ideal of Community and the Politics of Difference. In *Feminism/Postmodernism,* ed. L. Nicholson. New York: Routledge.

Zavella, P. 1992. "Feminist Insider Dilemmas: Constructing Ethnic Identity with 'Chicana' Informants." *Frontiers* 13, no. 3: 53–76.

Zhang, Z. 2000. "Mediating Time: The 'Rice Bowl of Youth' in Fin-de-Siècle Urban China." *Public Culture* 12, no. 1: 93–113.

Zhu, J. 1999. "Local Growth Coalitions: The Context and Implications of China's Gradualist Urban Land Reforms." *International Journal of Urban and Regional Research* 23, no. 3: 534–48.

Index

Ananya Roy is assistant professor of urban studies in the Department of City and Regional Planning at the University of California at Berkeley, where she teaches international and comparative planning. She was formerly executive coordinator of the International Association for the Study of Traditional Environments at the University of California at Berkeley. Her publications include articles on transnational approaches to the study of housing; social policy and poverty alleviation; feminism and planning theory; and the cultural politics of place.